MW00984704

THE HEALING OF THE GODS

The Magic of Symbols and the Practice of Theotherapy

By the same author

The Armageddon Script
Beyond All Belief
The Cosmic Eye
Gospel of the Stars
The Great Pyramid Decoded
The Great Pyramid: Your Personal Guide

THE HEALING OF THE GODS

The Magic of Symbols and
the Practice of Theotherapy

Peter Lemesurier

Element Books

© Peter Lemesurier 1988

First published in 1988 by
Element Books Limited

Longmead, Shaftesbury, Dorset

All rights reserved.
No part of this book may be reproduced or
utilized in any form or by any means,
electronic or mechanical, without permission
in writing from the Publisher.

Typeset by Poole Typesetting (Wessex) Limited, Bournemouth
Printed and bound in Great Britain by Billings, Hylton Road, Worcester

Designed by Max Fairbrother

Cover illustration by Belinda Downes

British Library Cataloguing in Publication Data
Lemesurier, Peter
The healing of the gods : the magic of
symbols and the practice of theotherapy.
1. Symbolism. Psychological perspectives
I. Title
153.6

ISBN 1-85230-033-7

The illustration on the front cover contains the following symbolism:

— the female figure is *Aphrodite,* Goddess of Love. She stands for the power of sexual attraction and her mirror symbolises her quest for beauty and allure and the moon within it suggests the reflection of her essential femininity.

— the seated figure is *Asclepius.* He is the God of holistic healing and medicine, as symbolised by the snake he is carrying.

— the mosaic floor shows the moon (as the feminine principle and the icon of the unconscious), the sun (as the masculine principle and the fire of conscious reason) and the circle which is the symbol of the Self.

— the wheat represents the harvest, reproduction and regeneration.

— the distant figure is *Apollo,* the Sun God. He embodies the typically male aspects of the psyche and he symbolises the triumph of the intellect as well as music and the arts.

CONTENTS

ACKNOWLEDGEMENTS

I am grateful to those who have kindly given permission for the reprinting of copyright material. Details are to be found in the Reference-Bibliography. I should also like to record my thanks to Liz Price for the spark of the idea, to John Major for adapting his *Memotext* word-processing program for my use, to the numerous friends who have kindly read and commented on the manuscript, and to Annie Walton and Simon Franklin for their editorial enthusiasm and collaboration.

P.L.

Author's Note

Any book in English concerned with the psyche of humanity is bound sooner or later to run into the problem of linguistic sexism. So male-orientated is our language that, short of performing the most incredible linguistic acrobatics, it is difficult to avoid giving the impression that the world is populated exclusively by men. The point is highly significant for the present study, in that it indicates the extraordinary extent to which the Anglo-Saxon world in particular is in thrall to one particular form of consciousness — the typically 'male' point of view — at the expense of all other possibilities. Those possibilities are the 'gods' of my title.

For my women readers, therefore, I should like to make it clear that, wherever I use the generic term 'man', it applies equally to woman; and that the associated pronominal forms 'he', 'his' and 'him' might just as well be replaced by the forms 'she' and 'her'. Which is an odd point to have to make at the beginning of a book whose aim is to help Western 'man' to rediscover the lost parts of 'himself', which by definition include 'his' feminine side . . .

PART 1
THE MAGIC OF SYMBOLS

. . . the magic of the symbol . . . contains those primitive analogies that speak to the unconscious. The unconscious can be reached and expressed only by symbols, which is the reason why the process of individuation can never do without the symbol. The symbol is the primitive expression of the unconscious, but at the same time it is also an idea corresponding to the highest intuition produced by consciousness.

CARL GUSTAV JUNG:
Commentary on Richard Wilhelm's translation of
The Secret of the Golden Flower[39]

INTRODUCTION

The magic of symbols is an all-pervading magic. In the deep wells of our innermost being it pervades our dreams, orchestrates our emotions, heals our psyche. When it emerges into conscious play it creates ideas, conceives philosophies, spawns new social orders. Under its potent spell the world is transformed, the universe reduced to order, nature herself brought to heel.

Yet that magic is also a terrible magic. No sooner have its services been consciously engaged than it can turn upon the magician just when he least expects it and rend him asunder.

And so those who would misuse it walk blithely into the jaws of hell, kingdoms are destroyed, whole civilisations go under. And with them, it may be, humanity itself.

But what strange magic is this? What arcane symbols can have such devastating power? Who, indeed, is the magician in charge?

The truth is that it is you and I who fulfil that fateful role. Not on special ritual occasions, but every day of our lives. Much of the time the process is purely unconscious. But it operates at the conscious level too. And here it does so not so much through any secret system of magic signs and spells, nor even through the wonders and terrors of science and technology, as through the potent magic of our everyday thought and language.

It is humanity at large that is the cosmic sorcerer's apprentice. And it is the magic of our conscious symbols that has both made the world we know, and could just as easily destroy it tomorrow.

•

Large claims, you may say. For surely the fate of the world depends not on anything so airy-fairy as symbols, but on hard, material facts. It is in the gift not of magic or the gods, but of politicians and generals, of administrators and scientists. Clearly, too, it is the plaything of economic forces and natural disasters, of plague and famine, population-growth, resource-depletion, pol-

lution and accidental nuclear Armageddon. Such, admittedly, is
the negative side of the coin of human destiny.

But what of its opposite? What are the positive forces that have
the ability to save us and secure our race's posterity?

Well, for a start there is idealism. There is reason. There is
goodwill. Contingency planning and good management have a
distinct role to play. Canny anticipation and philosophical
wisdom are clearly basic to our survival. The spirit of healing and
wholeness must inevitably underpin it.

But these are all abstract ideas, not hard, material facts — ideas
that are themselves born of word and concept, of dividing up a
seamless universe into watertight compartments that can have no
actual counterparts in raw reality. In a word, of symbols.

For the truth is that our very words are symbols, our very ideas
mere ciphers for the truth.

And perhaps it is because no cipher can ever *become* the truth
that our carefully constructed systems of artificial symbols, our
optimistic edifices of reason and thought, all eventually have to
fail. To fail, that is, in the face of the ancient gods — those primal,
unconscious human urges which they are powerless to resist or
even recognise. To fail in the face of major disasters which they
themselves have provoked. To fail, too, in the face of large-scale
natural cataclysms which they are too blinkered and too rigid to
understand or anticipate.

Symbolism, then, is nothing less than the triune god in our
pantheon of possibilities. At the level of the deep unconscious it is
Brahma, the Creator. At the level of healing and psychological
development, whether individual or collective, it is Vishnu, the
Preserver. At the more familiar, everyday level of thought and
language it is Shiva, the Destroyer and Regenerator.

And the mystic dance of Shiva, which is said to shape and
condition the whole universe as we know it, is none other than the
deadly dance which the conscious you and I, did we but know it,
are performing every day.

•

But what is the real nature of this fateful dance that we perform so
consciously and yet so unknowingly? What are its steps, and who
invented them? When and how did it begin? And how was it that
we joined it — indeed, as it now seems, actually choreographed it
in the first place?

These are among the questions that we shall need to begin by addressing. But there are others too.

Is there any hope for the dancers? Will the dance of the damned go on? And if so, can it possibly last until the first light of some new and more hopeful dawn?

Much depends on whether the dancers are prepared to wake up to their real situation. To a remarkable extent they are like a crowd of animated marionettes performing jerky, reflex actions to the predetermined rhythm of a music whose origins lie far back in the night of time. Somehow a douche of cold water needs to be administered, a breath of fresh air to be admitted into the stale atmosphere of the dance-hall.

A shock sufficient to enable the dancers to realise that there is a world beyond the dance-hall, a silence beyond the music, a starry firmament looking everlastingly down from far above the smoke and the chandeliers.

And that other powers, other gods — by no means all of them unfriendly — are yet abroad in the universe, bearing their healing symbols before them.

Are *you* prepared to stop dancing? Can you let go of your partner for a few hours? Will you switch off the music, open the windows, turn down the lights?

Are you prepared to break the spell, to trace the source of the magic? To follow it back on a long journey through the portals of consciousness, beyond the veils of projection and dream, to the deep wells of the unconscious?

Are you prepared, once that mysterious underworld has been attained, to confront the gods, to unmask the ancient beginning?

Are you ultimately prepared to face reality and perhaps discover . . . your Self?

1 SYMBOLS OF THE WILL

Far away in an unknown land, in an age long lost to time, there lived a race that knew reality. Or rather, it *was* reality.

Hope and regret were unknown to it. 'You' and 'I' were meaningless concepts. 'Here' and 'there' were one and the same, 'this' and 'that' undivorced because unidentified in the first place.

And all because the very words were lacking.

So, even if the concept 'you' chanced to float vaguely into awareness, it might as easily change into 'she', transmute itself into 'they', turn around and boomerang unexpectedly into 'I', simply because there was no means of fixing it. Reality refused to be tied down.

And so there was a feeling of magic about the place. Yet it was an autonomous magic, a magic that defied the efforts of anybody to control it or misuse it for purely selfish purposes.

As well it might, for the self that might wish to control it had as yet only the vaguest idea of its own selfhood, let alone any notion that that selfhood might in some way be separate from other selfhoods 'out there'.

•

That race, you will already have guessed, was our own race. It was a humanity as yet without language or conscious thought. It was a part of the animal kingdom that was as yet still groping its way towards what we call consciousness.

And for that reason it was neither happy nor unhappy, neither hopeful nor regretful, neither good nor evil. It simply *was*.

Possibly it was *unaware* that it was. That is to say, it had never turned its collective mind to the proposition. By the same token, it had never addressed the question of whether the universe *was*, either.

In other words, as far as those early ancestors of ours were concerned, *it wasn't*.

Or rather, there wasn't even an 'it' to 'be' or 'not be' in the first place. Nor even, for that matter, the basic time and space for that 'being' to take place *in*.

And so, with a race that (so far as it was concerned) didn't exist, paying no conscious attention to a universe that (so far as the race was concerned) didn't exist either, reality was good and whole and undivided and exactly as it had to be.

Which is as good a way as any of describing what we today might refer to as primal bliss.

•

Not that we have to look so far back to discover that state of being. You and I each experienced it, however briefly, in our infancy.

It was vague. It was woozy. It was miasmic. It was messy. It was smelly. It was gloriously irresponsible. It was everything-all-at-one-and-nothing-out-of-place.

It was lovely.

•

And then the magic began. Not at the hands of some witch-doctor or medicine-man. Runes and secret signs and occult formulae had nothing to do with it. The gods as such were not involved, for they had not yet even been invented. Neither rite nor ritual had any hand in its inception.

Just everyday living, a man or woman with an itch to tie down one small corner of experience.

And a noise.

Nobody knows, even today, what that noise was. Probably it arose many times, in different places. In which case there may have been many different First Noises.

But the important thing was that that First Noise, initially at least, had a definite exterior *meaning*. It applied to one aspect of experience, and to that aspect of experience only.

And from it, incredible as it may seem (and much as the occultists are prone to claim, if in a different context), the whole of our familiar, perceived universe was in due course to spring.

•

It is traditional to assume that the First Noise must have been the *name* of something. 'Wife', perhaps, or 'food', or even some personal name.

Yet this seems unlikely, partly because without the name it would have been difficult to be sure that you were talking about a 'thing' in the first place, and partly because such a name would not in any case have been very useful. Animal cries of the more instinctive sort, after all, hardly fit into the category of what we would call 'names'. They are intended to produce reactions — feeding, perhaps, or mating, or flight.

And the nearest equivalent in the new, invented code would thus have been some kind of simple command — 'fetch', possibly, or 'go', or 'come'.

And so the conscious symbol was born. It was a personal acoustic tool, a willed cipher whose magic produced actual, tangible results. Thanks to a mere noise, people started to fetch, or go, or come when they were told, instead of merely when they felt like it.

Or indeed, to refuse to do anything of the kind.

So sounds for 'yes' and 'no' cannot have been slow to follow.

But if some people were likely to be more co-operative than others, the obvious next step was to direct your orders at particular people, rather than to the world at large.

The naming of names began.

Yet if you could use names to identify who was to perform the task in hand, you could extend the technique to apply to the other end of the process as well. You could use your new sound symbols to indicate *what* was to be fetched, *where* it was to be taken. With the aid of a few more noises, you could start to control events even well out of range of your pointing finger. You could distinguish between similar objects on grounds of size, or colour, or texture. You could lay down just *how* they were to be fetched or taken.

And then — an astonishing development, this — you could start to apply your by now thoroughly familiar noise for 'no' to almost anything that you were now capable of saying. You could perform the extraordinary philosophical feat of telling people what *not* to do, of imposing upon them a non-existent obligation, or even an existent prohibition.

The negative had started its baleful march through human thought and history.

Possibly this development marked the beginning of human *abstract* thought. Certainly there can be few things more abstract than a non-existent obligation, or even an existent prohibition. It needed only the development of the trick of making statements *about* what was going on, rather than merely issuing orders to bring it about in the first place, to open the floodgates. John's fetching, or Mary's coming, could now be crystallised into a single noise-complex. So, even more significantly, could John's *not* fetching or Mary's *not* coming. A single word could start to stand not merely for an event, but for a non-event too. Soon words could start to symbolise whole clutches of both, whole complexes of abstract possibility and impossibility. Not to mention possibilities long past or yet to be.

And in the process a new world started to grow-up alongside the seamless world of basic, integrated sense-impressions – a world which, far from being seamless, was divided up into the distinct categories represented by the words that were now being used to symbolise it. On the one hand, the world of reality. On the other, the world of illusion.

It was words, then, the relatively new technology of human sound-symbolism, that had created that world of illusion. And it was words that now went on to ensure that the world of illusion would loom ever larger in human awareness, to the point where the real world, that it was designed to symbolise started to disappear little by little from human view.

It is to that inexorable process that we today are the eventual, indeed, possibly the ultimate heirs. The world in which we live is a world that is almost entirely of our own devising. We see what we see primarily in terms of the language that we use to describe it. And since the very basis of that language lies in the identification of *differences* (John is not Mary, fetching is not taking), the world we live in is fundamentally fragmented. This is particularly true of the modern Western world. Its very commerce is based on the distinction between 'I' and 'you', its politics on the gulf between left and right, its morality on the divide between good and evil, its religion on the dichotomy between God and Devil, its despair and anxiety on the gap between 'now' and 'then', between 'here' and 'there', between 'I' and 'me'.

So it is no surprise to find that the fundamental questions of our time increasingly concern the ultimate distinction between our race's very survival or non-survival.

It seems, then, that that question will be decided not so much by nuclear bombs or famine, by disease or pollution or over-population. It will be decided by the extent of our willingness to persist in the obsessive symbol game to which we today are heirs, our proneness to divide the world up into 'us' and 'them', to put 'I want' before 'we need', to imagine that by siding with the half of the universe that we choose to label 'good' we can blithely ignore, or even destroy, the other half of it that we choose to label 'bad'.

Such are the gifts of the goddess Reason, whom we ourselves have created out of our divisive words and thoughts. Such are the perils of ignoring all the other, darker gods that we have thereby unwittingly let loose upon the world.

Yet kicking an old habit is never easy. How are we to begin to escape the ancient magic of language? Are we to stay entirely mute? Does the world have to become one big Trappist monastery? Or is there some alternative language that could heal the wounds? A language less committed to the notion of division, and whose roots lie not in the wilful illusions of dualistic discrimination, but in the seamless robe of primal reality?

Fortunately, the answer seems to be 'Yes'.

2 Mystic Involvement and the Dream Time

Long before language arrived on the scene, our primitive ancestors were managing to cope very successfully with reality – a good deal more successfully, it could be said, than we ourselves seem to be doing today.

We have various reasons for believing this. In the first place, *they survived.* (Otherwise they would not have been our ancestors.)

In the second place, they had successfully adapted to their own special ecological niche, just as every other known animal species has. (Otherwise they would not have survived.)

In the third place, that adaptation, that total oneness with their environment, was so complete that it evidently continued uninterrupted for some millions of years. (Otherwise their descendants would not have survived long enough for language to appear on the scene to start with.)

And in the fourth place, that adaptation was strong enough to survive even the introduction of language itself, so that it is still possible to observe it at work in the newly-discovered primitive tribes of our own day.

Again and again anthropologists find themselves amazed (those who have not long since become inured to the phenomenon, that is) at the sheer perfection with which supposedly primitive, Stone Age tribes have adapted to their circumstances. Their ability to relate to their surroundings, to cope with death, disease and natural enemies, to find food and clothing and shelter, to devise appropriate survival technologies — all this puts us to shame.

For the truth is that there is scarcely one in a hundred modern Westerners who would have more than the faintest inkling of how to survive in such circumstances. Scarcely one in a hundred, indeed, who would do much better even in their familiar home environment if our entire civilisation were suddenly to collapse about our ears.

And yet how do these primitives arrive at their astonishing ability to cope? Do they rely on books or university experts, on sophisticated systems of schooling and medical research, on hi-tech agricultural and construction industries? Do they, for that matter, rely on rational analysis and what we regard as logical, conventional forms of linguistic explanation at all?

Not in the slightest. What baffles the anthropologists perhaps above all are the positively lunatic complexes of belief upon which the whole edifice of primitive life and survival seem to depend. For these strange patterns of consciousness bear little relation to our familiar way of looking at the world, and none at all to what we call logic.

A term coined long ago by the philosopher and ethnologist Lévy-Bruhl to describe this primitive attitude to existence was *participation mystique*. In English the expression might perhaps be best rendered as *mystic involvement*.

•

Typically, the true primitive perceives the whole of reality in an undivided light. Admittedly, in all cases known to us, language has already entered the picture. And not 'primitive' language, either. Every known language is at least as sophisticated and subtle as our own, no matter how socially backward its speakers may appear to us to be.

A fact which suggests that language has been around and developing for a good deal longer than we often suppose.

Yet, despite this powerful influence for disintegration, the sense of essential unity has somehow prevailed. And its ultimate manifestation shows up in the sheer oneness of the primitive tribe with its environment.

But how is this unity achieved? Or rather, how is it that it was never lost?

The answer seems to lie in the very nature of primitive perception. Astonishing as it may seem, the true primitive *makes no distinction between himself 'in here' and perceived reality 'out there'.*

This is no philosophical trick. It is not a question of deducing, after long thought, that perceived reality is actually only an inner event generated by our own psyche — roughly the position, say, established by modern neurology and quantum physics, not to mention traditional Buddhism. Nor can it realistically be described as a case of psychological projection, an unconscious foisting of inner psychological states onto events, objects or people 'out there', even though that is how modern psychologists are apt to view it with the benefit of hindsight. (To label such an attitude as 'projection', after all, you need to start by assuming that there is a basic separation between subjective experience and objective reality in the first place. *But that is merely our own 'modern' view of things*.)

To the true primitive, the very basis of such distinctions is meaningless. There is no such division. There is no 'outer' world. There is no 'inner' world. There is simply reality, the whole of it infused with spirit, permeated by psyche.

And so sunrise is joy, and joy sunrise. Cloud is depression, and depression cloud. Spring is new vigour, and new vigour is spring. Winter is death, and death winter.

If disease is hyena, then hyena is disease. Therefore if I am ill, my soul is hyena's. If strength is lion, then lion is strength. Therefore when I am strong, I too am truly a lion (the idea still survives into our modern speech, but has by now become devalued into a mere metaphor). Gazelle is my fleetness of foot, bull my fertility, spider my cunning. Trees are my security, plants my survival. All are therefore indivisible aspects of myself. And if I would have healing, or secret wisdom, or longevity, or even death, then I must respect and worship my brother snake, who is the embodiment of them all.

As for the world of nature, so for the world of humanity. And so it goes without saying that my human brothers and sisters are as much a part of me as I am — which means that tribal unity is a quintessential condition of my existence.

The point is of obvious survival value, and may indicate an actual reason in genetics for this whole tendency to what we have termed *mystic involvement*.

However this world of 'inside out' comes to me, that is how it is. There is nothing fixed or logical about it. Yet because I am living in close community, my visions and intuitions are shared. So are those of others of my people. There arises a tribal view of reality and experience — a view totally different, it may be, from the view of the tribe across the river. Yet for me and my brothers and sisters it is valid. It works. And so it survives. Much to the astonishment of the anthropologists.

Yet this supposedly 'backward' cultural paradigm characterises and spells out the true Dream Time, the earthly paradise so wistfully recalled to this day by the Australian Aborigines. It is the state of bliss before language separates the world into distinct natural kingdoms. It is the magic of the ancient beginning, when the gods are creating humanity and humanity is at the same time creating the gods . . .

•

At this primitive stage it cannot truly be said that symbolism has yet entered the picture. Nothing *stands for* anything else, since there is no distinction between them in the first place. Winter *is* death, lion *is* strength, bull *is* fertility.

The original Greek *symbolon* was a single coin or token. A circle. A whole. When two friends parted, it was broken in two. Each kept one perfectly fitting part, in witness of the unity that had been lost and might one day be restored. It was thus a token both of trauma and of eventual healing.

It was only when the *symbolon* was broken that true symbolism began.

And so it seems to have been with the consciousness of our early ancestors. Yet the process of separation which lies at the basis of symbolism did not happen all at once. Even among the pre-classical Greeks, the word *ouranos* (Uranus) did not merely refer to the god who ruled over the sky. It *meant* 'sky'. Sky and Earth, Ocean and Sun, Moon and Dawn were still just as much personal encounters with the gods 'in here' as inanimate objects or events 'out there'. To the Egyptians, too, the inner god and his outer manifestations were still one and the same, the pyramidion atop the sacred obelisk no more and no less solar than Ra himself. And the souls of the dead could live quite happily on *painted* food, in *model* houses, through *sculpted* bodies.

It was not a question of reality versus representation. 'Art' just did not exist. Experienced reality *was* reality.

Yet already the distinctions were beginning to creep in. Analytical, conscious thought was on the march. The human intellect was showing signs of becoming rampant. By classical times the Greek philosophers were gleefully dismissing the ancient gods of Homer and Hesiod, much to the trepidation of the more credulous common folk. And totally unaware of the fact that they were unconsciously still deferring to them in almost every respect —

whether in their choice of subject-matter, their chosen approaches or even their general conclusions.[13]

Possibly the change was slower to come in the dogmatic climate of monolithic Egypt. Yet here, too, it had to come in the end. And so, as first Greece, then imperial Rome took over the leadership of the known world, the remaining sanctuaries of mystic, integrated consciousness fell one by one to the onslaught of applied classical thinking, with its associated armoury of powerful tools and technologies and its inbuilt rejection of the strictures of ancient taboo and tribal inertia.

The friends had parted. Inner consciousness and outer awareness had been sundered. The great ship of psychic wholeness had foundered. And only the symbolic associations of the former world of mystic involvement were left swimming about, scattered and largely unrecognised, amid the wreckage of the communal psyche, each bearing with it not only a sensory image, but a whole complex of ideas, inner feelings and emotional loadings as well.

And it is this world of symbols, this country of our dreams, that alone seems capable of restoring the coin of our former wholeness and reinstituting that state of bliss which ultimately reflects the nature of our true selves.

3 Symbols of the Unconscious

The ancient symbols, then, are far older than the language-based, separative consciousness with which we now choose to consider them.

Yet they are still alive, still vigorously working their magic within the human psyche.

Not necessarily in terms of any particular images that could be listed and tied down. But as a range of instinctive (and often unexpected) psychic responses to inner and outer circumstances — responses capable of invoking any one of a number of 'outer' images or sense-impressions as their 'objective' vehicles.

There are, it is true, a number of basic visual images that do seem to be almost universal. The symbolisms of Sun and Moon, Tree and Tower, Eagle and Serpent, Circle and Square, Phallus and Cave, Sacrifice and Scapegoat, Seed and Egg, Cross and Star are, in the broadest terms, common to most cultures. Dreamers world-wide dream them. Artists paint them. Architects and sculptors embody them. Directors of art films and horror films and producers of fantasy video games constantly invoke them. Poets revel in them. Occultists manipulate them. Magicians live by them. And the world's encyclopaedias of symbols are crammed solid with illustrations of them.

Yet the air of deadness which patently surrounds such illustrations suggests that they lack something vital. There is, it seems, a kind of living essence, a direct emotional or psychic content, without which such images are little more than stuffed exhibits in a museum.

That essence, that content, is *meaning*. Yet it is a meaning which can arise only in a context of direct and intimate personal involvement.

It can never be said that a given image has a given, 'definite' meaning outside that special context. The merest glance at the welter of possible interpretations offered by the encyclopaedias is enough to make the fact plain. Indeed, the very word 'meaning' is perhaps misleading here.

For the symbols of the unconscious, unlike mere signs or signals, *do not have meanings in the conventional sense.* It is their very lack of exterior meaning that marks them out as symbols of the unconscious in the first place. Every symbol is a complex of image and personal inner response *which is its own meaning.*

Words of explanation may point the way to the experience, but they can never be equated with it. Which is perfectly logical. For if any such explanation were possible, the symbols would be transformed from symbols of the unconscious into symbols of the conscious mind. Whereupon their power to heal us, to put us back in touch with the deeper psyche, would be gone.

The mania for verbal explanations is a particular bugbear in any study of symbolism. For the fact is that you can no more explain a symbol or a sacred mystery than you can explain a joke. Any attempt at explanation immediately destroys what you are trying to explain.

True, an explanation can help if the symbol never had any noticeable effect on you in the first place. An explained symbol, too, can become a useful *conscious* tool in the service of reason, the will, or even wishful thinking — no less than can everyday words and language. But once this has happened, its spontaneous ability to operate at the unconscious level tends to be weakened, as the conscious mind brings its ever suspicious critical faculties to bear.

The explained symphony may be a better understood symphony, but somehow the music never sounds the same again.

It is as though a symbol were a kind of 'body-soul complex'. Try to examine the one in the absence of the other, and you are liable to find yourself looking at a corpse. Just as you know when you are walking, or cycling, or joyful, or sad, so equally you know when a symbol — be it inanimate or animate, a stone or a god — is at work within you. Simply because the working of the symbol *is itself the knowledge.* Analysing the muscular movements and/or neural feedbacks involved, whether physical or psychic, can only get in the way of the process.

That is why standardised systems of dream interpretation are for the most part both inappropriate and unhelpful. It is in dreams, after all, that most of us have our most vivid encounters with the symbols of the unconscious. Our personal dreamworld abounds with strange objects and events, with weird mixtures of everyday animals and fabulous beasts, of mighty gods and demons and the people next door. And it is only too natural for the preconditioned conscious mind to want to reduce them to impersonal order and 'make sense' of their apparent chaos and irrationality.

Yet, once again, all that any such exercise can do is reduce the living symbols to mere dead pawns of the conscious mind. Whereupon their vital power is lost.

All that is necessary, in fact, is that the dreams be *experienced to the full*. And that means acknowledging them, recalling them, reliving something of their inner power, their primal *frisson*. A number of techniques can aid the process, from painting them and acting them out, through recounting them to others, to recording them daily in a dream notebook — preferably in the present tense (the dream, after all, is a present experience) and in the first words that come to you.

But explanation is not of the essence. Subsequently, perhaps, you may wish to return to what you have written in search of clues to your current inner state and process. But it is important not to do this all the while the dream is still vivid in your memory, or you will disempower the direct inner experience which is its primary function and purpose.

The dream is for the benefit of the dreamer, not of the amateur psychologist.

It is possible, of course, that we dream all the time, only noticing the process when the noise of the senses and the chatter of the conscious mind are switched off at night. But in that case how can we stay in touch with our potentially healing world of symbols during the daytime?

In fact this poses few difficulties, since the symbols are constantly emerging from the woodwork around us.

We may not always realise it — and not all of us may be willing to accept the idea, for all its basis in research[12,40] — but the unconscious is careful to arrange virtually everything that happens to us in such a way as to give it something of the quality of a symbol or omen. We break a leg, so telling ourselves that we haven't a leg to stand on. We go down with bronchitis, apparently in order to tell ourselves that we need to get something off our chest. We suffer digestive problems, possibly as a way of establishing that we cannot stomach whatever is happening to us.

Disorders of the throat may suggest to us that there is something we cannot swallow. Respiratory difficulties warn us that we are sorely in need of a breath of fresh air. Fevers that force us to our beds bring with them the message that it is time to lie low. Diseases of eye or ear speak to us of an unwillingness to look or listen. And cancer threatens us when we are continually eaten up with suppressed rage or frustration.

The very words of the familiar idioms can, it seems, be a good deal more revealing that we sometimes realise.

True, the germs and microbes may have a role to play, too. But they are not particular about whom they attack. We are all crawling with them — all of us, quite impartially. Yet it is only some of us who, it seems, open the door, and whose defences unaccountably crumble. Not because of some conscious decision, but because of a combination of environmental and constitutional factors which seem to have more than a little to do with the symbolic workings of our unconscious, the state of our emotions, our stress levels, psychological resilience and general lifestyle.

As children, those factors may not be totally under our control. As adults, they are factors over which we have a considerable say.

Even Louis Pasteur, the original architect of the currently fashionable germ theory of disease, was careful to stress in his writings that people's mental and physiological states are at least as important to their state of health as the microbes themselves.[4] As ever, it was subsequent generations of disciples who tended grossly to oversimplify and even caricature the prophet's message.

Not that there is any question of *blaming* the patient, however. Feelings of guilt would be entirely out of place. It is actually axiomatic to the system of healing which I shall be expounding later in this book that *it is perfectly all right — indeed, perfectly normal — to be ill*, unpleasant though the experience may seem at the time. Contrary to the negative assumptions with which most of us are brought up, illness turns out actually to be a tool of healing, offering us valuable symbolic pointers as to how to redirect our lives for the better. Even death itself is far from the calamitous failure, the ultimate letting down of the side which modern medicine tends to portray it as being. Instead it is seen to be a perfectly valid part of life — indeed its ultimately validating culmination and completion.

So that the experience even of cancer — one of the most feared of all modern diseases — can be viewed positively rather than negatively, accepted rather than swept under the carpet. It is quite remarkable, for example, how many patients attending positively-orientated clinics and institutions such as the Bristol Cancer Help Centre have eventually felt moved to say (breaking all the accepted taboos) that they are actually *glad* to have contracted the disease, because of the way in which it has brought new validity, shape and purpose to their lives. At the same time such a positive attitude can, it seems, also contribute considerably to its successful treatment, whereas being eaten up with resentment ('Why did it have to happen to *me*?') is quite likely to make things worse. And the source of this success lies in the fact that patients can start to relate to their illness, to learn from it, *and above all to take responsibility for it.*

It is that taking of responsibility which, as we shall see, turns out again and again to lie at the basis of true healing. Whoever can cause his illness can *un*cause it too. Instead of seeing himself as the pathetic plaything of external circumstances, a mere helpless body being squabbled over for possession by malignant microbes and disease processes on the one hand and disease orientated and possibly power motivated medical specialists on the other, the patient himself takes control. Knowing that the human organism has remarkable healing powers of its own, he calmly chooses how *he* will approach the problem, what remedies *he* will seek, what changes *he* will make in his way of life, and ultimately whether he will live or die. His existence once again acquires meaning. Even through his suffering he starts to sense once more a deeper process at work, a connectedness with the very purpose of his being.

In short, he comes to himself.

Which, it has to be said, is one of the more important things that any of us can hope to achieve in our lifetime . . .

•

Not only our illnesses, meanwhile, but our accidents and even the events of our everyday life seem capable of having the same marked symbolic 'oracular' quality that I have just been describing — and all the more so to the extent that we fail to recognise whatever the problem is on the *inner* level. If, while motoring, we run into a brick wall, perhaps that is precisely what we are doing on the psychological level. If we fall down while running for the bus, possibly we are trying to run too fast in a more general sense too. And if we seem to be in perpetual conflict with our partners or our children, it is not beyond the bounds of possibility that we are also failing to relate to our own inner masculine or feminine sides, or to the various childhood personalities that are still alive within us.

Naturally, however, such an oracular view of everyday events may not appeal to everyone, particularly those of a more materialistic frame of mind. To them it may smack too much of magic or superstition.

So that it is just as well that the symbol-maker within us has more than one string to its bow.

Thus, we have only to stare at the pattern of the wallpaper or the embers of the fire for our symbols to emerge once more, this time confronting us with *visual images* to reflect our current inner processes. Outside, the clouds, and even unusually shaped trees and rocks, will perform a similar service — anything, in fact, that is vague and amorphous enough to allow our awareness to abstract from it the configuration that best corresponds to our current psychological state.

Which is why the psychologists find the imponderabilities of Rorschach's inkblot test so helpful in pinpointing our current inner concerns and obsessions.

The ancients were well aware of this approach. And so techniques were long ago developed by priests and shamans the world over for divining the contents of their own unconscious minds, and thus the 'will of the gods', in the random patterns of sheep's entrails and rune-sticks, of smoke and water and stars in the sky.

And if others were to read into them auguries for the future, who was to say that they were wrong?

Meanwhile you have only to engage in a much more everyday activity nearer to home to gain some idea of what is involved. Tearing yourself away from the dregs of your newly-drained teacup, you take a walk along the beach. And, lo and behold, suddenly certain stones virtually jump up at you and demand your attention without any conscious effort on your part. Examine them, and you are likely to find that they have a strictly limited number of themes in common. Or perhaps only one. Possibly they are all round, or near-perfect spheres, or vaguely egg-shaped, or long and thin, or divided neatly down the middle into dark and light halves. Possibly they are all a pristine white, or boldly striped; possibly they are black and misshapen, or pitted with holes.

You may wonder what all this means, what arcane message your unconscious is trying to convey to you. Once again, however, 'meaning' is not of the essence. Significant words and phrases may indeed spring to mind. But it is sufficient to recognise that the pebbles have somehow managed to reflect back to you the mood of your own inner moment, and then move on. Acknowledged, your psychic process will continue on its way, ready to throw up more symbols as it reaches the next stage on its journey of development and self-discovery.

Be assured, it is quite competent to undertake this task. It needs neither orders nor interference on the part of your conscious mind. It requires only that you acknowledge and accept its efforts at the appropriate time. It demands only that you attend when attention is due.

If you doubt it, *try* interfering. Instead of letting the pebbles find you, go in search of pebbles of the type which you think you *ought* to be discovering. You are likely to find it extraordinarily difficult and unrewarding.

Give the unconscious the credit for knowing what it is about.

•

All this is not to say, though, that humanity's symbolic images were somehow fixed and predestined in the very beginning. It might admittedly be thought that the stars in the night sky are immutably grouped into Lion and Goat, Hunter and Bull, Bear and Eagle, Archer and Scorpion, Scales and Fishes, Virgin and Ram and Heavenly Twins. But nothing could be further from the truth. The stars in the sky are totally random. Those within particular constellations are often in different regions of space entirely and only appear close together because of our particular terrestrial perspective.

Consequently you are at perfect liberty to group them in any way you wish, just as the inventors of the original zodiac did (and as, curiously enough, even the mythical records of the Greek gods seem to imply[9]). Being for the most part wandering herdsmen who wanted nothing more grandiose than something to tell the time by at night, they naturally saw a sky full of animals, and divided it up accordingly.

Which is why the word *zodiac* means nothing more arcane than a celestial *zoo*.

That the system would subsequently come to acquire a much

deeper and more esoteric significance is unlikely ever to have
entered their minds — consciously, at least — however much you
or I may now care to credit their communal unconscious with deep
prescience in the matter.

But if you are already familiar with the traditional figures, the
chances are that you will now find it extremely difficult to
exchange them for other visions of your own.

This phenomenon of what might be called *symbolic inertia* is a
well-known one. Examining the 'transparent box' below, for
example, you are likely to assume that you are looking at it either
from below . . . or from above. (You may also notice a certain
splaying of the parallel lines as a result of the deliberate absence of
perspective.)

But now attempt to reverse that assumption, and you may well
not find it too easy.

Again, the picture overleaf can be seen either as a hook-nosed
crone looking slightly downwards and to the left, or as a fashion
conscious young girl also looking to the left, but away from the
viewer. But once again, you may find it extraordinarily difficult to
discover the alternative image, once you have settled initially on
one or the other.

There seems, in other words, to be an inbuilt tendency for the
human psyche to perpetuate whatever basic patterns it detects in
'outer' events and objects. And it is then perfectly natural for each
succeeding generation to pass on its own perceived patterns to its
children. Clearly this tendency to symbolic inertia is a vital
prerequisite for the establishment of a common language and
culture in the first place. And so we may confidently date it to well
before the initial invention of language itself, i.e. to some two
million years ago at least.

But the case of the zodiac points up another, quite different
feature of the process — the quite arbitrary nature of the original

identification. The original wandering herdsmen, in other words, did not *have* to see the sky as peopled with circling animals at all. That they did so was merely a natural extension of their daily circumstances. Had they been architects, they might have established some kind of Heavenly City, much as later Judaeo-Christian visionaries were to do. Had they been carpenters they might have cluttered the sky with pieces of furniture. The Greeks, for their part, were to associate the stars with the gods themselves.

There was nothing inherently zoological about the stars in the night sky. The inventors of the original zodiac made a definite *choice*, however unconsciously.

The possibility, then, is actually there for any object of consciousness — any sense-experience of whatever kind — to draw to itself that numinous cloud of emotional and psychological responses which will turn it into a true symbol. This can happen either spontaneously or as the result of an act of will. But either way the symbol is determined, not necessarily inherent in nature. We could therefore use the term *symbolic determinacy* to describe the phenomenon.

And so *any* of life's experiences can take on a symbolic role for us. And not only visual ones. A piece of music, a child's laugh, can evoke feelings and attitudes in us which we had thought long forgotten. So, as Marcel Proust discovered, can the taste of a teacake or a simple smell. The feel of a baby's skin, or of that of our beloved, can conjure up memories, thoughts, moods that lie, in Wordsworth's words, 'too deep for tears'.

All have become symbols to us. And by 'all' I mean not only the tokens 'out there', but the responses 'in here' as well. Or perhaps 'responses' is the wrong word. For so closely integrated are the contents of the symbol, so much a simultaneous case of 'inside-out' and 'outside-in', that the process is just as likely to work in reverse. When there is a mood of profound sadness or religious ecstasy, you are quite likely to find an appropriate piece of music going round and round in your head. Teacakes and smells and babies' bottoms are likely to flash into your mind at the most unexpected moments.

Much as other symbolic objects do in your dreams.

Not, it seems, for any particular utilitarian purpose. Not for any obvious survival value. But simply because the ancient form of all-in perception has succeeded in surviving, much against the odds, into the very midst of our modern world.

The symbolic process, then, is a delicate yet powerful instrument. It can latch on to almost any object or event 'out there' as a symbolic tool almost in the twinkle of an eye. Yet once the vital connection has been made, symbolic inertia can be relied upon to preserve the resulting association not only throughout your life, but perhaps for generations to come.

And so the ancients had only to conjure up the faces of a pantheon of gods as symbols for their inner, psychic processes — their complexes, their neuroses, their various sub-personalities — for those gods to become truly immortal. Their cultural descendants would inevitably see the same gods as forever bestriding their inner and outer horizons. And we who (whether we realise it or not) are the ultimate heirs to the culture and consciousness of ancient Greece are fated to discover in our turn that it is the Greek gods who, under whatever name, continue to preside, determinedly and inexorably, over our inner Olympus.

We shall be considering these particular gods in due course. Their role, as we shall discover, is basically a healing one. But they are not unrivalled. Other, equally persistent gods are abroad, too — gods of division, of dualism, of destruction.

Whereas the Greek gods arose largely spontaneously out of the communal unconscious, with only their names and faces being consciously contrived after the event, the gods of dualism arose, as we shall see, directly out of our use of language. They are self-perpetuating symbols created by the wilful conscious mind to serve its own ends, its basic determination to divide and rule.

Since, consequently, the strife-torn world we live in today is largely the one which these latter gods have bequeathed to us, that is where any attempt to put matters right has to begin. We can only start from *here*.

And so, lest we merely repeat old mistakes, we should do well to take a look now at that inheritance in some detail, carefully observing the inner and outer havoc that can be wrought by the irresponsible creation and use of such blatant *symbols of power*.

4 SYMBOLS OF POWER

The symbols of language have always been potential symbols of power. Once determined — however haphazardly — in antiquity, they fixed man's perception of the universe around him. Thanks to symbolic inertia, that view of the nature of things was then to remain virtually unchanged for countless generations, increasing only in the intensity of its power over the human psyche.

Not only was reality divided up into 'things' and 'actions' and 'qualities' to fit in with the new categories of noun, verb and adjective. The ways in which these fictitious entities could interact with each other were themselves severely limited by the new rules of language. So totally do we rely on that language to tell us how things are — or rather how they are supposed to be — that most of us are quite incapable of experiencing reality in any other light. Our poets simply baffle us when they attempt to push back the barriers again. They are hounded, despised, ignored.

Worse, we have inherited a world that is subject to the dictates of several thousand *different* languages. Not only does this fact interfere with international communication, it also ensures that each group of speakers actually sees the world in a different way from the rest.

The power of language for good or ill is thus self-evident. If world-wide illusion and misunderstanding can result from the mere haphazard symbolic decisions of our ancient ancestors, what cataclysms might not result were anybody to hijack the process deliberately?

•

The question is, of course, purely rhetorical. The deed has been done long since. It has been done, once again, by people who imagine that they are separate and distinct from everybody else, that they can somehow thrive on others' misfortune, that they can win by ensuring that others lose. Which is a concept born of language, and one whose birth only the delusions of linguistic symbolism could ever have permitted in the first place.

It starts, as most things start, at a very basic and everyday level. I have a problem, let us say. It may be financial, or it may be emotional or psychological — in fact, in the last resort, it almost inevitably is. Since, thanks to language, all things are now distinct and separate from each other, the problem can be no part of me. Therefore I perceive it as coming from 'out there'. I organise myself to deal with it, to push it further away still, if possible to destroy it entirely. But the more I push, the more it seems to resist. Or possibly it *seems* to go away, but is immediately replaced by other, even more threatening problems. These I also push away from me as fast as I can. The world 'out there', in consequence, starts to turn into a universe full of threatening, rejected entities, all looking for their chance to destroy me. And since *you* are 'out there' too, you very quickly become associated with them.

By which time the sheer ludicrousness of the whole situation should be starting to make it quite clear that the root problem really lies somewhere within myself.

However, such suggestions are blasphemy under the laws of the new kingdom of language. 'I' can never be wrong since 'I' am the subject, the doer, the actor. If I am wrong, then the world has to be topsy-turvy. Redressing the balance can only mean destroying the world. Or else myself.

And so the next stage of the process swings into action. This is the stage of *projection.*

In the former world of mystic involvement, projection had no place. There was nobody to do the projecting, nothing to project, and nobody and nothing to project it onto. In an undivided world there is neither 'I' nor 'you', neither 'here' nor 'there'.

But with the appearance of language all that had changed. All things were now separate, I was 'I', and you were 'you'. And 'you' were just as much 'out there' as the problems from which I was so busily dissociating myself.

Yet the old instinct for mystic involvement still remained. Instincts cannot be waved away just like that. Despite the advent of language, the psyche still insisted on making links between what language described as 'out there' and what it described as 'in here'.

Even if, at the conscious level, I now refused to admit that anything problematical could be 'in here' at all.

And so the process of projection could swing into play.

•

Even in placing my problem 'out there' in the first place, I am of course already making use of the mechanism of projection. Or possibly it should merely be called 'rejection', as I have not yet settled on anything specific 'out there' to attach it to.

But at this point the penny drops. The lightswitch of realisation clicks. However prematurely.

If *you* are 'out there' and the problem is 'out there', perhaps you are not merely *associated with* the problem. Distance may lend enchantment, but it also lends perspective. The images tend to merge.

And so in no time *you are* the problem.

Now all sorts of symbolic possibilities can open up. Once I have established that you are the problem, all I have to do to get rid of it is to get rid of *you*.

For you and the problem are now aspects of a single symbol. Or rather, as we less accurately prefer to put it, you have become a symbol of my problem (a phrase which ignores the equally important fact that my problem has also become a symbol of you).

The further you go away, the less the problem bothers me. At the same time, thanks again to sheer perspective, the more obvious it is that you and the problem are indeed one and the same. And so eventually all my problems come to be seen as rooted in the far away — fundamentally associated with distance, whether personal, geographical, political, racial or moral. Near at hand, by contrast, all is sweetness and light. Especially within my own psyche.

Needless to say, the whole set-up is purely illusory. The more illusory it is, the more the problems 'out there' tend to turn nasty and threatening, or are replaced or even apparently connived at by further 'enemies within' — for all my efforts to boot them out of the door as quickly as possible. I become increasingly obsessed with projecting all my inner fears and insecurities onto a range of outside entities — from mere germs and microbes at one end of the scale, through everyday human enemies and imagined corporate foes, to vast nuclear conspiracies and extraterrestial and even supernatural powers at the other. And all the time the whole thing acquires ever more ludicrous proportions. Yet this state of continual projection (believe it or not) is the 'normal' state of affairs, and most of us unthinkingly wallow in it every day of our lives.

Heaven help us, then, when things go really wrong, and the problems start to take up obvious residence 'in here', while heaven is seen to lie exclusively 'out there'. For then we have fallen prey to neurosis, or worse. We know and are forced at last to acknowledge that we are sick within. And yet we now have long since given up the symbolic instruments which might bring us true self-healing.

So it is that we attempt to deal with our self-inflicted disease of dualism by creating even more dualisms. Roping in all our resources of projection and language, we inflict the maximum possible damage on all those aspects of our experience that we have finally rejected. We turn our fury on the rest of our perceived universe — or else on ourselves.

Either way, of course, it is we who are the losers. For though we may long since have forgotten it, *we are* the universe, as the universe is us. Like some planetary cancer, we have turned upon what is essentially our own body.

And lest we should forget it, we continually remind ourselves of the fact in the most literal, blood-and-guts ways. And notably through the media of politics and war.

•

The picture that emerges, it has to be said, is not a pretty sight. On the face of it, it has little to do with the healing that we and our race currently need. The battlefield and the hurly-burly of politics seem far from the concerns of the ancient gods of the psyche who, as I hinted earlier, seem capable of bringing us that healing.

Yet the ancient gods were *intensely* political. They were also incessantly at war — if not with each other, then with other races of beings. And perhaps it is for that very reason that dualism, too, has its gods. It is their cults, indeed, which are arguably responsible, even more than language itself, for the almost universal inner and outer crisis for which the present book attempts to offer one possible remedy at least. And consequently it may be that we should do well to take a good look at the cult of dualism as it manifests itself on the world stage.

For it is important to realise how even the gods can be misused. Re-fashioned and reclothed in the image of the rampant conscious mind, they can be saddled with all our waking concerns and wishful thinkings, made to speak words which we ourselves have deliberately chosen to put into their mouths and — the ultimate indignity — forced, like us, to take sides in our petty squabbles.

Which is why not only in war and politics, but also in morality and religion, we are often only too eager to invoke their authority — whether by name or merely by unconscious implication — for setting ourselves up in righteous opposition to our enemies, and for identifying those who disagree with us as the embodiment of all evil.

God, it seems — our particular god — is on our side.

Again and again, consequently, 'they' — those other people 'out there' — are seen as the very agents of iniquity, while 'we', by contrast, are on the side of the angels. 'They' are the problem, 'we' the solution. 'They' may be neighbours, Russians, blacks, Jews, drug addicts, homosexuals, AIDS victims, socialists or communists. Equally, 'they' may be Americans, whites, government officials, police, taxmen, moralists, Christians, capitalists or members of the Establishment. In wartime, particularly, it soon becomes almost a heresy to suggest that 'we' could be wrong in any way, while every citizen of the opposing nation turns into a devil in disguise.

Or possibly not even in disguise, if the reported belief of Joan of Arc's French contemporaries that the English actually had tails is anything to go by.

The illusion persists years after the event. Many a Briton still imagines that it was the Germans, and not the British, who invented the concentration camp, or asserts as a matter of common knowledge that it was Hitler who declared war on Britain, and not the reverse. Many an American is convinced that it was the Russians who invented the nuclear threat.

But this is not the half of it. The real crunch comes when the great manipulators enter the fray — convinced by their own linguistic symbolism that they are somehow personally unique and separate from everybody else, and above all *right*. For at this point we start to see the full-blooded use of what I have termed *symbols of power*.

•

We are all thoroughly familiar with such symbols of power and their baleful effects. Moved by the national anthem, we become emotionally wedded to the flag. Inspired by the flag, we are then surprised to find ourselves willing to perform deeds of astonishing heroism, not to say foolhardiness, in the name of the nation. For the sake of the nation we finally discover that we are prepared to lay down everything — even our very lives, if need be — for causes which, in our saner moments, we might have considered of little, if any, real importance. And so the road to Armageddon lies open before us.

Such is the insidious spell which our leaders are able to cast over us with the aid of such mere symbolic adjuncts. For anthem and flag are of course no more and no less than symbols, with no significance whatever outside the symbolic realm. And even the nation itself is a mere symbol, an abstract, collective entity with little more to unify it than any other, randomly chosen piece of the Earth's surface. Little to unify it, that is, other than a single government, a single body of tribal tradition and (theoretically at least) a single language — the language which made the whole self-destructive charade possible in the first place.

Yet such blatant symbols of power have several potential weaknesses. They can be seen through. They are self-evidently man-made and man-exploited. 'Nation' is, at best, a pretty woolly concept. A flag is self-evidently only a piece of cloth. The national anthem may stir the emotions, but the magic lasts little longer than the time it takes to perform it.

Perhaps, then, some even more powerful and all-pervasive symbol is called for, whose presence can be sensed at all times and in all places? A symbol that can be carried in the mind, so leaving the hands free to fight. A symbol which is* above all suspicion (rightly or wrongly) of being man-made, and so of having been cobbled together by crafty politicians for mere reasons of personal ambition. A symbol onto which, consequently, all your nation's ideals can confidently be projected.

At which point, enter the gods.

Or rather, the god. Already, after all, it is virtually axiomatic that your god is on your side in a general sense. But now the trick is to assert that that god — that one unseen, omnipresent, superhuman entity — is devoted specifically to the welfare of your particular nation. And since, by definition, your nation alone is supposed to be right, and everybody else's wrong, the same thing has to apply to the god in question too. Moreover, since you clearly want to *win* all your wars and petty international squabbles, that god has to become pre-eminent in whatever heaven he or she inhabits.

Being top dog demands having the support of a Top God.

I have of course described the process only in the crudest terms. Yet even in the most sophisticated ones, it is just something of this kind that seems repeatedly to have happened throughout human history. Again and again some perfectly normal and unexceptional deity from the home culture's traditional pantheon — the equivalent, perhaps, of the Greeks' Zeus — has been made to take on the role of national guardian and protector.

And from that moment megalomania has set in.

He has been made to set himself up against all other gods; to declare his own unlimited power and unsullied righteousness; to usurp the former Great Mother's natural claim to have given birth to the universe in the first place; even, in the most extreme cases, to declare his own total uniqueness, while denying that his former divine colleagues ever existed at all. Zoroastrianism, Judaism, Christianity and Islam alike — all of which started out as purely national or tribal creeds — owe a great deal to this particular phenomenon. And again and again it has proved disastrous.

Zoroastrianism, admittedly, turned out in practice to be remarkably tolerant of other gods, at least as it was applied by the ancient Persian rulers who eventually made it their state religion. But the other three religions, the so-called 'religions of the book', were to prove much less easy-going in this respect. Other gods of whatever kind, especially female ones, were to be resisted tooth and claw, destroyed, banished from sight. The true religion was to be continually affirmed and upheld, cost what it may.

As is the way of things, all three initiatives were to bear much positive fruit. Such single-mindedness is apt to focus human energies in a remarkable way on communal needs, reforming ideals, idealistic causes. Many of the characteristic achievements of Western civilisation — its systems of justice and morality, its public education, its mechanisms of public welfare, its abolition of slavery, even its art, architecture, music and literature — would have been unlikely ever to have developed as they did without the influence of Christianity and its associated activities. And this very largely because Christianity's god had always been the prime symbol for human will, and thus for the conscious, intellectual aspect of the human psyche that was largely responsible for bringing all this to pass.

And at the end of the road lay the Promised Land, the Kingdom of Heaven on earth whose very definition had always been enshrined in the words 'Thy will be done.' 'Thy will', that is, as enshrined in man-made Holy Writ.

Yet all this was to be bought at a price. Focusing the human will has its dangers. In promoting a single, almighty godhead to serve as a symbol for the rampant conscious mind, triumphant over all its enemies and determined to destroy them for ever, you inevitably banish all the other aspects of the human psyche to outer (or inner) darkness, the place of wailing and gnashing of teeth. As the church traditionally maintained, you can't have a God without a Devil.

And so it was to prove. The wailing and gnashing of teeth duly took place. The rejected side of human nature was cornered, battened down, pushed under. The lid was screwed down. And as the inner, psychic pressure increased, the unholy mixture started to burst out at the seams in a paroxysm of mass-projection.

Not for nothing do focusing and projection go hand in hand in today's cinematic industry.

The result was a series of almighty bloodbaths. Religion and its symbols came to be seen as sufficient causes for conflict in their own right. There were wars of conquest, crusades, inquisitions, persecutions — even wars between different factions of the *same* religion. Indeed, if the various great monotheistic faiths have a particular claim to fame, it is that they have possibly given rise to more and bloodier wars than almost any other cause apart from simple, honest-to-goodness territorial disputes. One of the prime roles of the One God has become to act as the Lord of Hosts, the Commander of the Armies. Repeatedly it has been his symbolic banner that has led the troops into battle. Even though the blessing of the self-same god — under whatever name — has often been sought by the other side, too, in support of its own apparently satanic military efforts.

In the very nature of things, meanwhile, the intensity of the outer conflict was in due course to be reflected in the inner world, too. From about the time of the Middle Ages in particular, a ferocious battle started to be waged within the human psyche itself — a battle characteristic above all, perhaps, of the Christian West. In effect, it was a war to the death between the now familiar god of the conscious mind on the one hand and the ancient, irrational gods of the unconscious on the other. And it was stoked up by the

Church to an unprecedented degree with dire threats of eternal damnation and bizarre images of the most excruciating torments in the afterlife.

We today may have shaken off the more gruesome symbols of the inner conflict — or at least we have banished most of them to the modern battlefield, horror film or video nasty. Yet we are still pursued by the ghost of that obsession. Christian or non-Christian, most of us still spend our lives enmeshed in an eternal conflict between a righteous 'I' on the one hand and a subversive 'me' on the other. We suffer agonies of guilt, crises of conscience, as we try to satisfy the supposed demands of the still active inner godhead, even though we may long since have forgotten his name or replaced it with another — be it 'duty', or 'honour', or 'good', or 'right', or even 'conscience' itself.

Meanwhile the rejected gods have acquired new names, too. We call them neuroses and psychoses, and they besiege our lawcourts and consulting rooms no less determinedly than they formerly stalked the medieval streets. In times of war, it is true, we may feel rather better, slightly more 'together'. All evil seems to lie out there across the borders, not here at home. And so for a while, thanks to the familiar magic of group projection, we imagine that defeating our enemies will produce a land fit for heroes, peace in our time. But then the conflict ceases — and the problems return. The *angst*, the psychological illness, the inner and outer unrest, the social turmoil, the political chicanery, the crime, the drugs, the rape, the sheer inhumanity of man to man. All reminding us of the eternal gap between the ideal and the actual, the 'good' and the 'bad', God and humanity, conscious and unconscious, 'I' and 'myself'.

Of course it has long been so. But perhaps — just possibly — there was a time when happier counsels prevailed. A time when all the gods of the psyche could co-exist in relative harmony — or at least when it was unthinkable for any one deity, any one single inner complex or archetype, to get such an exaggerated idea of his own importance as to set himself up as an exclusive paragon of virtue and the sole arbiter of universal morality. The Greece of antiquity seems to offer just such a historical context of healthy pluralism.

And so the inevitable question poses itself: just how are we to get from here to there — from enforced, but failed unity, to spontaneous but fruitful diversity? How are we to make the conceptual journey from the obsessive dualism of our current culture, with all its evidently disastrous effects on our psyche and thus on our general health, to a more healthy, pluralistic psychological climate such as the Greeks seem to have managed to maintain through the medium of their myths?

Clearly there is a transformation of attitude to be undertaken, a personal and communal healing to be undergone. That healing in turn needs tools and a technology. And it is just such a technology that the world's major religions and spiritual cults — apparently sensitive to the urgent need that some of them themselves helped to create — have long claimed to supply, while the occultists and esotericists, for all their suspicions of such claims, have nevertheless turned to very similar tools of healing.

5 IN QUEST OF WHOLENESS

Nowhere is symbolism more blatantly or more consciously used than in the sphere of the spiritual and the occult. In the age-long quest for inner wholeness and transformation, in the search for arcane healing and regeneration, the symbol reigns supreme.

So vivid and disturbing is this symbolic world of gods and spirits, of ritual gestures, secret talismans and words of power, that its fame has penetrated well beyond the locked doors of the cultic sanctuaries. Mention symbols to the man in the street, and more likely than not he will think of witches and black magic, of upturned crucifixes and five-pointed stars. Or possibly of the secret ceremonies of the Freemasons and Rosicrucians.

And this notwithstanding the fact that in politics, too, the image is all, or that the same man in the street unconsciously allows the symbols that he sees every night on the television to influence his choice of car or his wife's choice of groceries at the supermarket (I refer, of course, to sex-roles as they are, not necessarily to sex-roles as they ought to be).

I have already referred briefly to a number of primal symbols of the collective unconscious which are co-opted by occultists, magicians and others in their arcane rites and ceremonies. Sun and Moon as divine tokens of the archetypal masculine and feminine, of activity and passivity, of constancy and fluctuation, of intellect and intuition, of life, death and rebirth; the Tree as the cosmic link between Underworld, Earth and Heaven, and thus as the ancient, shamanic 'Jacob's Ladder' between physical and spiritual, conscious and unconscious; the Tower as the phallic representation of firmness and stability, of determination and idealism; the Eagle as the lordly embodiment of the unfettered Divine and the ultimate triumph of spirit; the Serpent as the manifestation of the dark powers of the Underworld and of the unconscious, whether for self-renewing life or for death, whether for health or for sickness, for good or evil; the Circle as a prime icon for eternity and infinity,

for spiritual wholeness and perfection, for healing and completeness; the Square as the sign of the physical, of rationalism and
materialism; the Phallus, Club or Wand as the very image of
masculine drive and aggression, of male sexuality and fecundity;
the Cave as the vaginal or uterine repository of the dark, feminine
mysteries surrounding birth and regeneration; the Sacrifice and
the Scapegoat as tools for manipulating the powers of the psyche
through sheer projection; the Seed and the Egg as universal
talismans of hidden life and magical rebirth; the Star — whether
five- or six-pointed — as the image both of the Divine and of the
Satanic, as well as of the human soul itself; the Cross, in its myriad
forms from swastika to ankh or crux ansata, as a prime symbol of
humanity amid the cosmos, standing at the crossroads of spirit
and matter, of space and time — all these and more are not only
universal symbols, thoroughly familiar (largely through the
medium of dreams) to the deeper psyche of humanity world-wide,
but also have their immemorial place in the magical pharmaco-
poeia.

And this because, given the right psychological context, their
very universality virtually guarantees a vigorous response —
whether it be an uncontrollable crawling of the spine, the hair
standing on end, or merely an overwhelming sense of excitement,
awe or dread.

The method of application varies with the tradition involved.
But the basic principle is both clear and common to all traditions
— and by no means confined to the sphere of healing. It is the
familiar principle of 'bad out; good in'. Just as we immemorially
send away from us as fast as possible all those things (and people!)
that have become symbols for what we reject — our suppressed
emotions, our fears, our ideas of 'wrong', our problems and
illnesses — so we avidly bring near to ourselves whatever symbols
seem to us to stand for what we approve of desire — our
acceptable emotions, our cultural ideals, our ideas of 'right', our
health. It is the very presence, the sheer, intimate closeness of the
healing symbol, in other words (be it a thing or a person) that in
itself makes us feel whole.

That having been said, the perspectives and procedures of
medieval alchemy are not necessarily the same as those of African
tribal lore, Siberian or North American Indian shamanism,
ancient Greek cultism, traditional Hinduism or Tibetan Buddhism. All have their preferred rites, ceremonies and healing-

techniques. Yet towards the end of the nineteenth century a group made up largely of Freemasons and Rosicrucians, welded together under the banner of the enormously influential Theosophical Society, managed to bring some of these traditions — notably the oriental ones — together under a single, if rather loosely defined umbrella.[25] Subsequently a whole range of splinter groups, ably abetted by the efforts of occultists such as Aleister Crowley, did much to promulgate and publicise them further. And the results are still to be seen today in the literature, rites and ceremonies of a variety of cults and organisations ranging from AMORC (the Ancient Mystical Order of the Rosy Cross), through post-theosophical groups such as the Lucis Trust and the Anthroposophical Society, to the Atlanteans, the Aetherius Society and a host of other, relatively harmless esoteric coteries which operate far from the public view and come to the fore only at the various Mind-Body-Spirit festivals and Psychics-and-Mystics jamborees.

In all of these movements, symbols of various kinds — ranging from those already listed to the actual, apparently flesh-and-blood figures of supposed Himalayan Masters and extraterrestrials — are used as points of focus, tokens of new possibility, catalysts of transformation. Somehow they serve to anchor the awareness of participants, however briefly, in a much deeper level of the psyche than usual, so permitting them new insights and new perspectives, much after the manner both of dreams and of the now-familiar psychotropic drugs such as LSD. And onto them, consequently, can be projected the particular grace of healing.

Moreover, the symbols of the occultist had, and still have, their undoubted effects. People are changed, their attitudes revolutionised, their whole being charged with new energy. But at this point the subject of motive insists on rearing its inconvenient head. Certain questions need to be asked. Why do the occultists undertake their extraordinary work? For whose benefit is it? Who, if anyone, is transformed? What is the motive for such transformations? And what, in practice, are the results of such endeavours?

Unfortunately the answers ar not universally encouraging.

The occultist who uses symbols in an effort to work his will on others is clearly, from the outset, a deluded soul in the grip of egomania. The occultist who uses them to transform *himself* may seem more honest, but is in fact just as deluded. For a start he is assuming that he is somehow separate from the self whom he would transform. Yet this means that either one or the other has to be illusory — a fact which necessarily knocks the legs from beneath the whole project. And in the meantime this very attempt to pull himself up by his own bootstraps reveals him to be intrinsically divided down the middle, fundamentally flawed, and thus in no position to impose on himself — still less on others — symbolic cures and other measures whose effects are likely (as we shall see) to be temporary at best, if not actually harmful in practice.

The apparent personal changes, in other words, are just that — apparent rather than real. The aura of knowledge and power, of authority sanctioned by higher intelligence, is largely a mirage, even though the occultist himself may be totally convinced that it is all the genuine article.

The only way out, then, would seem to be to seek some archetypal sage or guru 'out there' who *has* managed to make the grade. Some being so patently suffused with wholeness and psychic perfection as to be able to confer the benefits of such symbolic exercises on oneself *without any suspicion of self-seeking or danger of basic illusion.*

You may look for such a being, but the paradox is that you are most unlikely to be able to find him. From time to time, it is true, you may come across some would-be guru with such pretensions. But unless you are so addicted to your own delusions as to be unable to see what is in front of you, it will soon become clear that he is not what he seems. And despite the familiar conviction that somewhere, somehow, the ideal Perfected Being must exist — despite, too, persistent second-hand reports that *others* have found such a saviour — somehow you yourself never manage to find him.

Or perhaps, in the teeth of all probability, you *do*, only to discover that, while his sheer presence helps — as that of a true symbol of healing always will — he absolutely refuses to perform the definitive magic that will send you away whole and perfect, and with your problems banished forever. And so you are reduced either to staying with him for the rest of your life or to collecting what relics of him you can, taking his picture home with you, perhaps even making a symbolic sanctuary to contain them and so 'enshrine' his continued healing presence . . .

•

Perhaps, then, this is the natural point for religion to enter the picture. For, typically, the world's great religions tend to assert that the Perfect Being who can transform and heal you *did* exist once, or perhaps still exists, but in purely spiritual form — the god, the avatar, the redeemer. And so you can happily persist in your beloved, projection-based delusion of a saviour from 'out there', since you can now explain why you cannot perceive him physically. Moreover, his symbols are still there, only waiting to bring you what you desire. Your quest, it seems, is over.

So it is that the popular religions duly claim their share of devotees, all anxious for self-healing, self-transformation, self-justification. And at this point the age-old magic of symbols swings into action once more.

But in virtually no case are those symbols the exclusive copyright of the religion concerned. Surprisingly, perhaps, they are merely the old, familiar symbols of the collective unconscious in a new — or even a very old — disguise.

Almost every symbolic feature of the Roman Catholic mass, for example, has its roots in an antiquity far more remote than Christianity — in some cases far more remote than the evolution of modern conscious thought itself. The candles, the incense, the bells, the chalice, the wafer and the ritual movements all pick up themes that were as universally present in the ancient primal psyche as they still are in the dream activities of the modern human unconscious, be it Christian or otherwise. The words, for obvious reasons, do not go back so far, yet many of them derive directly from ancient Middle Eastern antecedents in the dying-and-rising saviour cults of Mithras and Adonis, Attis and Tammuz,[8] and in turn conjure up primal associations which *were* around before language appeared on the scene. The chanting has a similarly ancient ritual pedigree. The church's symbolic year, for its part, follows closely the pattern of the former pagan calendar. And the symbolisms of its buildings, its organisation and its vestments all derive directly from earlier cults whose own symbolisms were rooted firmly in the former dispensation of total mystic involvement.[24]

It might, of course, be thought that the cross at least is something new and original. But no. Even that — like the crescent moon of Islam and the Buddhists' swastika — is firmly rooted, as we noted earlier, in the natural workings of the unconscious. Regular manifestations of all three are to be found both in primeval antiquity and in the present-day dreams and obsessions of people of all cultures and spiritual traditions.[5,15]

Baptism and marriage, confession and absolution, penance, litany, prayers, hymns and eucharist — there is not one of them that is not pregnant with the symbolisms of an age long before the coming of Christ, and even of civilisation itself.

Such is the antiquity of the tools with which the Church seeks to transform and heal the soul, or deeper psyche.

Yet sheer age, it seems, is no drawback. These primal symbolisms, many of which were already thoroughly familiar to the cults of ancient Greece, are still very much alive and active. For the faithful they still retain much of their ancient power. In their presence, at least, many do feel healed, uplifted, strengthened, however much the problems tend eventually to resurface and the symbolic cures themselves to become addictive. For such people at least, their chosen god is still hard at work, his ancient and at first sight preposterous claims of omnipotence and exclusivity amply justified by the apparent power of his acts and the manifest effect of his co-opted symbols within the suffering soul.

But what of the *un*faithful? What of those who have long since come to regard the Church as old hat, Christianity as a bygone creed, Holy Writ as a mere dead letter?

Ever avid for symbols, such doubters tend to turn in ever greater numbers to other symbolic systems, especially to those of the Far East. *Mantras* (spells and sacred incantations), *mudras* (ritual hand gestures) and *mandalas* (meditative designs), the language and ritual and exotic accoutrements of Hinduism and Buddhism — such symbols have found a new lease of life in London or New York or San Francisco. A good deal more so, indeed, than the actual teachings or philosophical ideas which lie at the basis of either system. Far from actually changing the way I think and act in my daily life, it is far more important (or so it seems) that I say the right words, chant the right chants, wear the right clothes, perform the right ritual gestures. For these are symbols of salvation, tokens of enlightenment, which allow me to transform myself as though by magic and so spare myself the disagreeable necessity of actually doing anything practical about my problems and inadequacies on the ground.

And even those who drop out of religion altogether, opting instead, it may be, for any one of a number of materialistic and/or socialistic sects, find themselves falling into exactly the same trap, which in this case is compounded by the unconscious conviction that they can somehow change themselves by operating on the world 'out there' (otherwise why would they wish to change it?).

Meanwhile, in the religious sphere, all manner of alternative cults take advantage of the new situation to raise their ugly — and sometimes shaven — heads, all eager to jump on the symbolic bandwagon. Borrowing symbols from left and right as the frenzy takes them, they assure their devotees that truth and wholeness can be attained merely by the use of magic — the magic of joining the right crowd, of donning the right garb, of performing approved types of meditation, singing the right songs, and above all using the correct jargon.

For some, of course, even this is too much. So obviously fake is the whole 'alternative', 'New Age' group-phenomenon, so obviously doomed to failure the materialistic and/or socialistic alternative of trying to transform the world — and thus the human psyche itself — by purely physical means, that they would rather sit at home and read a book.

Not realising, of course, that they are now in danger of turning *the book itself* into a symbol. Which is no doubt why, in the end, even the reading of books seems incapable — any more than any other of the activities I have mentioned — of bringing about any real and permanent changes in myself.

True, I may feel temporarily uplifted, elated, justified, even saved. But unless I frantically substitute symbol for symbol, magic for magic, book for book, in the end it all comes crashing down about my ears again.

Leaving me, if anything, worse off than before.

•

Why is it that the symbolic process, apparently full of potential and pregnant with possibilities, so often seems to fall down in this way? Why does it seem incapable of bringing me permanent salvation, definitive transformation? Why is it apparently incompetent to bring me the healing that even the humble family doctor claims to provide?

Perhaps the contrast is more imagined than real. Looked at more closely, the work even of the family doctor is seen to suffer from many of the same drawbacks as its more esoteric counterparts. And this because — surprising as it may at first seem — much of what goes on in the doctor's surgery is itself purely symbolic in nature. The doctor, with his proverbial bedside manner, fulfils much the same role as that of the immemorial priestly confessor, ready to take on the burdens of your soul. As for the fact that the doctor is able to *name* your illness, this has an almost immediate palliative effect. True, all that has generally happened is that he has told you in Greek and/or Latin what you yourself have just told him in English. ('Doctor, doctor, I've got a rash on my skin and it won't go away!' — 'Don't worry, you've just got chronic dermatitis.') Yet the naming of names has had one important benefit. It has turned the illness from an unknown inner process into a known *thing* — a thing which can be be projected 'out there' and consciously related to (i.e., in this case, rejected). Hence the sudden feeling of relief, of being back in control, of renewed hope for the future.

The production of the regulation pills is even more effective. Often it is immaterial what the pills actually contain, as the well-known 'placebo effect' demonstrates. What is important is less that they are powerful drugs than that they are recognised as symbols of recovery and wholeness, that the power of healing has been projected into them. And so, in giving you your pills, the doctor has 'given you healing'.

What more natural, then, than that you should immediately feel better?

But then you run into the usual problems. Not only may there be unwanted side-effects. There may also be the problem of relapse. The next week, unless some real changes have taken place within you, you are back at the surgery. Evidently you have not been healed after all. The symptoms were merely given a brief holiday.

The same problem bedevils symbolic healing of the more religious sort. Visiting the sacred grotto, kissing the saint's icon, bathing in the holy spring, embracing the divine statue, lighting the blessed candle, receiving the sanctified host — all can have quite magical effects, for a while at least. Yet unless something else changes as well — something deep within the psyche of the sufferer — the symptoms will come back again. And so the time will eventually come for a return visit. The habit of the annual pilgrimage will have begun.

•

Virtually all healing therapies suffer from this general drawback, a fact which is enough to suggest in itself that the therapies themselves are all basically symbolic in nature. Conventional and 'alternative' therapies alike, in other words, seem to work at least as much through the mechanism of symbolic projection as they do through any presumed chemical or neurological adjustment.

And especially is this so in the case of the 'alternative' therapies.

If your preferred treatment is herbalism, then the herb is the outer token; if acupuncture, then the prick of the needles; if chiropractic, the pressure of the healer's hands on your back; if acupressure or shiatsu or reiki or reflexology or the metamorphic technique, the more localised pressures of the healer's fingers; if radionics, the celebrated Black Box (which even most practitioners admit works just as well if full of nothing but sawdust); if rebirthing, the breath; if psychosynthesis, in all probability the healer's own person; if Jungian psychotherapy, the insights of the therapist; if psychiatry, the scratching of the doctor's pen; if colour therapy, the coloured light; if aromatherapy, the various smells with which you are assailed . . .

Or whatever other symbolic images you care to abstract from what actually goes on at any given session.

The very fact that all these therapies will quite happily claim to treat *one and the same complaint* helps to emphasise their essentially symbolic nature. The healing comes not so much from the technique itself as from the natural healing process — hitherto, it may be, unaccountably 'blocked' — which it sparks off in the patient.

And this it seems to do by basically symbolic means.

How else could it be that therapies with such fundamentally different understandings, approaches and techniques could all apparently achieve the same result?

How else, too, could it be that the familiar pattern of relapse nearly always follows (as we have already seen) unless the patient has in the meantime changed his or her way of life — or is merely suffering from some everyday, short-term ailment?

How else is it, in consequence, that the healers manage to make such a steady living?

•

What emerges, then, is that permanent and effective healing, i.e. true wholeness, is not to be achieved by partial approaches of any kind whatsoever. The only satisfactory answer has to be some kind of *holistic* approach, one which involves healing the whole person, *complete with his lifestyle, his attitudes and his relation-ship to the perceived world around him.*

As indeed most of the alternative healers are only too ready to admit, at least in theory.

If there is no such change, any healing is likely to be both partial and illusory — and, where deep seated illnesses are concerned, only temporary into the bargain.

The symbol, it seems, has its place — be it pill or mixture, herb or gismo, icon or ritual or god — but it is not sufficient in itself to bring about healing. Something further is needed.

Where, then, to begin?

•

First of all it is clearly important to ensure that the healing symbol itself is *appropriate* — preferably one which has arisen naturally and spontaneously out of the patient's own unconscious, rather than one that has been imposed arbitrarily by a healer or a religion with a particular axe to grind. Left to itself, the unconscious is perfectly capable of indicating what symbol is appropriate through dreams and other symbolic activities — including those of everyday life — *and it is in fact far better left to do so.*

Step one, then, is not to use symbolic violence on yourself, or to allow anybody else to do so on your behalf. Instead, allow the healing symbol to arise of itself out of your own dreams, symp-toms and other spontaneous experiences. In this way you can be sure that you are using the right tool for the job — a symbol which has meaning *for you.*

It is precisely this approach that is followed by the healing method that I shall be describing later in this book.

This having been done, the next vital step has to be to *take responsibility for your own healing* — for if you are to be changed, then it is you who must do the changing.

The point may seem obvious. But actually it lies at the root of the whole problem.

Properly chosen, the symbol will do its job. But that job is merely to make it possible to see 'out there' what is really going on 'in here'. By manipulating the symbol you may even be able to disturb and shift the inner problem a little — for a while, at least. But if you push the process too far and too fast, the outer token will no longer truly reflect the inner reality, and the symbolic link will break down.

The secret, then, seems to lie in using the symbol as a kind of lever to shift the problem for a little while. Then, while it is temporarily off-balance, you can slip a new piece of 'psychic muscle' underneath it, so that it cannot fall back into exactly the same place as before. That new 'psychic muscle' will be the direct result of deliberate changes of lifestyle, attitude and thought-habit on your part. Repeat the process a few times, possibly changing the original symbol for another, and eventually you will have the problem exactly where you want it — or rather the space formerly occupied by the problem will be totally taken up with 'new psychic muscle'.

In short, you yourself will have changed. And in changing you will have ensured that the problem no longer has anywhere to lodge.

This approach, too, is basic to the general healing technique apparently pioneered by the ancient Greeks, and which I shall shortly be going on to describe.

•

While symbolism, then, is not itself a panacea, it can prove a valuable catalyst in the healing process. Possibly this is precisely the way in which the unconscious uses it all the time, whether through our dreams or through our everyday waking experience.

For it goes almost without saying that the two have long since become almost interchangeable. Even our waking world, as we saw earlier, is nowadays peopled almost entirely by our own unconscious projections, which duly show us what we are doing to ourselves and in what direction salvation consequently lies.

We do not see the world as it is. We see it as we are.

Which makes all the more important our efforts to heal ourselves. For if we fail to do so, the world of our projections can only grow sick, and fail, and die.

As, indeed, it is currently showing itself only too liable to do.

6 EXORCISM AND THE SCAPEGOAT

Among primitive tribes there is one almost universal technique of healing — a technique which bears a direct, if uneasy, relationship to what I shall be describing as the Greeks' *theotherapy*, or 'healing of the gods'. A technique, moreover, which at its best combines well-tried techniques of projection with the prime healing requirement of change of lifestyle. And it starts in a familiar way.

Today, just as long millennia ago, the tribal witch-doctor or shaman performs an intricate ceremony, full of smoke and sound and herbs and magic words and ritual, to encourage the patient to project his sickness onto some unsuspecting entity 'out there'. Enveloped in a social womb of throbbing co-humanity, the patient, close as he still is to the primitive form of awareness which we have described as a state of mystic involvement, is generally only too willing and able to oblige.

And lo! Suddenly, amid a paroxysm of muscular twitching and screaming on the part either of patient or of healer, the disease — or the entity held to personify it — is seen (at least by those present) to transfer to whatever entity has been designated by the witch-doctor to receive it.

Often this will be a carefully chosen animal. And not just the species in general. An actual goat or pig or chicken is brought into the tribal arena. Once the sickness has been symbolically inflicted on it, the creature may be shouted at, beaten or tortured. Then it is sent away, chased far into the bush. Or else ritually slaughtered.

Such is the nature of the scapegoat phenomenon. Whence, of course, the term.

Alternatively, the blame for the disease may be laid on some malign ancestor, generally in terms of his or her surviving spirit. In this case, once the symbolic transfer has been made, the spirit is bawled out, insulted, pleaded with, banished — and eventually, by hook or by crook, persuaded to go away.

At other times the spirit in question may be deemed to have no special connection with anybody or anything present. It is merely a malicious demon or god that has wandered in from the wild — or been summoned thence by some evil sorcerer — and so must be persuaded to depart again in the shortest possible order. Or, to put it another way, the projection mechanism has been refined to the point where the disease can be focused not just on something physically present or visible, either now or formerly, but on a mere abstract concept which never related directly to anything tangible in the first place.

There is, as we shall see, much mileage to be gained from such an approach, if treated with due circumspection.

All of these forms of exorcism — for that is what they amount to — are to be found in today's primitive societies world-wide, a fact which suggests that they represent a kind of inbuilt, instinctive healing mechanism to which we all are heirs. A mechanism which projects onto objects 'out there' not so much healing as the *illness itself*.

This technique is one which is even reported in the Bible in connection with the healing ministry of Jesus. Again and again we find him casting out 'devils' in the name of healing, and in one case at least the supposedly malign entity involved rends and tears its victim — just as in the more primitive, tribal context — before departing in the universally approved manner. In another case we find an illness, or rather the 'devil' associated with it (the entity insists on being called 'Legion' because, it says, 'there are so many of us'[31]), being projected onto a herd of two thousand pigs, which duly rush — or possibly are pushed — over a cliff to their watery doom.

Exactly as traditional scapegoat symbolism requires.

(This incident carries with it an obvious hint that there is actually a possibility of 'multiple haunting', much as our later consideration of theotherapy will also suggest.)

What is even more interesting is that Jesus, after his various cures, generally recommends to his patients that they alter their subsequent lifestyle for the better in some significant way (the practice once again reflects the best shamanic tradition).

As well he might. For, once again, the familiar problem of relapse is likely to arise if the symbolic exorcism is not accompanied by some additional effort at personal change on the part of the patient.

'Go, and sin no more,' are his most frequent and well-known words on such occasions. The injunction clearly recognises that feelings of guilt are one of the commonest causes of mental, and thus psychosomatic illness in highly moralistic societies, such as that of Jesus clearly was.

Jesus himself on one occasion (Mt. 12:43) dramatised the phenomenon of post-exorcismic relapse in unmistakable terms. 'When an unclean spirit comes out of a man it wanders over the deserts seeking a resting place, and finds none. Then it says, "I will go back to the home I left." So it returns and finds the house unoccupied, swept clean, and tidy. Off it goes and collects seven other spirits more wicked than itself, and they all come in and settle down; and in the end the man's plight is worse than before.'[31] (Once again, it seems, we have a reference to the possibility of 'multiple haunting'.)

Such has always been the risk where exorcism is concerned. The symbolic act itself merely provides a breathing-space. *If nothing else is done*, the patient's condition is in due course liable to worsen again, possibly even to a far more serious degree than before the treatment was undertaken.

Clearly, then, to play with exorcism is to play with fire, unless the mechanics of the process are fully understood. The scapegoat phenomenon has its uses, as we shall see in our consideration of theotherapy, but only as a temporary prophylactic, a tool to create space for a real effort at self-transformation. Blaming everything on *Them* is all very well, but it is *We* who need to change.

What, then, if a method of exorcism and healing were to be discovered *whose very performance necessarily involved a change of lifestyle*? Certainly such an approach would, *prima facie* at least, have a real chance of success. In practice there is evidence that such things are possible, even in quite primitive societies. Where the witch-doctor or shaman has sufficient power and social clout to insist that patients change their food, their habits, even their abode and way of life, real cures seem to happen.

To such good effect that the 'traditional healers', i.e. the witch-doctors of Nigeria, have long been officially reckoned by the

World Health Organisation to have a higher rate of cures than their 'Western' counterparts, the local psychiatrists and psycho-therapists.

And it is to a similarly primitive, but world-renowned tradition of healing that we shall therefore now turn our attention.

7 THE HEALING OF THE GODS

The Greeks of pre-classical times were as prone as any other primitive people to project their illnesses onto spirits and other entities 'out there'. Yet it was an 'out there' which, thanks to the phenomenon of mystic involvement, was still held to be inseparable from 'in here'. And so the free spirits that inhabited the rocks, trees, streams and other aspects of the natural world around them were at the same time recognised to be identical with their own familiar, inner daemons.

At basis, these spirits were wild and untamed. And it was the very fact that they were out of control that actually constituted the various illnesses.

How, then, to control them?

From the start it became clear that controlling them was in fact out of the question. What *was* perhaps possible was to propitiate them. They were, after all, powerful beings. Even banishing them might prove dangerous, lest they return in even more dangerous mood than before. The perennial lesson of the scapegoat was one that could not lightly be ignored. But by propitiating them, bribing them — going along with them, even — perhaps their goodwill might be gained, their co-operation achieved, their baleful spell to some extent mitigated. The symbol of illness might actually turn into a talisman of healing.

The scapegoat, in other words, must simply be allowed to be itself.

It was a very gentle, subtle idea. Basic to it was the notion that there was, as it were, a continual interplay between you and the spirits, between conscious and unconscious, as between human life itself and the life of the wild. Illness and healing were, in some mysterious way, one and the same. And so there was a balance to be struck, a dynamic equipoise to be maintained, if human health and happiness were to be assured.

Softly softly catchee monkey.

We do not, of course, have to credit the Greeks with the invention of the idea. The spirits that were eventually to be elaborated into the Hellenic gods had their origins all over the Middle East — from Crete, through Egypt, to Palestine and beyond. Some of them went back to misty, archetypal originals from out of the ancient Aryan steppes or the early tribal life of the lower Danube basin. Possibly they went back even further still. All of them were the stuff of dreams, symbolic entities which the primal unconscious had thrown up as natural symbols of illness — and thus of potential healing too.

And with them, no doubt, this same concept of propitiation, of wary co-operation. For how were you to oppose what was essentially part of yourself?

So that, by the time the gods as we now know them were finally assembled in pre-classical Greece, there were already some fairly clear ideas of how they might most profitably be dealt with.

Anyone suffering from a serious illness, whether of body or of soul, might present himself to a healer, who would apply what first aid he could. If the illness proved too deep-seated for him to deal with, he would then identify from the symptoms which god or goddess was feeling offended or neglected, and send his patient off on a pilgrimage to the appropriate divine sanctuary.* Here, in exchange for suitable goods or services, the sufferer would be initiated into the Mysteries of the local cult in an effort to placate the divinity involved and gain his or her favour.

He might be dunked in cold water, serenaded with the music of flutes or lyres, fumigated with aromatic smoke, treated with herbs of varying toxicity, stoned out of his mind with magic mushrooms, subjected to sessions of supervised sleep and guided dream-interpretation, frightened out of his wits, left for dead in a coffin, half-starved, kept awake all night, mercilessly teased, sworn at, harangued with verses from the sacred scriptures, forced to watch ritual dramas and ballets, presented little by little (and however symbolically) with every aspect of the cultic myth, muttered at, prayed upon, gesticulated over — and eventually brought before the god or goddess (or rather a symbolic substitute) in the innermost shrine of the temple. Then he would be sent away with some daunting long-term task to perform — one that

---

*At least until the advent (c. 500 BC) of the cult of Asclepius, the 'Divine Healer', whose centres may perhaps have corresponded to our modern teaching hospitals.

would actually entail changing his life in such a way as to conform
with the myth.*

The Mysteries, in other words, were essentially initiations, rites
of passage, celebrations of new beginnings.

Alternatively, or possibly as a diagnostic prelude to all this, the
sufferer might be presented to the local oracle — generally a
dishevelled, half-crazed priestess in a state of mediumistic trance
— who, with the aid of entrails, dice, mirrors, clouds, smoke,
dreams, flights or calls of birds, or mere chance overheard
remarks, would either point him towards the right treatment or
ordain a similar task or change of lifestyle, at the same time
throwing in some idea of his likely prospects for good measure.

Not all of this happened at once, of course, nor necessarily in
every respect. But all these activities and more are known to have
been performed, at one time or another, at the many Greek cult-
centres and oracles in the name of healing and regeneration.

Such, at least in part, was the *therapeia* — the 'therapy' — of
ancient Greece. The word, of course, meant 'healing'. But it also
meant 'worship' and 'service'. The three ideas were in no way to be
separated. Worshipping the god also meant *serving* the god. And
only out of that service could true healing ultimately come.

•

The whole thing was, of course, a regular industry. Much of it,
inevitably, was sheer hocus pocus. The priests and temple servants no doubt did very well out of it. It was their living, after all.

Especially was this so at Eleusis — sacred to the Corn Goddess
Demeter and her daughter Persephone, Queen of the Underworld.
Virtually overshadowed by the nearby city-state of Athens, this
celebrated cult centre was run by two priestly families who at
some point hit on the brilliant commercial expedient of throwing
open its Mysteries to all Athenians — indeed, in due course, to all
Greeks — of good standing and repute, more or less on demand.

The result was perhaps predictable. Making the pilgrimage to
Eleusis soon seems to have become socially *de rigueur* for cultured
Athenians, whether or not they had the slightest interest in what

*In the Egyptian and Greek worlds, no less than elsewhere, re-enacting the god's myth
was always, as it still is today in the case of the Christian Mass or Holy Communion, a
central feature in the process of enlisting the god's favour and regaining personal
wholeness.

the rite actually meant. It was all rather reminiscent of members of
the London social set making the annual visit to Glyndebourne.
And what they learnt from it, too, was of almost exactly compar-
able value. For virtually no information of any practical importance was imparted. A number of fanciful reports notwithstanding, the ritual secrecy traditional on such occasions in no way
implied the presence of any kind of 'secret doctrine': by and large
— and with the notable exception of the so-called Orphic Mysteries and the later school of Pythagoras, both of which seem to have
been the result of Egyptian or Asiatic influence, rather than of
native Greek thought — the Greeks did not go in for such arcane
antics. The real purpose of initiation into the Mysteries of Eleusis
was the same as at any other cult centre — simply to win the
favour of the divinity concerned.

Or, in the case of the socialites, to enjoy the 'experience' and be
seen.

For those few who *were* seriously interested there was, it is true,
something special about being initiated at Eleusis — for the
goddess Persephone was herself the female initiator *par
excellence*, her myth of death and rebirth the very myth of
initiation itself. But then the same applied wherever Demeter and
Persephone were worshipped, and not merely at fashionable
Eleusis.

Most of the other centres simply got on with what they were
designed for. As a result, they were often less famous. But at all of
them healing was definitely in the air. A sometimes violent and
startling form of healing, admittedly. But also a healing of a
particularly promising kind.

None of your ten-minute consultations, your instant pills, your
hastily written prescriptions. Instead, you were encouraged to
take extended time out, to experience a totally unfamiliar pattern
of living, to look at things from an entirely new perspective, to
have a break well away from the friends and family who might
well have more than a little connection with the causes of your
problem. And above all to make permanent changes in your way
of life, of a type capable of transforming it into a form of service to
the god.

Meanwhile you were given a massive psychic shock (very much
after the manner of birth itself) to symbolise a totally new
beginning. The vividly presented cultic myth that you were
henceforth urged to live out assured you that you and the universe

were engaged in a process that was far bigger than you alone. Your inner process mattered, just as the outer world mattered. And the success of the one reflected directly on the success of the other.

It was symbolism again, but symbolism of a kind which promised directly to alter your life for good or ill.

If only because, having once committed yourself to the god's mercy, you were unlikely to want to incur the divine wrath if you subsequently ignored his advice.

•

The gods were not concerned only with healing, of course. Their cults were involved in everything from ritual athletics, through agricultural development and power politics, to ceremonial atonement on a cosmic scale. Yet it was in the field of the psyche that they were always acknowledged to have their primary playground. And if so, then sicknesses of soul — what we should nowadays call neuroses (minor psychological problems) and psychoses (major ones), together with their psychosomatic manifestations in the form of actual physical diseases — were very much their business.

Now one of the marvels of the ancient Greeks' observation of such phenomena was the acuity with which they had isolated the typical symptoms of the various psychic disorders and projected them onto appropriate gods. Not only that, but it seems at some stage to have occurred to them that these symptoms rarely occurred in isolation. What seemed to happen when patients were stricken with a neurosis — and even more so in the case of a thorough-going psychosis — was that a whole panoply of symptoms (what Freud was to call a 'complex', and Jung was later to describe as an 'autonomous fragmentary psychic system') suddenly descended on them, both directly and as reflected in their social and family relationships. These various symptoms seemed to fit together so neatly and inevitably that it was almost as if a kind of autonomous sub-personality had temporarily taken over — a sub-personality which, like all personalities, had both its negative and its positive sides.

There were, indeed, actual flesh-and-blood people walking around who displayed given groups of symptoms *more or less all the time*. Here, perhaps, carrying her tightly-closed basket, was a heavily-veiled young woman who was both gullible and naive, who had both menstrual problems and a horror of sex, who was often depressed and possibly alcoholic, yet who was also incredibly beautiful and attractive to men. At the same time, possibly, she was incorrigibly shy and retiring, and liable both to lead them on and to back away in fright if ever she was taken seriously.

Across the street, on the other hand, there might be a young man who, having been seduced by his stepmother (whether literally or merely emotionally) and perhaps wrongly accused of rape, was now a refugee far from home, and prey to a fierce compulsion to drive horses and chariots with such reckless abandon as to be involved in many a dangerous spill. At the same time, by way of compensation for his earlier experience, he might be of a distinctly religious turn of mind, inclined to purity and chastity, severe of countenance, and an excellent athlete and hunter into the bargain.

To an ancient Greek observer, each of these individuals must clearly have been 'taken over' by the god or goddess whose projected characteristics most closely corresponded to their particular group of symptoms.

Their obvious vocation, therefore, was to become a priest or a priestess in that god's cult, or a servant in the nearest official sanctuary — in this case, the woman in that of Selene, the man in that of Hippolytus (see Part 2).

Meanwhile there were other individuals whose behaviour seemed perfectly normal most of the time, but who at odd and unpredictable moments — or, in some cases, perfectly predictable ones — could be 'taken over' by a completely unexpected set of symptoms associated with a given god or goddess. (Such people still exist today. Most of them insist, quite naturally, that their various sub-personalities are in reality 'spirit guides'. We call these people 'mediums' — a term which is particularly apt, since it reveals the role of the sub-personality in mediating between the deeper psyche and the conscious mind.) The obvious career for such people — most of them women, it has to be said — was thus to become a temple oracle, through whom the god himself might be expected to speak more or less on demand, possibly with the judicious assistance of suitable drugs or aromatic fumes.

Both 'priests' and 'oracles' could thus in due course find their predestined niche in society. Their various neuroses would no longer be problems, but positive professional advantages. They would be eccentrics, but in suitably eccentric situations; square pegs in square holes.

But to the ordinary man or woman in the street or, more likely, in the field, such oddities were often less welcome, especially if they appeared as it were out of the blue in what had previously been an apparently perfectly normal life-situation. At the psychotic end of the spectrum, particularly, they actually threatened to make that life impossible.

Which meant that these people, too, duly found their way into their inevitable role.

They became patients. Or rather postulants, neophytes, candidates for instruction . . .

•

In the course of time the foibles and peculiarities of the gods became better and more intimately known, as more and more of their human representatives could be identified and observed. The intellectually brilliant Apollo, with his homosexual tendencies. The dark and dangerous Artemis, the predatory virgin. Athene, the redoubtable embodiment of civilised values and the very pillar of society. Zeus, the rumbustious and over-sexed dictator, ever squabbling with Hera, his powerful but scolding wife. Dionysus, the noisy, irrepressible drunkard and sexually ambivalent adolescent. Hestia, the modest guardian and protectress of hearth and home. Aphrodite, the seductive and promiscuous sex-goddess, ever flaunting her considerable charms. Hephaestus, the lame smith, labouring at his forge. The distraught Demeter, mother and provider, desperately searching for her abducted daughter Persephone. Poseidon, the ever-menacing embodiment of sea and earthquake, and thus of irresistible subterranean rumblings generally. Ares, the brutal and churlish warrior. Hermes, the cunning, deceitful spirit of journeys and transitions. To say nothing of Pan and Eros, of Uranus and Gaia, and of a host of other gods, nature-spirits, nymphs, Titans, demons and translated heroes.

For all their divine or semi-divine splendour, all were portrayed with brutal frankness, in their true colours. There was no attempt at a whitewash or blackwash, as in theocratic Palestine or Egypt, still less at transforming the gods into metaphysical entities, walking thesauruses of philosophical concepts, as in equally theocratic India.

In relatively anarchic Greece the gods were revealed as gloriously and irrepressibly human (as, indeed, they actually were and always had been) and subject to few, if any, normal human conventions or inhibitions — as might be expected of true representatives of the unconscious.

The oddities and ailments of the psyche were displayed for all to see.

And those who would learn to cope with them now had the opportunity to learn to walk with the gods.

•

Thanks to the relatively early rise of lay literacy in Greece, we have an enormous amount of information on the natures of the various gods, dating (directly or indirectly) from as far back as the eighth century BC to the later Roman period. The poet Hesiod (c. 750 BC) left us a particularly copious body of information on the subject.

But if Hesiod was already able to assemble all this information at the time, then it is clear that the oral tradition on which he was basing his work went back even further into the past. The mighty Homer had himself been part of that long tradition. While putting precise dates on this archetypal and semi-legendary 'blind bard' is a matter of vast conjecture, not to say dispute, it is fairly safe to deduce that he lived at some point between the tenth and the eighth centuries BC. Yet on archaeological grounds alone it is clear that the events he describes in the *Iliad* and (if he in fact composed it) the *Odyssey* belong to a much earlier time even than this — say around the thirteenth century BC. Indeed, the *Iliad* in particular seems in its turn to be based very closely on earlier sagas dating from much nearer to the ancient epoch it purports to describe.

But this is not the half of it. For it is clear from the texts (which in all other respects seem to be remarkably free of 'cultural editing') that the originals of Homer's ancient characters *themselves* deferred to a whole pantheon of gods and goddesses who had, it seems, already been settled in their lofty mountain fastnesses since long before anybody could remember. So long, indeed, that they were seen to be just as much a fact of nature as Olympus itself.

The gods, in other words, were already ancient even in that remote age. And so it seems that we are talking of a tradition which dates not merely from the Bronze Age, but possibly from long before it. Comparative mythology confirms the conclusion.

Much of the mythical material, it is now clear (and as we suggested earlier), has its origins far back in the mists of Indo-European prehistory.

Yet not necessarily all of it. It is almost inevitable that a long process of accretion had occurred even by Homer's time. And the process is known to have continued since then.

It seems safe to assume, though, that no given accretion would have survived for long had it not been accepted by the various cults involved, and found to fit in with what else was known about the particular complex of characteristics that was represented by any given god. Only in the case of very late and purely scholastic additions to the various myths — additions with no possible relevance to actual ritual or healing practice — are we bound to bring a certain amount of scepticism to bear on the literature.

The word 'myth' is significant. For the accepted way of transmitting oral traditions in ancient Greece, as in other primitive cultures world-wide, was via the medium of story-telling. Often in the form of poetry, this not only ensured maximum attention on the part of the listeners. The very regularity of its verse structure made it far easier to remember the text, and far more difficult to omit odd words or phrases.

The practice still continues in remote rural communities even today, whether in the west of Ireland, in Turkey or in the Far East.

Our surviving information on the gods of ancient Greece, in other words, takes the form not of catalogues of positive and negative characteristics, but of connected narrative. We are presented with vast collections of stories, once oral, now recorded for all time.

And thanks to these stories, we are now able to reconstruct much of the healing system apparently practised by the ancient Greeks, and to apply it directly to our own lives.

•

It is, of course, a considerable undertaking. We have to decide how the various myths should be interpreted. Should we take them literally, or analyse them psychologically in the light of deep Jungian symbolism? How much of a given story has to survive to make it useful?

And — the central question — how accurate or practical are its insights likely to be anyway?

To such questions the information itself, once abstracted and tabulated, gives, as the following pages show, its own very clear answers.

For a start, it is evident that no very complete picture of the characteristics of any given god can emerge unless a fairly full biography has been preserved in the literature. Given a reasonable account, however, it is soon obvious that — unlike the case where little more than a name and a natural association survive — very little symbolic interpretation is necessary. The myths are for the most part remarkably direct in what they have to say. However valuable an in-depth symbolic analysis, a virtually literal approach seems to be both possible and desirable.

A fact which reduces considerably the risk of subjective 'editing' on the part of the interpreter.

In no way, meanwhile, does such an approach contradict the more 'psychological', Jungian attitude, since it is axiomatic to Jung's own teachings that the unfinished business of our inner life inevitably manifests itself, sooner or later, in what appear to us as literal, physical events and symptoms 'out there'.

As for the validity and accuracy of the system presented in the following pages, readers are invited to examine for themselves the Reportory of Treatments on pages 122 to 191. It is sufficient to choose a god whose characteristics under 'A' correspond to one's own problems — or those of any given friend or relation — to reveal how accurate or otherwise the other details are. Not only the symptoms, but also the suggested therapies, may well turn out to correspond in remarkable detail to what can actually be observed in practice. Indeed, the experience of those who have applied the system suggests that the 'hits' are far more frequent than one might expect — sometimes even quite astonishing in the broad spectrum of their accuracy and the depth of their insight.

And, that being so, there is at least a good chance that the proposed therapies may also be relevant, since they, too, are firmly rooted in the literary record.

In point of fact, simple observation suggests that the therapies and approaches offered are often what the more intuitive sufferers actually turn to of their own accord anyway, without the benefit of any such consciously-applied system. Many a literary biography also attests to this fact. Where the system promises to be especially useful is thus in encouraging such sufferers to persist with their current endeavours, while enabling the vast majority who are less intuitive, and more inclined to ignore their symptoms

— especially their inner ones — to benefit from such treatment too.

A fact which raises the possibility that the *therapeutic* content of literary biographies may be one of the factors that lie, if unconsciously, at the basis of their popularity with the reading public.

True, the sphere of psychic experience is not easy to be objective about (which is one good reason for humanity's use of projection to objectivise it in the first place). But the experience of therapists and patients world-wide is that the problems and illnesses of the human psyche continually reveal themselves in forms which accord closely with the recorded natures and deeds of the Greek gods.

Pure accident this may of course be. Yet, to the extent that it is the case, there is clearly no earthly reason why it should not be admitted and, in our case, put to good use.

•

The view originally put forward by Jung was that the gods are particular expressions of what he called the *archetypes* — primal, instinctive behaviour-patterns, common to the entire human race, which are forever active within the psyche, and which surface at particular moments of life in order to push us in this direction or that, according to the psyche's current developmental needs. Where these needs have a distinct personal, therapeutic component — in response to particular traumas and environmental pressures, for example — the archetypes often collect around themselves a whole galaxy of further, symptomatic behaviours which are not strictly archetypal (i.e. not built-in from the beginning). Yet even these, once constellated, tend to behave as perfectly cohesive and consistent entities, or complexes, and are comprehensive enough to be regarded almost as sub-personalities or — to use Jung's term — 'autonomous fragmentary systems' in their own right. The temptation is thus irresistible to give them a face — whereupon a further group of 'gods' comes into being.

In this way each complex, each family of symptoms, tends to throw up its own god or divine therapist. His or her function is both to embody and to compensate for our current psychic needs and problems.

Consequently the various psychic illnesses — perhaps *all* illnesses — should actually be seen as *paths of healing*. They arise in order to point the way towards our eventual attainment of wholeness.

Whenever a given archetype or complex surfaces, we can be sure that something needs to be done, some new initiative undertaken. The god needs to be recognised, acknowledged, deferred to. Not only in his or her negative aspects, but in his or her positive aspects too. Indeed, it is in encouraging those positive aspects that we are most likely to avoid the most damaging effects of their more negative counterparts.

The god, in short, needs to be honoured and served.

The obvious alternative approach would of course be to attempt to 'send the god away', somewhat after the manner of the traditional scapegoat. To the extent that this would necessarily involve recognising the entity involved, there might even be some degree of initial success. Yet, short of an almost miraculous and instantaneous change of attitude and lifestyle on the part of the sufferer, this path can lead only to disaster. The emerging contents of the unconscious are far more primal and powerful than the relatively Johnny-come-lately conscious mind, and will quickly return with renewed vigour and vastly worsened symptoms, much as has already been outlined in Chapter six.

There is, however, a 'third alternative'. This is the option which most Westerners nowadays pursue. And it is by far the most dangerous of all.

Briefly, it involves *denying* that the archetypes and complexes exist at all — whether as gods or in any other form. The conscious mind rules OK. And in its tightly-run kingdom there is no room for other principalities or powers — unless it be a single, monolithic Deity modelled very largely on the conscious mind itself.

The world is logical. Things are as they seem to be. There is a reason for everything. For every problem there is a rational answer. And Good will always triumph in the end.

Unrecognised and unrelated to, the emergent forces of the unconscious are, by this very act of denying them, freed (as we saw earlier) to wreak the utmost inner havoc. They start to behave rather like unidentified night-time intruders, or bulls in the proverbial china shop. It becomes impossible to guess where they will strike next. The patient is overwhelmed by forces that he cannot understand, struck down by dark, nameless fears which are dark only because he will not let them emerge into the light, nameless only because he will not name them, and fears only because he will not face them for what they are.

Yet this is an inadmissible state of affairs. The conscious mind, like the jealous Supreme Deity onto which it so often projects its wishes and desires, cannot accept that its authority is other than absolute. And so the patient turns to a familiar technique of the psyche, and projects all his symptoms onto people and objects 'out there'. An 'out there' which, thanks to language and the activities of the conscious mind, is now seen as totally and irremediably separate from the psychic 'in here'.

So it is that everything is seen to be *Their* fault. And out of that conviction a whole Pandora's box of disputes, confrontations, revolutions, wars and nuclear threats duly comes into manifestation, along with all their further, associated insanities.

Such, indeed, is the way of our world today. And consequently defusing the situation is not primarily a matter of peace conferences and hard-fought bargains and protracted negotiations. By far the most useful thing we can do is to start — each of us — by *withdrawing our external projections*. And this in turn means recognising what is going on within our own psyche, acknowledging once more the presence of the archetypes and autonomous psychic contents within us — in short, acknowledging and deferring to the gods. Which means taking responsibility for the only thing that, ultimately, we *can* take responsibility for — namely ourselves.

And so we come back to the realisation that it is all really *our own inner problem* — a function of the ever-changing psychic dynamic that is common to all of us, a manifestation of the additional distortions and imbalances that we as individuals have superimposed upon that inner programme in response to our personal circumstances. And of our need for some kind of inner therapy.

•

But just what form is that therapy to take?

As far as archetypal psychology is concerned, the typical post-Jungian approach has been first to identify the god in question, and then symbolically to interpret and re-express the various features of the appropriate myth as the patient's symptoms reveal them. Finally, other, known features of the same myths — again interpreted in terms of the symbolisms of depth-psychology — are used to work towards an eventual resolution. The myths, in other words, are treated very much as though they were the patient's own dreams — a procedure largely justified by the fact that much the same thematic material often turns up in both.

There can be no doubt that the approach is valid. Certainly it is capable of producing remarkable results. There are many ex-patients alive and flourishing today who have good reason to be thankful for it.

An *ex*-patient, after all, has to be a good sign for *any* system of healing.

There are a good many would-be Jungians, meanwhile, for whom even this approach is too direct and obvious. Having identified the myth currently being enacted by the patient, they proceed to treat the myth as if it were a kind of Rorschach test — a series of random inkblots onto which they can then project *their own* deeper insights.

Even this approach doubtless has its uses and produces its due quota of cures. But if it does so, the fact has little directly to do with the original myth, and even less to do with ancient Greek initiatic practice — except, possibly, in its oracular version.

At which point it is somewhat reassuring to recall that Jung himself was, in this respect, almost certainly not a Jungian.

•

Yet even the authentically 'Jungian' approach, with its careful exploration of the unconscious through the medium of the patient's projections, can never have been the one used by the ancient Greeks. The unconscious — in the Freudian or Jungian sense — was not even recognised as such until the early years of the present century. The *psychological* interpretation of ancient myths can have played no part in the ancient Mysteries, simply because the very idea of psychology had not yet been born.

To the ancients, the myth was simply the myth. Its effects on those who were involved in enacting it were direct, immediate and externally obvious. It was sufficient to dramatise it, to ritualise it, to bring its various aspects into objective form so that they could be related to emotionally, physically and mentally by the patient. Given only this, healing could come of its own accord.

It would be true to say, then, that the psychic healing of the ancient Greeks was conducted *almost entirely in terms of projections*.

This may seem a highly primitive and rather dubious state of affairs, until it is realised that the same is in fact true of psychiatry and most related forms of psychotherapy even today. Keen though their advocates may be to believe that they are dealing with 'real' meanings, in fact they operate almost totally in terms of *words* — which are, of course, every bit as symbolic in nature as the *non*-verbal symbols of the Greeks, and even further removed from reality itself.

The words, after all, are purely arbitrary symbols devised by the conscious mind, not natural products of the unconscious. Moreover, they operate, by their very nature, in terms of a divided universe and a divided consciousness — both of which are notions inherently inimical not only to the way in which instinctive symbols of healing naturally operate, but to the very nature of healing, i.e. wholeness itself.

Making the processes of the unconscious understandable to the conscious mind may *seem* a good idea — especially as true healing ultimately has to imply the construction of some sort of bridge between the two — yet the result of the operation can only be to present to the conscious mind not the true unconscious, but a verbal analogue of it that is really just as much a child of the conscious mind as of the unconscious itself.

This of course immediately raises the question of how it is that traditional psychiatry and psychotherapy ever manage to work at all. Possibly such success as they do enjoy is due largely to the fact that patients are encouraged not merely to consider, re-live and above all accept their problems, but to do so *in the presence of a healer.* Possibly, in other words, it is the placebo effect of the therapist's 'bedside manner', together with his enthusiasm for his own approach, that has at least as much to do with the healing as the particular therapy used. (Much the same applies, for example, to the relative success or otherwise of rival teaching methods in schools.) Quite conceivably almost any other technique would do as well.

As, indeed, the very existence of a whole mass of 'alternative' approaches would seem to imply.

•

It is neither the 'alternative' approaches, however, nor even the psychologically sophisticated and highly interpretational Jungian one, but the simple, direct, ancient Greek approach to psychic healing — or at least those aspects of it that can be recovered from the surviving records — that lies at the basis of what I refer to as *theotherapy*, as outlined in Part 2 of this book.

The method makes no deep psychological assumptions. It eschews profound symbolic interpretation. It imposes no violence. It employs no drama, no ritual, no special effects. It simply recognises that a given myth *is already being expressed* in the patient's own symptomatic behaviour. It goes on to suggest areas in which further, associated, symptomatic behaviour might be allowed space to happen quite naturally. It recommends specific activities that might help to facilitate such new behaviour. And it offers a range of appropriate symbols for contemplation, all of them drawn from the myth of the relevant god and the cultic practices formerly associated with it.

•

Meanwhile the gods themselves, the apparent actors in this whole drama, are of course entirely illusory. They are mere faces which our ancestors imposed on their own inner experiences — *and not, note, on other people*. Yet those experiences were, and still are, indubitably real and actual. And if we who live in a largely illusory world choose to put a further (and this time quite harmless) illusion to good effect in our attempts to cope with those experiences, who is to blame us?

Thanks to that ancient exercise in projection, we ourselves can now recognise our inner Olympus. The nameless within us can be finally and fearlessly named. And so the gods can come to us bearing the gift of healing.

We need do no more than accept the gift with both hands.

PART 2
THE PRACTICE OF THEOTHERAPY

We are still as possessed by our autonomous psychic contents as if they were gods. Today they are called phobias, compulsions, and so forth, in a word, neurotic symptoms . . . Where the god is not acknowledged, ego-mania develops, and out of this mania comes illness.

CARL GUSTAV JUNG:
Commentary on Richard Wilhelm's translation of
The Secret of the Golden Flower[39]

We are learning what other cultures always knew: to know ourselves we must know the Gods and Goddesses of myth.

JAMES HILLMAN:
Preface to
Facing the Gods[13]

We must do what the gods did in the beginning.

Ancient Brahmin text[7]

THEOTHERAPY:
INTRODUCTION AND GUIDE

The basis of the Greeks' practice of theotherapy lay, as we have seen, in associating given symptoms with given gods and goddesses. Thus, there was virtually nothing arbitrary about the initial choice of healing symbol. The god was no more than a traditional face that had been fitted to the symbolic symptoms *which the patient himself was producing.*

Already, then, the therapy was on the right lines, if our earlier analysis is to be regarded as valid.

Once the correct identification had been made, the divinity concerned now had to be propitiated, soothed and so eventually persuaded that he or she had been heard and duly co-operated with.

The method, in other words, was essentially homoeopathic. It was a case not of fighting the illness but of recognising and co-operating with it, in the realisation that all illness is essentially a tool of healing. More than that, the method involved fully accepting the emergent symbols of the unconscious and thus, by extension, the dark and often repressed parts of the psyche. Once again, then, the therapy was a psychologically healthy one, encouraging the further development of the inner human being in the direction that the illness itself had the function of suggesting.

The result of all this was not only a patient who, having listened uncritically to the messages of his deeper psyche and taken responsibility for changing his life accordingly, could return home potentially healed. It was also a human being who had taken a further, important step in his life-journey towards eventual psychic wholeness.

In neither case, however, was the process to be regarded as in any sense over and done with. The purpose of the therapy was not to confer instant 'normality' — whatever the term might mean.

Inwardly, the patient was simply taught, through recognising his god, to accept himself fully and unconditionally just as he found himself at that moment, so achieving the inner balance and integrity which alone could allow him to go on to the next stage of his inner development, unencumbered by inner blocks and conflicts. Outwardly, meanwhile, he was encouraged, not to try and 'fit back into' his familiar social niche, but to seek a new one entirely.

The blatant violence to the person that is involved in modern psychiatry's attempts to 'normalise' the patient was thus almost entirely lacking. There was no effort to abolish Olympus in favour of Zion. Healing was regarded as a step along the way, not as the end of the road. And so, as symptoms came and went and god succeeded god, initiation must forever succeed initiation.

•

Basic to our own application of the method, then, has to be the identification of our symptoms and other personal characteristics with the appropriate god. I include in the term 'god' the whole range of demigods, heroes, immortals, nature spirits and other mythical and semi-mythical entities of ancient Greece, since all of them were in due course to be absorbed into the general body of myth which not only lay at the basis of ancient Greek healing but also lies, thanks to the work of thinkers such as Plato and Aristotle, at the basis of a good many of our everyday thoughts and assumptions even today.[13] The *Directory of Symptoms* on pages 86 to 121 is designed specifically to aid that identification.

Using this diagnostic tool is extremely simple. It involves no more than glancing through the directory of symptoms and, as you come to your current symptoms and characteristics, reading off the names of the gods or goddesses associated with them. By and large, male gods to apply to male subjects, goddesses to females — but transexual 'hauntings' also occur quite frequently, especially where the more androgynous gods and goddesses such as Hermes and Dionysus are concerned. In such cases the gender terminology should of course simply be reversed.

The list is a long one. There is no need to be daunted, however. Just as 'your' pebbles are quite capable of finding you from among the millions of others on the beach, so 'your' symptoms and characteristics are quite capable of identifying themselves from the list. You can safely trust the unconscious, in other words, to do what it does best — namely, to present you with the right symbols at the right time.

And so you need do no more than focus your mind for a moment on your current problems or inner state — then allow your eye to skim lightly down the list in as relaxed and playful a way as possible, and without deliberately concentrating on each heading in turn. Almost at once, certain headings should start to jump out at you, almost of their own accord. And with them, the names of the appropriate gods.

As the process gathers momentum, you will normally find that the name of one god or goddess in particular comes up more often than the rest in connection with your most obvious symptoms and characteristics. Or possibly two or three of them seem to be primarily involved. Their names should quickly become quite obvious to you. Keeping a mathematical tally is normally unnecessary, though reading them aloud could help fix them in the mind. In fact, you will almost certainly have discovered your particular gods long before you have reached the end of the list. At which point you may be surprised to find that there are up to half-a-dozen of them. Perusing the list further may succeed in narrowing them down somewhat, or equally they may insist on maintaining their multiplicity. If so, there is no need to worry. The phenomenon is in fact a quite common one, particularly among people with complex personalities (or, alternatively, with very well balanced ones). There may even be positive advantages in this, since any suggested therapies that are common to all the gods involved can be virtually relied upon to be helpful.

This phenomenon of 'multiple haunting' may reflect the fact that all the archetypes are, by definition, forever present, if latent, within us. Their actual appearance together at any one moment may merely be a function of the fact that there is a considerable overlap between the characteristics of the various gods, just as there is between those of different people — not least because a single archetype can lie at the heart of a whole family of related complexes. Especially is this true of the major goddesses, almost all of whom seem to have started off life historically as Moon Goddesses or Earth Mother figures.

That having been said, however, your task at this point is merely to note the names in order of their apparent relevance to you. Which gods, in other words, most clearly speak to you from the list?

If some of your symptoms are missing from the directory, there is again no cause for alarm. The surviving records (even as somewhat amplified in the present directory) cannot possibly cover all possible symptoms and problems. (Nor, incidentally, is the list necessarily designed to work in reverse, i.e. as a reliable indicator of all the characteristics of any given god. For this, simply refer to the alphabetical listing on pages 124 to 192.)

And do bear in mind that your god or gods will almost inevitably change with time, in line with your changing symptoms — at which point it will be time for another consultation of the directory of symptoms.

•

Now the time has come to turn to the *Repertory of Treatments* on pages 122 to 191. But before doing so, be warned: when you turn to your prime god or goddess (or his or her runner-up) you may well find yourself confronted by aspects of yourself that you would rather not be reminded of. That, indeed, is quite likely to be a prime reason why that entity is currently 'haunting' you. You therefore need to decide at this point whether you can face that prospect.

If you are not at present ready to be totally honest with yourself, it could well be that you are not ready for therapy. Many people identify so closely with their problems that they actually become attached, even addicted, to them. It is as though they feared that, without them, they would cease to exist as people, or at least lose their current identity. If this is the case, then no therapy can possibly be of any use. There is nothing to be done but to wait for the symptoms to worsen — as they surely will — to the point where something *has* to be done. And that will be the time for therapy.

The decision is yours. Is the time for therapy now, or later? Are you prepared to be totally honest with yourself? Are you prepared to accept responsibility for yourself, to assert your power over your own destiny? Are you ready to make actual changes in your life?

If the answer to these questions is 'yes', then you should turn now to the *Repertory of Treatments* and find the god or goddess that you most frequently encountered in the *Directory of Symptoms*.

•

Under the name of that deity you will find two lists of characteristics labelled 'A' and 'B'. List A contains a broad spectrum of characteristics which most frequently appear as 'problems'. They are, so to speak, *negative* characteristics.

List B, by contrast, contains further characteristics that may strike you as *positive* qualities.

The first task, then, is to look through list A. How well do these characteristics correspond to your current problems?

You should not, of course, expect a 100% correlation — you are, after all, a unique individual. Indeed, it may be that what you have hitherto thought of as your main symptom does not appear at all. Even this is quite normal, since ultimately it is not individual symptoms, but the overall syndrome or complex that is producing them, which theotherapy seeks to address. It is sufficient, then, that the *majority* of the 'negative' characteristics should apply to your case. If they do, then you may well have found your current god. In fact, the very extent of your negativity towards these characteristics is itself an index of your resistance to the god in question, and thus of the urgency of the need for some corresponding *positive* therapy.

This having been said, it is probably as well at this stage to check your second and third choices of god as well. If either makes a better fit, transfer your primary allegiance. (There are further checks to come, so you can still keep a careful eye on your original choice as well.)

Bear in mind, meanwhile, that this part of the therapy, along with your perusal of the directory, corresponds to the doctor's diagnostic session. Be prepared to allow at least as much time for the whole process as you would for a visit to your local surgery.

•

Now turn to list B of your chosen god's characteristics. By and large, you are likely, as we have seen, to experience these as *positive* characteristics. Check whether these also fit your experience.

Bear in mind, at the same time, that one person's vices can be another person's virtues. It is possible, though relatively unlikely, that you will find characteristics in list A which seem 'positive' to you, and others in list B which seem 'negative'. This would be entirely acceptable.

It is important only that your characteristics should be listed *somewhere*. If they are, then you have found your god.

At the same time it is important to realise that not every god and goddess in the Greek pantheon can possibly be listed. The surviving records are not, in the nature of things, complete. Only those gods and goddesses have been included whose biographies are full enough to permit a reasonably reliable analysis of their main characteristics. Consequently, should you have any difficulty in identifying your god, this could well be the main reason. In such cases (which happily are rare) there is unfortunately next to nothing that can be done about it, short of seeking other forms of therapy.

•

Having identified the god who is associated with your symptoms, you are now ready to go on to the stage of *treatment*.

Bear in mind at this point that the object of the exercise is not to banish or suppress the god or goddess concerned, but to co-operate. And so, even before you consider the various direct therapies on offer, it is important to take a look at those characteristics that you have *not* identified as negative, i.e. in all probability, those in list B. Most of these, after all, are aspects of the god that are likely to be relatively acceptable and congenial to you, and which you could therefore happily express without in any way doing violence to yourself.

Ask yourself, then, how you can change your life to encourage or make room for more of these qualities. Are there new activities that you could take up? Are there old relationships, expectations, duties or habits that might better be dropped — especially ones imposed on you, whether consciously or unconsciously, by your parents? Are you really giving yourself a chance?

It is, after all, *you* who need that chance, not they.

Allow time to ponder these questions — and perhaps to raise with yourself the possibility of suitable new initiatives — before going on to the next stage of the treatment.

•

We now come to the various *therapies* on offer. In doing so, it is again important to realise that *all* the aspects of each god are really therapies. Every symptom of every disease is, as I pointed out earlier, really a tool of healing — whether because it has a direct healing effect on the underlying disease itself, because it fulfils some deep-seated psychic need (possibly rooted in childhood) or because it forces us to take appropriate remedial action.

Nevertheless, there are some actions which are more in the nature of acts of deliberate will than others — matters of choice, rather than of compulsion — and it is these that are listed here as therapies.

On inspecting the list, you will see that the therapies can be either few and far between, or rather overwhelming in their diversity. Be assured, this has nothing whatever to do with the hopelessness or otherwise of your case. It is simply that the amount of detail is determined almost exclusively by how well documented the myth of your particular god is.

So relax — and consider the various therapies in turn.

The first and most important of these is always to name and acknowledge the god or goddess in question — just as, in conventional medicine, the doctor almost always starts off the healing process by naming the illness. As we have already noted, this helps the patient to objectivise and relate to the symptoms — or, in this case, to the particular god or goddess involved. Use your own powers of projection to imagine the deity as a living, three-dimensional being. Name him or her. Welcome them into your life.

In this way you will allow your natural instinct for projection to work for you. Having projected your symptoms onto an entity 'out there', however imaginary, you have a better chance to come to terms with them.

But there is another beneficial result, too. For now you can start to use your god as a direct healing symbol, much as you might your personal guru. In the latter case the basic technique, you will recall, involves spending as much time as possible in his presence — the closer the better. And the whole thing inevitably starts with finding out all you can about him.

Similarly, then, you could read up everything you can find about the god in question (see, for example, the titles by Graves and Kerenyi listed in the Reference-Bibliography), to the point where you feel that you are really getting to know him or her. If you can plan your holiday itinerary to take in Greece or Turkey, you could then (where applicable) visit the god's traditional birthplace, explore the sites of the relevant temples and cult-centres. (Your therapy is likely to involve you in some kind of transition anyway, and so travel — the province of Hermes, the *god* of transitions — would be entirely appropriate at this stage.) You could collect pictures, figurines or statuettes of your god — however cheap, tatty or tourist orientated they may be. On your return home, taking a further leaf out of the guru-hunters' book of well-tried symbols, you could even use these and other mementos and souvenirs to set up a small shrine to that particular divinity in a corner of your room as a constant token and reminder of his or her healing presence (see Appendix B for details).

None of these further activities is essential, of course, but any or all of them could help.

Having brought your god as fully to life in your imagination as possible, you are now ready to go on to the other therapies listed. Consider each in turn, and establish whether or not you are drawn to it — or at least whether you are prepared to have a go. (You may even find that you have already taken up some of them intuitively — such is the archetypal power of the gods.)

Do not in any case be tempted to undertake any therapy that repels you, or with which you feel genuinely unhappy. Any such therapy is likely to do you more harm than good. You are a unique individual, and not every therapy is likely to be right for you.

By the same token, though, not every therapy that is right for you is necessarily listed here. You may discover that changing your diet, for example, has unexpected benefits. So, in the short term, may a brief fast, a long holiday or a complete rest. You may be drawn to particular colours (whether for clothes or for decor). You may find particular smells both attractive and soothing. You may find yourself captivated by forms of music other than those already listed (and in this connection it is perhaps worth pointing out that the word 'flute' in the lists could well include *any* kind of woodwind, and possibly even the organ, while 'plucked instruments' may well take in *all* types of stringed instrument, including the piano).

All can serve as therapies.

Again, many of the therapies listed can take forms today that were unimaginable to the ancient Greeks. 'Sailing' can nowadays take in power-boating, windsurfing and presumably other wind-based sports such as parachuting, parascending, gliding and hang-gliding. At this point they start to merge into 'flying', which can clearly involve much more than the mere flapping of wings. And 'hunting' may include bird-watching, big-game camera safaris, television nature programmes, detective work or even visits to the sales (i.e. bargain-hunting), and not merely the traditional bloodsports.

In all cases, however, it is your own natural preferences that should decide the issue. It is not for others to tell you which forms of therapy you *ought* to be using. What is conventional or expected has nothing whatsoever to do with it. You alone are responsible for yourself. Experiment, be open-minded, turn a totally deaf ear to what other people think. And if they persist, avoid them.

Trust your own feelings in the matter.

But then act. This is not a mere academic exercise. Careful consideration is needed, of course. But once you have chosen your therapy or therapies, that is the road for you. In which case follow it.

•

A special word, meanwhile, about the herbs that are occasionally listed. These, like all the therapies mentioned, are based on surviving accounts of the corresponding myths and of the cultic practices that formerly attended them. *It needs to be stressed that their effectiveness is no more guaranteed than is that of any single, given detail of the accounts themselves.*

It is possible that the herbs — whether tasted, smelt or applied externally — were originally designed as a kind of first aid, intended to treat certain of the symptoms until the main therapy could be set in train. But it is equally possible that their choice was based on pure association or sympathetic magic. Add to this the fact that their *modus operandi* appears to swing almost at random from the homoeopathic, via the allopathic, to the completely unknown, and it is difficult to avoid the conclusion that the herbal treatments are probably best avoided if possible. *Certainly they should be attempted only under the supervision of a reputable herbalist* (the term may well include qualified naturopaths and homoeopaths).

Indeed, their real function may in many cases be to act as *symbols* rather than as physical treatments. Many of them, after all, are frankly poisonous, and so may reflect on the physical level what the archetypal complex in question is liable to do to you on the *psychic* level if you fail to respond to it adequately. In which case the prime role of the herbalist may well lie not in prescribing the herb, but in telling you what it would do to you if you were actually to take it.

•

We now come to the gods' various *symbols* as such. Most of these are living creatures — plants, animals or birds. That is to say, plants, animals or birds are their outward expression. Inwardly they are designed to have their expression too. And so you may find that merely contemplating one or other of the images listed may have a soothing or otherwise helpful effect, especially if it is one to which you feel some natural affinity.

You may, if you wish, do this purely in the mind. But you will almost certainly gain a good deal more by obtaining, visiting or observing an example of it in the flesh, and then using *all* your senses on it — not merely sight, but hearing, taste, touch and smell too. If it helps, repeat the exercise regularly, especially last thing at night, to the point where the symbol in question actually starts to appear in your dreams.

Once again, though, if the effect is entirely negative, choose another symbol. It is the health of *your* psyche that is at stake.

Even then, it is quite possible that you will notice very little effect at all. We twentieth-century human beings — so far removed from the primal state of mystic involvement — have become almost as insensitive to natural symbols (in the waking state, at least) as we are to natural smells, changes in the weather and the position of the sun in the sky.

What we have instead, though, is a relatively highly developed intellect.

Failing any direct symbolic effect, therefore, the next step is not merely to *contemplate* the god's various symbols, but to *consider* them. Consider the implications of their size and shape and texture. Consider the way in which they move (if at all). Especially consider their life-cycles, the speed of their development, the stages of their transformations. For you, too, have some developing and transforming to do.

And from this consideration you may find some useful hints beginning to emerge.

•

The admittedly speculative notes which round off each god's or goddess's details are designed to help put that entity into some sort of context, and especially to help you bring him or her to life in your mind.

It is, after all, the human imagination which created the gods (as opposed to the pre-existing psychic realities which they embody). And it is *your* imagination that is above all important in establishing your relationship with your god or goddess, and so in setting in train the healing which he or she can ultimately bring.

'Ultimately' is the word to remember, though. Do not expect the healing to be instantaneous. The psychic neglect of a lifetime is not to be repaired overnight. The cure may take months rather than weeks, even years rather than months. The therapy may need, for that matter, to be persisted with for the rest of your life.

For its basic purpose, as we noted earlier, is not so much to 'make the god go away' as to enable you to co-operate. The therapy's job is to help you live with your problem, to accept it as part of yourself, to realise that it is in reality no problem at all unless you choose to think of it that way.

The therapy, in fact, could be seen as a kind of Olympian equivalent of the Buddhist Eightfold Path. Like its oriental counterpart, it involves the adoption of Right Views, Right Motive, Right Speech, Right Conduct, Right Livelihood, Right Effort, Right Mindfulness or Attention, and Right Meditation. But there is a major difference. For in this case the word 'right' means not some unchanging, previously laid down and virtually unattainable code of conduct — what today is often referred to, curiously enough, as an 'Olympian ideal' — but, quite simply, *what is right for you.*

By altering your life to accord with the particular myth that you yourself have chosen to express through your symptoms, you learn to accept yourself for what you currently are. You take responsibility for the whole of yourself, and not merely for those aspects of yourself which you consciously approve of. You put yourself back in touch with your own reality. And it is on that basis of acknowledged reality that your development as a human being — so long blocked, it may be, by your inner and outer

inconsistencies — can then go forward towards ultimate wholeness.

•

Finally, remember that theotherapy's function is not to enable you
to pigeon-hole other people according to their 'type' — tempting
though that prospect may seem to an ego still obsessed with its
own separateness. Nor, in the reverse direction, can anybody else
do your healing for you.

True, sensitive parents may well find it possible to apply
theotherapeutic methods to their children as a guide to suitable
forms of upbringing. Most mothers, in particular, understand
their children's true characteristics and motivations far better than
the children themselves — not least because the young (and
adolescents especially) are only too prone to fall prey to the Walter
Mitty syndrome. The result is that they are then incapable of
identifying their own true characteristics, and can pinpoint only
those which they would *like* to have.

Walter Mitty, it could be said, is the one 'god' who is totally
proof against theotherapy.

Outside the context of child-rearing, however, the system is
simply not designed for analysing and treating other people. The
chances are negligible that I, for example, could ever know what
makes you 'tick' in sufficiently close and intimate detail to make an
accurate identification of your various gods from the symptoms
list, even after years of acquaintance. Only you have that detailed
knowledge. The chances are equally negligible that you could ever
know which of the therapies listed would actually feel right to me.

The upshot is therefore inevitable. Theotherapy is essentially a
do-it-yourself job. Just as you are ultimately responsible for your
own illnesses and problems, so you are responsible for your own
cure. That responsibility cannot be delegated to others.

Admittedly, the world of ancient Greece had its fair share of
priests and priestesses, all of them devoted at least as much to the
cult of the middleman as to the service of the god. They have their
direct counterparts in today's would-be healers and psychothera-
pists. All have insights and explanations to offer, many of them
quite valid and highly interesting. And all will demand their share
of the benefits — whether pecuniary or emotional — which you
will eventually gain.

But symbols, as we established earlier, need no explanation.

They carry their own meanings. Whoever puts his explanations between you and your symbols gets between you and the truth.

And this for the very simple reason that those explanations are mere words, *which themselves are merely symbols for reality* — and arbitrary, artificial ones at that. And so, with symbol being substituted for symbol, truth flies out of the window, and meaning is no nearer than it was before.

Learn, then, from one aspect at least of the practice of the ancient cults. Unless there are compelling reasons to the contrary, *keep secret* the tryst with your god.

A theotherapist is a contradiction in terms. The healers are the gods themselves.

And therefore there is nothing to be done but to welcome the gods into your life — and turn to page 86.

NOTE

It is of course possible to be 'taken over' by gods other than the Greek ones. The human psyche world-wide has always thrown up a vast variety of gods, and continues to do so right up to the present day, whether through the medium of fiction or of actual history — exactly as was the case in ancient Greece. These archetypal psychological entities are often recognisable by the fact that their names can nowadays be preceded in English by the indefinite article. Thus, they can appear not only in expressions such as, 'He's a regular Hercules', or 'She was a perfect Venus'. They also crop up in more up-to-date forms such as 'She's a regular Lolita/Joan of Arc/Shirley Temple', or in more accusatory vein, 'Who do you think you are — Tarzan/Stirling Moss/Adolf Hitler?'

Yet the whole point is of course that there is no call either for condemnation or for self-accusation. It is perfectly acceptable at the individual level — and in most cases at the social level too — to manifest any one of the more modern 'gods', whether of stage, screen, sport, the arts or actual history. What is called for is not rejection (which can only make any problems worse), but acceptance — acceptance, that is, not merely of the more positive aspects of the complex involved, but also of its more quirky and uncomfortable characteristics, together with the advice for dealing with it which is generally expressed quite clearly in the story of the character concerned. These 'lesser gods', in other words, beg to be treated in much the same way as the 'major gods' of whom most

can be seen as simple variants. Even the appropriate healing
symbol is often prominent in the biographical account — whether
it be Cinderella's broom and slipper, St. George's spear, Joan of
Arc's male armour, Robin Hood's bow and arrow, Falstaff's
alcohol, Sherlock Holmes's cocaine, violin and magnifying glass,
John Wayne's hat, boots and gun, John McEnroe's tennis racket,
or Churchill's cigar.

Biography, then, is the key. Having once identified, imagined
and welcomed the 'god' involved, carefully studying his or her
story — reading the book, watching the film, following the series
— will often reveal suitable therapies to apply.

Or rather, a suitable life to live. For as the educational revolutionary A. S. Neill discovered from practical experience in the
course of his teaching, 'When the children are allowed to live out
their complexes, no therapy is necessary' — by which he meant no
additional, Freudian analysis. Allowed to be themselves, it seems,
people are naturally whole.

Much the same applies in the overtly religious context, too —
the one context where gods and other divine and semi-divine
entities continue to be allowed to act out their true natures in the
full light of day, even amidst the otherwise sceptical climate of
modern Western civilisation. Here one can as easily be hijacked by
Yahweh (Jehovah) or Allah, by Jesus or Mary, by John the Baptist
or Muhammad, by Satan or St. Paul, as inhabitants of the ancient
world regularly were by Isis, Osiris or Mithras, as a good many of
the Germans quite recently were by Odin/Wotan, or as present-
day Indians are by Shiva, by Vishnu in his incarnation as Krishna,
by Kali, or by any one of a multitude of local Mother Goddesses.
The *orishas* of West and Central Africa and of Brazil — often
disguised as Christian saints — likewise have their modern devotees.

Yet most of these cases to some extent represent 'willed hauntings' rather than naturally occurring archetypes. They are generally the result not so much of unconscious urges, as of deliberate,
conscious decisions, whether on one's own part or on that of one's
parents or compatriots.

Nevertheless, the recommended treatment follows the familiar
pattern.

First, identify the negative aspects of your involvement, be they
moralistic anger, bigotry, judgemental attitudes towards others,
narrow-mindedness, po-faced puritanism, scriptural legalism,

self-righteousness, feelings of superiority, elitism, over-paterna-
lism, ethical rigidity, extravagant ritualism, sentimental religio-
sity, idolatry, incense-induced feelings of sanctity, attachment to
psychic powers, delusions of invulnerability, paranoia, disrupted
social life, mistrust of the body, horror of sex . . . or whatever.
(And bear in mind that, unless the negative characteristics are
recognised as negative, no healing is possible, since there is no will
for it in the patient.)

Next, identify the *positive* aspects of the entity involved and its
associated teachings — and especially those aspects which you are
not currently experiencing in your own life. These may include
compassion, forgiveness, understanding, willingness to mix and
to listen, humility, self-sacrifice, healing, comforting, charitable
work, social reform, a capacity for fun and/or a love of music and
dance.

Suitable therapies might then involve taking concrete steps to
express these positive aspects in practice, whether individually or
within the framework of some suitable religious community.

And the traditional symbolic adjuncts of the faith in question
will duly help to focus and anchor the process within your psyche.

THEOTHERAPY: DIRECTORY OF SYMPTOMS

NOTE: This directory is designed to offer pointers to the various treatments listed in the next section, rather than exact descriptions of the gods concerned. See pages 71 to 85 for instructions.

abandoned as child   Eumolpus, Oedipus, Pan, Perseus
abandoner of own children   Tyro
absent from work   Demeter, Pan
absent-minded   Demeter
abused as child   Hippolytus, Niobe, Pelops, Tyro
accident-prone   Actaeon, Demeter, Helius, Hippolytus, Orion
acquisitive   Earth Mother, Midas, Niobe, Poseidon
actor   Dionysus, Muses, Narcissus
adaptable   Athene, Dionysus, Hermes, Thetis, Zeus
adder of insult to injury   Achilles
addicted to danger   Achilles, Caenis, Dioscuri, Heracles, Odysseus,
   Perseus, Theseus
administrator   Ares, Ariadne, Athene, Cronus, Hermes, Minos,
   Pelops, Perseus, Zeus
admirer of spirited women   Zeus
adolescent   Adonis, Apollo, Artemis, Dionysus, Eros, Ganymedes,
   Narcissus, Pan, Perseus
adolescent male beauty   Adonis, Eros, Ganymedes, Narcissus
'adrenalin junkie'   Dioscuri, Odysseus, Perseus, Theseus
adulterer   Aphrodite, Hippolytus, Zeus
adventurous   Achilles, Caenis, Dioscuri, Heracles, Hermes, Odysseus,
   Perseus, Theseus
aerial joy-rider   Ganymedes
aeronautics   Daedalus
afraid of change   Cronus, Hestia
afraid of dark   Pan
afraid of drowning   Tantalus
afraid of men   Daphne
afraid of own sexuality   Actaeon, Daphne, Selene, Thetis

afraid of rejection   *Narcissus, Niobe*
afraid of spiders   *Athene*
afraid of the future   *Cronus*
afraid of the new   *Cronus, Furies*
afraid of women   *Actaeon*
ageing   *Cronus*
aggressive   *Achilles, Ares, Artemis, Athene, Atlas, Caenis, Eris,*
    Uranus, Zeus
aggressive only when provoked   *Heracles, Perseus*
alcohol abuse   *Ares, Ariadne, Aristaeus, Centaurs, Dionysus, Fates,*
    Polyphemus, Selene, Silenus
alcoholic   *Ares, Ariadne, Dionysus, Selene, Silenus*
alienated from society   *Achilles, Demeter, Polyphemus*
all-concealing clothes   *Athene, Hera, Hestia, Selene*
all-devouring love   *Amazons, Artemis, Great Mother, Rhea*
all-knowing   *Zeus*
alluring   *Circe*
all-rounder   *Athene, Heracles, Hermes*
always counting   *Cronus*
always in erection   *Dionysus, Eros, Hermes, Pan, Silenus*
always laughing   *Hermes, Pan*
always on the go   *Adonis, Athene, Helius, Hephaestus, Hermes,*
    Perseus
always washing   *Artemis, Daphne, Furies, Hestia, Orestes, Tyro*
ambitious   *Achilles, Atreus, Caenis, Medea, Minos, Niobe, Tantalus*
ambitious for own children   *Medea*
ambivalent   *Artemis, Great Mother, Hermes, Persephone*
ambivalent to healing   *Asclepius*
anaemic   *Artemis, Hades, Hecate, Medusa, Persephone, Selene,*
    Sirens
analytical   *Apollo, Prometheus*
anarchic   *Artemis, Dionysus, Eros, Hermes, Pan, Polyphemus*
angered by male chauvinism   *Amazons*
angry   *Achilles, Furies, Great Mother, Hera, Odysseus, Poseidon,*
    Typhon
animal passions   *Eros, Hera, Pan, Silenus*
anorexic   *Aphrodite, Artemis, Daphne, Demeter, Furies, Midas,*
    Narcissus, Niobe, Orpheus
antagoniser of sons   *Uranus*
antagoniser of women   *Heracles, Perseus, Poseidon, Theseus*
anti-authority   *Amazons, Atlas, Eros, Pan, Prometheus*
anti-brother   *Ariadne*
anti-domestic   *Amazons, Cyrene, Heracles*
anti-hero   *Hephaestus, Hermes, Typhon*

anti-housework   *Cyrene*
anti-male   *Amazons, Artemis*
anti-marriage   *Artemis, Athene, Daphne, Demeter, Hestia*
anti-monogamy   *Amazons, Zeus*
anti-sex   *Athene, Daphne, Hestia, Selene, Thetis*
anti-sleep   *Dionysus, Zeus*
anti-spiritual   *Earth Mother, Heracles, Polyphemus, Typhon*
anti-washing   *Pan*
anxious   *Epimetheus, Furies, Orestes, Prometheus, Selene*
'a place for everything, and everything in its place'   *Apollo, Cronus,*
   Hestia
appeaser   *Hestia, Orion*
architect   *Apollo, Athene, Daedalus, Hestia*
arrested adolescent   *Adonis, Artemis, Eros, Ganymedes, Narcissus*
arrogant   *Apollo, Athene, Caenis, Zeus*
arthritic   *Centaurs, Cronus, Hades, Hephaestus, Hera, Prometheus,*
   Rhea
artistic   *Apollo, Athene, Earth Mother, Hephaestus, Muses, Orpheus*
ascetic   *Daphne, Hestia, Odysseus, Orpheus*
assertive   *Achilles, Athene, Caenis, Heracles, Medusa, Perseus,*
   Prometheus, Theseus, Uranus, Zeus
asthmatic   *Ares, Eris, Odysseus, Medusa, Poseidon, Typhon, Tyro*
athlete   *Cyrene, Dioscuri, Hera, Heracles, Hippolytus, Theseus*
at loggerheads with husband   *Artemis, Hera, Thetis*
at turning-point   *Hermes*
attached to dogs   *Actaeon, Artemis, Hecate, Hippolytus, Orion*
attempting to buy love   *Orion*
attender at glittering social events   *Niobe, Tantalus*
attention-seeker   *Niobe, Tantalus, Theseus*
attentive to omens   *Earth Mother, Great Mother, Hecate, Heracles,*
   Hermes, Rhea
attracted to priesthood   *Daphne, Eumolpus, Hermes, Hestia,*
   Hippolytus, Orpheus
attracted to water   *Daphne, Midas, Narcissus, Orestes, Poseidon,*
   Thetis, Tyro
attractive   *Adonis, Aphrodite, Dionysus, Eros, Ganymedes,*
   Narcissus, Selene, Tyro
authoritarian   *Aristaeus, Athene, Medusa, Uranus, Zeus*
auto-erotic   *Aphrodite, Ariadne, Dionysus, Eros, Hermes, Narcissus,*
   Pan
avoiding sex   *Actaeon, Daphne, Eumolpus, Hestia, Hippolytus,*
   Selene, Thetis
aware of approaching death   *Cronus, Fates, Hades*
aware of own body   *Aphrodite, Dionysus, Eros, Narcissus, Thetis*

aware of place in society   *Athene, Atreus, Fates, Niobe, Tantalus*

bachelor   *Apollo, Hippolytus, Ganymedes, Narcissus*
back-problems   *Atlas, Hera, Prometheus, Zeus*
backstairs politician   *Prometheus*
bad dreams   *Pan, Typhon*
bad experiences with women   *Orestes, Orion*
bad influence on own children   *Niobe, Tantalus, Uranus*
barbarian   *Polyphemus*
bearer of others' problems   *Athene, Epimetheus, Prometheus, Rhea*
believer in just deserts   *Furies, Nemesis, Orestes*
believer in others' rights   *Athene, Prometheus*
believer in principles   *Aristaeus, Athene, Epimetheus, Prometheus*
believer in progress   *Apollo, Aristaeus, Athene, Prometheus*
belittled   *Hephaestus*
belligerent   *Achilles, Amazons, Ares, Artemis, Athene, Atlas, Caenis,*
     Heracles, Perseus, Prometheus, Uranus, Zeus
bereaved   *Demeter, Erigone, Niobe, Orpheus*
bereaved through childbirth   *Atreus*
berserk   *Achilles, Amazons, Ares, Atlas, Heracles, Typhon*
big eater   *Heracles, Polyphemus, Tantalus*
big-hearted   *Athene, Demeter, Earth Mother, Great Mother,*
     Poseidon, Zeus
bickerer   *Achilles, Ares, Eris, Hera*
bisexual   *Aphrodite, Apollo, Ariadne, Dionysus, Eros, Hermes,*
     Narcissus, Orpheus, Pan
bitchy   *Apollo, Ares, Eris, Furies, Hecate*
'bites off more than he can chew'   *Zeus*
bitter   *Achilles, Demeter, Heracles, Niobe*
black dress   *Demeter, Hades, Persephone, Rhea*
blind   *Oedipus, Orion, Polyphemus*
blind rage   *Achilles, Amazons, Ares, Artemis, Demeter, Hephaestus,*
     Oedipus, Orion, Prometheus, Typhon, Zeus
blind to higher truth   *Hades, Heracles*
bloodthirsty   *Achilles, Ares, Eris, Medea*
'bloody but unbowed'   *Athene, Atlas, Prometheus*
bloody-minded   *Achilles, Artemis, Eris, Heracles, Poseidon*
blows hot and cold   *Artemis, Great Mother, Odysseus, Persephone*
blusterer   *Ares, Eris, Zeus*
boaster   *Achilles, Atreus, Niobe, Odysseus*
body-organ fetishist   *Aphrodite, Dionysus*
bold   *Achilles, Artemis, Caenis, Dioscuri, Heracles, Odysseus, Pan,*
     Perseus, Prometheus, Theseus
borrower of others' ideas   *Perseus*
bossy   *Medusa, Nemesis, Uranus*

boxer   *Dioscuri, Hermes*
brave   *Achilles, Artemis, Athene, Caenis, Heracles, Odysseus,*
    Perseus, Theseus
brave talker   *Actaeon, Eris*
breast-cancer   *Amazons, Hera*
breathing-problems   *Ares, Eris, Medusa, Odysseus, Pan, Poseidon,*
    Typhon, Tyro
brilliant   *Apollo, Athene, Muses, Silenus*
brimmed hat   *Hermes*
brinkmanship   *Apollo, Ares, Athene, Eris, Hermes, Prometheus*
broad-shouldered   *Athene, Atlas*
brutal as a father   *Tantalus, Uranus*
brute force   *Heracles, Odysseus, Polyphemus, Theseus*
brutish   *Polyphemus*
builder   *Hephaestus, Hestia, Polyphemus*
bullfighter   *Theseus*
bull-like   *Uranus, Zeus*
burnt out   *Heracles*
bustler   *Helius, Hephaestus*

calamitous downfall   *Achilles, Atreus, Niobe, Odysseus, Tantalus,*
    Theseus
calculating   *Apollo, Atreus, Medea, Perseus*
campaigner   *Amazons, Aristaeus, Athene, Orpheus*
campaigner for women's rights   *Amazons*
cancer   *Amazons, Artemis, Cronus, Epimetheus, Niobe, Orestes,*
    Pelops, Prometheus, Tantalus, Typhon
canny   *Centaurs, Pelops, Perseus, Rhea*
capricious   *Artemis, Eros, Great Mother, Pan*
career woman   *Amazons, Artemis, Athene, Caenis, Cyrene, Daphne*
careless   *Helius, Hippolytus*
careless with property   *Helius*
caring   *Artemis, Demeter, Earth Mother, Great Mother, Orpheus*
casual affairs   *Artemis, Eros, Poseidon, Zeus*
cat-lover   *Hecate*
cattle-rustler   *Dioscuri, Hermes*
catty   *Artemis, Eris, Niobe, Sirens*
cause of female jealousy   *Adonis, Dionysus, Ganymedes*
cautious   *Athene, Odysseus*
cavalier treatment of women   *Heracles, Theseus*
celibate   *Artemis, Athene, Cyrene, Hestia, Hippolytus, Narcissus,*
    Selene
centred   *Aristaeus, Hestia*
centre of attention   *Achilles, Adonis, Aphrodite, Dionysus, Hecate,*
    Orpheus

chameleon *Dionysus, Hecate, Hermes, Nemesis, Thetis, Zeus*
'champion' complex *Achilles, Caenis, Cyrene, Heracles*
changeable *Artemis, Eros, Great Mother, Persephone*
changed appearance *Demeter, Furies, Hippolytus, Odysseus, Orestes*
characterless *Hestia*
charismatic *Achilles, Athene, Atreus, Minos*
chaste *Amazons, Artemis, Hippolytus, Selene*
cheat *Atreus, Eros, Hermes, Medea, Pelops*
child-abuser *Amazons, Atreus, Cronus, Tantalus*
child-carer *Artemis, Hermes*
childhood abuse by father *Niobe, Pelops*
childhood disfigurement *Hephaestus, Pelops*
childhood incest *Hippolytus, Niobe, Tyro*
childhood seduction by older male *Ganymedes, Narcissus, Niobe,*
    Pelops, Tyro
childhood trauma *Eumolpus, Hephaestus, Hippolytus, Nemesis,*
    Niobe, Odysseus, Pelops, Perseus, Tyro
childhood wasting disease *Hephaestus, Pelops*
childhood weakness *Hephaestus*
child prodigy *Heracles, Hermes*
chip on the shoulder *Nemesis, Orestes, Perseus, Prometheus*
chronic digestive problems *Midas, Prometheus, Tantalus*
civic-minded *Aristaeus, Athene*
civil engineer *Apollo, Hephaestus, Heracles*
clear-headed *Apollo, Athene*
clever with hands *Athene, Daedalus, Demeter, Earth Mother,*
    Hephaestus
clumsy *Cronus, Polyphemus*
combative *Achilles, Ares, Athene, Caenis, Dionysus, Eris, Heracles,*
    Perseus, Theseus
'come into my parlour' *Circe*
commanding *Achilles, Athene, Caenis, Medusa, Odysseus, Zeus*
commando *Odysseus, Perseus*
compassionate *Asclepius, Athene, Earth Mother, Great Mother,*
    Orpheus, Zeus
competent *Achilles, Aristaeus, Athene, Caenis, Orestes, Perseus,*
    Zeus
competitive *Achilles, Ares, Caenis, Cyrene, Eris, Pelops*
complicated *Ariadne, Epimetheus, Minos, Prometheus*
compromiser *Athene, Hestia, Odysseus*
comrade in arms *Achilles, Amazons, Centaurs, Dioscuri*
conciliator *Athene, Hestia*
confrontational *Achilles, Artemis, Ares, Athene, Hercules, Medusa,*
    Odysseus, Perseus, Theseus, Uranus

conscience-stricken   *Aphrodite, Epimetheus, Furies, Helius, Minos,*
   Orestes, Tantalus, Tyro
conscientious   *Athene, Helius, Heracles, Orestes, Orion*
consistent   *Hades, Hestia, Orion*
constipated   *Cronus, Hades, Midas, Tyro*
constrictive   *Athene, Cronus, Medusa, Uranus*
contemptuous of law   *Ares, Dionysus, Eris, Eros, Pan*
contented housewife   *Hestia*
contradictory   *Actaeon, Artemis, Great Mother, Persephone, Selene*
contrary   *Aphrodite, Ares, Atlas, Cronus, Furies, Prometheus*
conventional   *Apollo, Athene, Furies, Hera, Hestia, Orestes*
convivial   *Centaurs, Dionysus, Hestia, Pan, Silenus*
courageous   *Achilles, Amazons, Aristaeus, Artemis, Athene, Caenis,*
   Heracles, Orpheus, Perseus, Theseus
courter of danger   *Achilles, Caenis, Dioscuri, Hermes, Perseus,*
   Theseus
coward   *Zeus*
coy   *Actaeon, Amazons, Artemis, Cyrene, Hippolytus, Selene*
craftsmanlike   *Athene, Daedalus, Earth Mother, Hephaestus, Hermes,*
   Prometheus
crafty   *Hermes, Medusa, Odysseus, Perseus, Prometheus*
creative   *Athene, Daedalus, Eros, Hephaestus, Hermes, Muses,*
   Orpheus
critical of others' sexuality   *Artemis*
cruel   *Achilles, Aphrodite, Artemis, Atreus, Eros, Medea, Perseus,*
   Sirens, Tantalus
cruelly treated by stepfather   *Tyro*
cuckolded   *Hephaestus*
culturally eminent   *Apollo, Athene, Hephaestus, Muses, Orpheus,*
   Sirens
cunning   *Eros, Hermes, Medea, Odysseus, Perseus*
cutter-down-to-size   *Atlas, Nemesis, Prometheus*

dancer   *Apollo, Artemis, Muses, Narcissus, Silenus*
danger to own children   *Demeter, Niobe, Tantalus*
danger to wife   *Atreus*
daring   *Achilles, Caenis, Dioscuri, Heracles, Perseus, Theseus*
dark clothes   *Cronus, Demeter, Hades, Persephone, Rhea*
dark-skinned   *Pan*
death-defying   *Achilles, Caenis, Dioscuri, Heracles, Perseus, Theseus*
death-orientated   *Ariadne, Hades*
death-obsessed   *Hades*
debauched   *Eros, Pan, Silenus, Sirens*
deceitful   *Eros, Hermes, Medea, Pan*

decisive   *Aristaeus, Caenis, Orestes, Perseus*
defective vision   *Hades, Hecate, Oedipus, Orion, Persephone,*
   Polyphemus, Rhea
defender of own   *Achilles, Earth Mother, Great Mother, Perseus,*
   Poseidon, Uranus
deliberate disguise   *Demeter, Furies, Hades, Medusa, Orestes, Pelops,*
   Perseus
deliberately unattractive   *Athene, Medusa, Odysseus*
delirium tremens   *Dionysus*
delusions   *Aphrodite, Hecate, Typhon*
delusions of invulnerability   *Achilles, Dionysus, Heracles, Theseus*
depressed   *Aphrodite, Artemis, Cronus, Demeter, Dionysus, Erigone,*
   Hera, Heracles, Narcissus, Niobe, Orpheus, Polyphemus, Selene,
   Theseus
deserted by husband   *Ariadne, Thetis*
deserter of husband   *Hera*
deserter of wife   *Odysseus, Theseus*
designer   *Athene, Daedalus, Hephaestus, Prometheus*
desperate   *Erigone, Orestes*
destroyer of family   *Medea, Niobe, Tantalus*
destroyer of men   *Amazons, Artemis, Circe, Dionysus, Sirens*
destructive   *Achilles, Ares, Athene, Eris, Furies, Great Mother,*
   Medusa, Nemesis, Orion, Perseus, Poseidon, Typhon
determined   *Achilles, Aristaeus, Artemis, Athene, Heracles, Hestia,*
   Odysseus, Perseus, Theseus, Zeus
determined virgin   *Artemis, Athene, Hestia, Selene*
devilish   *Dionysus, Eros, Pan*
devious   *Atreus, Eros, Helius, Medea, Odysseus, Pan, Perseus,*
   Prometheus
devoted to partner   *Aphrodite, Ariadne, Dionysus, Selene*
diabetic   *Tantalus*
dictator   *Athene, Atlas, Atreus, Caenis, Eumolpus, Zeus*
difficult childbirth   *Ariadne, Artemis*
difficult courtship   *Hippolytus, Pelops, Selene*
difficult marriage   *Ariadne, Artemis, Epimetheus, Hera, Theseus,*
   Thetis, Zeus
digestive problems   *Midas, Prometheus, Tantalus*
diplomat   *Athene, Hermes, Zeus*
diplomatic trickster   *Athene, Atreus, Hermes*
dirty tricks   *Atreus, Eros, Pelops*
disabled   *Centaurs, Hephaestus, Hera, Prometheus, Tantalus, Typhon*
disbeliever in own good fortune   *Nemesis, Orpheus*
disguised   *Demeter, Hippolytus, Orestes, Perseus, Selene*
dishonest   *Atreus, Eros, Hermes, Medea*

dislike of snakes   *Apollo, Persephone, Zeus*
dismissive of unconscious   *Apollo, Epimetheus, Heracles, Prometheus*
disregarder of warnings   *Achilles, Theseus*
disruptive   *Achilles, Atlas, Dionysus, Eros, Typhon*
dissembling   *Atreus, Eros, Hermes, Medea*
dissimulator   *Atreus, Dioscuri, Hermes, Medea, Perseus, Zeus*
dissolute   *Aphrodite, Centaurs, Dionysus, Pan, Silenus, Zeus*
disturbed by sex   *Actaeon, Amazons, Artemis, Daphne, Medusa,
     Selene*
doctor   *Apollo, Asclepius, Athene, Centaurs, Hermes, Rhea*
dog-lover   *Actaeon, Artemis, Hecate, Hippolytus, Orion*
dogmatic   *Athene, Cronus, Uranus, Zeus*
domesticated   *Erigone, Ganymedes, Hera, Hermes, Hestia, Perseus*
dominant female   *Athene, Caenis, Great Mother, Medusa*
dominant male   *Achilles, Ares, Heracles, Minos, Theseus, Uranus,
     Zeus*
'don't do what I do; do what I say'   *Helius*
'don't just sit there, do something!'   *Odysseus*
doom-and-gloom merchant   *Cronus, Fates, Nemesis*
'do stop arguing together!'   *Hestia*
down-to-earth   *Earth Mother, Great Mother, Hephaestus,
     Prometheus*
'do you know what *he/she* did?'   *Athene, Eris, Helius*
dragon   *Athene, Medusa*
dragon-slayer   *Heracles, Perseus, Theseus, Zeus*
driving personality   *Athene, Atreus, Caenis, Minos, Pelops,
     Prometheus, Zeus*
drop-out   *Pan*
drug-pusher   *Circe, Hermes*
drunkard   *Ares, Aristaeus, Centaurs, Dionysus, Fates, Silenus*
drunken rapist   *Orion*
dutiful   *Aristaeus, Eumolpus, Furies, Hera, Hestia, Hippolytus,
     Nemesis, Orestes, Orion, Tyro*
dynamic leader   *Achilles, Aristaeus, Atlas, Caenis, Heracles,
     Odysseus, Theseus*

early homosexuality or pederasty   *Apollo, Minos, Tantalus*
earth-scientist   *Apollo, Daphne*
easily embarrassed   *Actaeon, Hera, Hippolytus, Selene*
easily flattered   *Athene, Furies*
easily wounded emotionally   *Achilles, Adonis, Orion, Selene*
easy-going   *Ganymedes, Pan, Silenus*
eccentric   *Circe, Hades, Hecate, Medusa, Minos, Muses, Orpheus,
     Sirens*
ecologist   *Daphne*

effeminate   *Dionysus, Ganymedes, Silenus*
egotistical   *Apollo, Athene, Atreus, Caenis, Eris, Hecate, Hera,*
     Medea, Narcissus, Niobe, Odysseus, Theseus, Uranus, Zeus
eloper   *Ariadne, Theseus*
eloquent   *Athene, Hermes, Muses*
elusive   *Eros, Hermes, Selene*
elusive enchantress   *Selene, Sirens*
emasculator of men   *Amazons, Artemis, Great Mother*
emotionally vulnerable   *Adonis, Muses, Odysseus, Selene*
emotional ups and downs   *Adonis, Amazons, Aphrodite, Artemis,*
     Demeter, Dionysus, Great Mother, Orpheus, Persephone, Selene
emotionally wounded by women   *Adonis, Orestes, Orion*
empire-builder   *Apollo, Aristaeus, Athene, Caenis, Heracles, Minos,*
     Perseus, Poseidon
enemy of civilised values   *Eros, Dionysus, Pan*
energetic   *Achilles, Aristaeus, Artemis, Athene, Atlas, Caenis,*
     Dionysus, Dioscuri, Eros, Hera, Heracles, Pan, Pelops,
     Persephone, Perseus, Prometheus, Theseus, Thetis
enthusiastic   *Aristaeus, Artemis, Dionysus, Heracles, Pan, Perseus*
entertainer   *Dionysus, Hermes, Muses, Narcissus, Orpheus, Pan*
entrepreneur   *Apollo, Heracles, Hermes, Midas, Pelops, Poseidon*
envious   *Achilles, Ares, Atreus, Eris, Niobe, Tantalus*
epileptic   *Orpheus, Pan*
erotic   *Adonis, Aphrodite, Eros, Narcissus*
esotericist   *Artemis, Circe, Eumolpus, Hecate, Hermes, Medea*
esprit de corps   *Amazons, Centaurs, Dionysus, Dioscuri*
ever-young   *Adonis, Artemis, Dionysus, Ganymedes, Hermes,*
     Narcissus
exaggerated show of masculinity   *Achilles, Dionysus, Heracles,*
     Theseus
exiled   *Aristaeus, Circe, Hippolytus, Oedipus, Orion, Perseus, Sirens*
expeditions   *Daphne, Heracles, Odysseus, Orestes, Perseus, Theseus*
experienced   *Cronus, Rhea, Silenus*
explorer   *Daphne, Odysseus, Perseus*
exposer of mother's faults   *Orestes*
extramarital affairs   *Aphrodite, Poseidon, Zeus*
exuberant   *Dionysus, Zeus*

failed lover   *Hephaestus, Sirens, Zeus*
failure to understand own children   *Niobe, Rhea, Uranus, Zeus*
faithful   *Dionysus, Hera, Orpheus, Persephone*
falling apart psychologically   *Actaeon, Artemis, Dionysus, Hermes*
'falls on his/her feet'   *Ariadne, Hermes, Midas*
false hopes of longevity   *Fates*
falsely accused of rape   *Hippolytus*

falsely hopeful   *Epimetheus*
family curse   *Atreus*
family tyrant   *Uranus*
fanatic   *Amazons, Dionysus, Pan, Zeus*
fascist   *Caenis, Zeus*
fast learner   *Apollo, Hermes, Muses*
fat   *Earth Mother, Silenus*
fatalist   *Cronus, Fates, Nemesis*
fatally soft   *Hera, Niobe, Rhea*
father-admirer   *Athene, Heracles*
father-figure   *Minos, Uranus, Zeus*
father-hater   *Cronus, Oedipus, Pelops, Zeus*
fatherless   *Hephaestus*
fear of unconscious urges   *Apollo, Minos, Muses*
feats of endurance   *Artemis, Cyrene, Heracles, Odysseus, Orestes,
     Theseus*
feigned madman   *Odysseus*
female adopter of male role   *Artemis, Caenis*
female prostitute   *Aphrodite*
feminine charmer   *Circe, Sirens*
feminist   *Amazons, Artemis, Persephone*
fertile   *Aphrodite, Ares, Ariadne, Athene, Demeter, Earth Mother,
     Eros, Great Mother, Nemesis, Niobe, Pelops, Poseidon, Selene,
     Zeus*
feverish   *Pelops, Typhon*
fickle   *Artemis, Great Mother*
fierce   *Achilles, Athene, Atlas, Heracles, Medusa, Perseus, Zeus*
fighter   *Achilles, Ares, Athene, Caenis, Dioscuri, Eris, Heracles,
     Oedipus, Theseus*
figure of fun   *Hephaestus, Hermes, Pan*
'finders, keepers'   *Hermes*
fire-raiser   *Eros, Hephaestus, Typhon*
flamboyant   *Apollo, Niobe*
flatterer   *Athene, Eros, Furies, Hermes*
flight from female advances   *Actaeon, Narcissus*
focus of female squabbles   *Adonis, Dionysus, Orpheus*
focus of male squabbles   *Aphrodite, Daphne*
fond of city-life   *Apollo, Artemis, Athene*
fond of darkness   *Pan, Persephone*
fond of gardening   *Aphrodite, Artemis, Daphne*
fond of living it up   *Cyrene, Niobe, Tantalus, Zeus*
fond of mountains   *Daphne, Prometheus, Uranus*
fond of own voice   *Athene, Narcissus*
fond of pets   *Aphrodite, Artemis, Orion*

fond of running water   *Daphne, Orestes, Poseidon*
fond of wild creatures   *Artemis*
fooled by own arguments   *Athene, Atreus*
forceful   *Achilles, Aristaeus, Artemis, Athene, Caenis, Minos, Pelops,*
     Perseus, Prometheus, Zeus
foresight   *Apollo, Aristaeus, Athene, Circe, Earth Mother, Hecate,*
     Hermes, Muses, Orpheus, Silenus, Sirens, Uranus
forgiving   *Athene, Hephaestus, Zeus*
fostered   *Eumolpus, Oedipus*
fratricidal   *Ariadne, Atreus, Medea*
fraud   *Atreus, Eros, Hermes, Tantalus*
friend of younger males   *Aphrodite, Apollo, Hermes, Orestes,*
     Persephone
friendly   *Dionysus, Hermes, Hestia, Orpheus, Silenus*
frightened by sexual advances   *Actaeon, Selene*
frightened of men   *Daphne, Selene, Sirens*
frigid   *Niobe, Persephone*
frivolous   *Cyrene, Rhea*
fruitful   *Aphrodite, Demeter, Earth Mother, Great Mother, Poseidon,*
     Selene, Zeus
frustrated   *Actaeon, Aphrodite, Epimetheus, Orion, Polyphemus,*
     Prometheus, Tantalus
full of nervous energy   *Adonis, Dionysus, Eros, Pan*
full of own importance   *Hecate, Niobe, Tantalus, Uranus*
furious   *Achilles, Atlas, Poseidon, Typhon*
furious at men   *Amazons, Artemis, Great Mother*

gambler   *Hermes*
gammy leg   *Centaurs, Hephaestus, Odysseus*
gangster   *Dioscuri*
gardener   *Aphrodite, Aristaeus, Artemis, Daphne, Demeter, Hera,*
     Persephone
gauche   *Aristaeus, Daphne, Dionysus*
general health problems   *Epimetheus*
generous   *Athene, Great Mother, Hades, Hephaestus, Poseidon, Zeus*
gentle   *Asclepius, Hermes, Orpheus, Selene*
genocidal   *Amazons, Perseus, Zeus*
geologist   *Daphne*
get-rich-quick   *Midas*
getting old   *Cronus, Rhea, Hades*
gift of the gab   *Atreus, Hermes, Muses*
giving away money   *Hades, Hephaestus*
glaring eyes   *Athene, Medusa, Typhon*
gloater   *Achilles, Atreus, Niobe, Tantalus*
gloomy   *Cronus, Erigone, Hades, Persephone*

glory-hunter   *Achilles, Caenis, Perseus*
goal-orientated   *Achilles, Aristaeus, Artemis, Atreus, Hephaestus,
    Orion, Perseus, Prometheus, Tantalus*
go-getter   *Achilles, Athene, Atreus, Caenis, Perseus, Poseidon*
golden boy   *Achilles, Atreus*
Golden Mean   *Athene, Hestia*
golden touch   *Hermes, Midas, Perseus*
good appetite   *Polyphemus, Sirens, Zeus*
good eyesight   *Helius, Hermes, Pan*
good general knowledge   *Apollo, Athene, Hermes, Silenus*
good humour   *Pan, Zeus*
good judge   *Minos*
good lover   *Aphrodite, Demeter, Eros, Great Mother*
good-natured   *Aristaeus, Hestia, Silenus*
good relations with daughters   *Demeter, Earth Mother, Great Mother,
    Oedipus, Zeus*
good speaker   *Athene, Hermes, Muses, Narcissus*
good voice   *Artemis, Eumolpus, Narcissus, Orpheus, Sirens*
good with animals   *Artemis, Hermes*
good with children   *Artemis, Demeter*
good with hands   *Daedalus, Demeter, Earth Mother, Hephaestus*
good with language   *Muses, Narcissus, Orpheus*
gossip   *Actaeon, Athene, Eris, Helius, Tantalus*
gracious   *Persephone*
grandmother   *Rhea*
greedy   *Atreus, Dionysus, Polyphemus*
grieving   *Erigone, Niobe, Tyro*
group aggression   *Amazons, Centaurs, Dionysus*
group mischief-maker   *Dionysus, Dioscuri*
group seductress   *Sirens*
growth-orientated   *Ares, Caenis, Eris, Poseidon*
guilt-ridden   *Epimetheus, Eumolpus, Furies, Minos, Oedipus, Orestes,
    Tantalus, Tyro*
gullible   *Atlas, Hera, Persephone, Polyphemus, Selene, Zeus*
gymnast   *Cyrene, Hermes, Theseus*

hander-on of received culture   *Apollo, Artemis, Athene, Hestia*
'hands off my children'   *Demeter, Earth Mother, Great Mother*
handsome adolescent   *Adonis, Ganymedes, Hermes, Narcissus*
handy   *Daedalus, Demeter, Earth Mother, Hephaestus*
happiest among young people   *Artemis, Daphne, Dionysus, Hermes,
    Orestes, Silenus*
happy in female company   *Ares, Daphne, Dionysus, Great Mother,
    Hephaestus, Persephone*

happy with routine   *Cronus, Hades, Polyphemus*
hard worker   *Apollo, Athene, Prometheus, Hephaestus, Polyphemus*
hard-to-get   *Narcissus, Selene, Thetis*
harsh to sons   *Tantalus, Thetis, Uranus*
hateful to own children and underlings   *Hera, Medea, Tantalus*
hater of clothes   *Hermes, Pan*
hater of cruelty   *Earth Mother, Great Mother, Orpheus, Rhea*
headaches   *Dionysus, Orion, Pan, Tantalus*
head-orientated   *Apollo, Athene, Prometheus*
headstrong   *Achilles, Ares, Athene, Atlas, Eris, Epimetheus, Perseus,*
     Poseidon, Prometheus
healer   *Aristaeus, Artemis, Asclepius, Centaurs, Hermes, Medea,*
     Muses, Rhea
hearing problems   *Achilles, Athene, Cronus, Hades, Narcissus,*
     Odysseus, Rhea
heartbroken   *Narcissus, Niobe*
heartless   *Achilles, Ares, Eris, Perseus, Sirens, Zeus*
heart-problems   *Atlas, Poseidon, Prometheus, Typhon*
heavy-handed   *Ares, Cronus, Perseus, Zeus*
hedonist   *Cyrene, Midas, Tantalus, Zeus*
helmeted   *Ares, Athene, Dioscuri, Eris*
henpecked   *Helius, Heracles*
hepatitis   *Prometheus*
herd-member   *Amazons, Centaurs, Dionysus*
hernia   *Atlas, Prometheus*
hero   *Achilles, Amazons, Hercules, Odysseus, Oedipus, Perseus,*
     Theseus
herpes   *Heracles, Typhon*
hidden powers   *Circe, Hecate, Hephaestus, Hermes, Medea*
high aimer   *Achilles, Atreus, Caenis, Pelops*
highly feminine   *Aphrodite, Demeter, Earth Mother, Great Mother,*
     Hera, Selene, Thetis
highly masculine   *Achilles, Ares, Perseus, Poseidon, Prometheus,*
     Theseus, Uranus, Zeus
hoarder   *Hades, Midas*
'hoist by own petard'   *Athene, Atreus*
home rule for women   *Amazons*
homeless   *Oedipus, Orion, Pan*
home-loving   *Hestia*
homosexual   *Apollo, Dioscuri, Ganymedes*
homosexual escapades   *Apollo, Dionysus, Heracles, Minos, Pan,*
     Poseidon, Silenus, Zeus
homosexual jealousy   *Apollo, Minos*
honest   *Athene, Orion*

honour-motivated   *Achilles, Athene, Orestes*
hooligan   *Dionysus*
horror of ageing   *Adonis, Artemis*
horror of blood   *Furies*
horror of sex   *Actaeon, Selene*
horrors   *Typhon*
horsey   *Amazons, Athene, Cyrene, Dioscuri, Hippolytus, Poseidon, Selene*
hospitable   *Circe, Hestia, Zeus*
hot-headed   *Achilles, Apollo, Ares, Eris, Prometheus, Typhon, Zeus*
hounded   *Actaeon, Hippolytus, Orestes*
house-proud   *Hestia, Niobe*
housewife   *Hera, Hestia*
humorous   *Aphrodite, Demeter, Hermes, Silenus, Zeus*
hunched shoulders   *Atlas, Hephaestus*
hunter   *Actaeon, Apollo, Aristaeus, Artemis, Centaurs, Dionysus, Eros, Heracles, Hippolytus, Orion*
hunter of unattainable male   *Artemis*
hurt by own children   *Ariadne, Rhea*
hygienic   *Aristaeus, Athene, Hestia*
hyperactive   *Adonis, Dionysus, Eros, Pan, Perseus*
hypersensitive   *Achilles, Heracles, Medusa, Orpheus*
hypnotist   *Circe, Hecate, Hermes*
hysterical   *Achilles, Ariadne, Dionysus*

'I am psychic'   *Hecate*
iconoclast   *Dionysus, Medusa*
idealistic   *Eros, Eumolpus, Hippolytus, Narcissus, Orpheus, Orion, Perseus*
'if it grows, cut it; if it moves, kill it'   *Cronus*
'if only . . .'   *Cronus, Epimetheus, Orpheus*
ignorant   *Polyphemus*
imaginative   *Daedalus, Hephaestus, Muses*
imagined invulnerability   *Achilles, Dionysus, Heracles, Theseus*
immature   *Achilles, Adonis, Dionysus, Eros, Pan*
impetuous   *Achilles, Adonis, Apollo, Ares, Eris, Eros, Great Mother, Hephaestus, Zeus*
implacable   *Achilles, Atlas, Fates, Furies, Orestes, Perseus*
impotent   *Cronus, Hades*
impractical   *Helius*
impulsive   *Achilles, Adonis, Artemis, Athene, Pan, Poseidon, Typhon*
'I'm quite all right, thank you'   *Narcissus, Tyro*
in a rut   *Cronus, Polyphemus*
incest with father   *Niobe*

incest with son   *Rhea*
incest with stepmother   *Hippolytus, Orion*
incest with uncle   *Tyro*
incestuous   *Eros, Eumolpus, Hephaestus*
incompetent   *Epimetheus, Helius*
inconsistent   *Artemis, Great Mother, Hermes*
inconspicuous   *Hades, Hestia, Odysseus, Perseus, Selene*
in danger of dying   *Artemis, Dioscuri, Hades, Hera, Rhea*
indefatigable   *Amazons, Athene, Atlas, Caenis, Helius, Zeus*
independent-minded   *Amazons, Apollo, Artemis, Athene, Cyrene,*
    Epimetheus, Hestia, Narcissus, Pan, Perseus, Prometheus
individual   *Artemis, Pan*
ineffectual   *Epimetheus, Hestia*
infant hardship   *Oedipus, Pelops, Perseus*
infanticidal   *Cronus, Tantalus*
infectious illnesses   *Apollo, Artemis*
inflexible   *Cronus, Furies, Hades*
influential connections   *Atreus, Tantalus*
ingenious   *Apollo, Ariadne, Daedalus, Hephaestus, Perseus*
ingenuous   *Actaeon, Orion, Polyphemus*
inhospitable   *Atlas*
initiative   *Aristaeus, Athene, Caenis, Heracles, Odysseus, Perseus*
in love with own body   *Aphrodite, Narcissus*
in love with the sea   *Aphrodite, Poseidon, Thetis*
in love with wilderness   *Actaeon, Artemis, Daphne, Pan*
'in *my* day . . .'   *Cronus*
inner blindness   *Heracles, Midas, Oedipus, Polyphemus*
inner conflict   *Artemis, Asclepius, Orestes, Orpheus, Persephone*
inner contradictions   *Apollo, Artemis, Asclepius, Dionysus, Hermes,*
    Persephone
inner torment   *Demeter, Epimetheus, Erigone, Minos, Orion,*
    Persephone, Prometheus, Tantalus, Tyro
in pursuit of the unattainable   *Artemis, Narcissus, Orion*
inquisitive   *Actaeon, Athene, Daedalus, Eris, Helius, Odysseus*
insane   *Artemis, Dionysus, Epimetheus, Furies, Orestes, Pan*
insanely jealous   *Hera, Minos*
insecure   *Actaeon, Hermes, Odysseus, Pan, Selene, Thetis*
insensitive   *Apollo, Ares, Athene, Cronus*
insightful   *Apollo, Athene, Circe, Demeter, Great Mother, Medea,*
    Oedipus, Zeus
insistent on others' rights   *Furies, Theseus*
insistent on own rights   *Achilles, Earth Mother, Fates, Hades, Hera,*
    Odysseus
insomniac   *Cronus, Epimetheus, Furies, Orestes, Prometheus, Zeus*

insufferable subordinate   *Atlas, Epimetheus, Prometheus*
integrated   *Apollo, Athene, Centaurs, Hephaestus, Hestia, Orpheus,*
    Rhea, Silenus
intellectual   *Apollo, Athene, Cronus, Muses*
intellectually brilliant   *Apollo, Athene, Muses*
intelligent   *Apollo, Athene, Hermes, Muses, Perseus*
intensely loving   *Artemis, Demeter, Great Mother, Orpheus, Rhea*
interpreter   *Hermes*
intolerant   *Ares, Athene, Cronus, Eris, Hades, Zeus*
intolerant of heat   *Orion, Prometheus*
intriguer   *Eris, Hera, Medea, Tantalus*
introverted   *Cronus, Narcissus, Selene, Tyro*
intuitive   *Atlas, Artemis, Great Mother, Hecate, Zeus*
inventor   *Athene, Daedalus, Hephaestus, Hermes*
involuntary nocturnal orgasms   *Poseideon, Zeus*
inward-looking   *Cronus, Narcissus, Selene, Tyro*
inwardly torn apart   *Actaeon, Athene, Epimetheus, Minos,*
    Prometheus, Tyro
inwardly tortured   *Epimetheus, Minos, Prometheus, Tantalus, Tyro*
'I ought to . . .'   *Aristaeus, Furies, Orestes, Orpheus, Orion*
irascible   *Athene, Atlas, Odysseus, Poseidon, Typhon*
iron-willed   *Achilles, Aristaeus, Artemis, Athene, Atlas, Caenis,*
    Heracles, Odysseus, Perseus, Theseus
irrational   *Achilles, Aphrodite, Ares, Artemis, Dionysus, Eris, Eros,*
    Great Mother, Pan, Poseidon, Typhon
irrational fears   *Actaeon, Artemis, Daedalus, Furies, Orestes, Selene*
irrational urges   *Earth Mother, Great Mother, Poseidon, Typhon*
irresponsible   *Cyrene, Dionysus, Eros, Helius, Pan*
'I try my best'   *Athene, Orion, Prometheus*
'it serves you right'   *Nemesis*
'it's all my fault'   *Eumolpus, Furies, Minos, Oedipus, Orestes, Tyro*
'I used to have problems, but now . . .'   *Daedalus*

jealous   *Achilles, Aphrodite, Apollo, Ares, Circe, Eris, Hera, Medea,*
    Minos, Niobe, Poseidon
jealous of rights   *Achilles, Earth Mother, Hades*
jeweller   *Hephaestus*
'jobs for the boys'   *Tantalus*
jovial   *Pan, Rhea, Silenus, Zeus*

keen on challenges   *Achilles, Caenis, Cyrene, Dioscuri, Heracles,*
    Odysseus, Theseus
keen on expeditions   *Daphne, Heracles, Odysseus, Orestes, Perseus,*
    Theseus
keen on outdoor pursuits   *Actaeon, Cyrene, Heracles, Perseus,*
    Theseus

keen sense of smell   *Hecate, Hermes, Polyphemus*
keen sight   *Helius, Hermes, Pan*
'keep off my patch'   *Ares, Daedalus, Earth Mother, Poseidon, Uranus*
kind   *Artemis, Demeter, Hermes, Hestia, Orpheus, Rhea*
kleptomaniac   *Hermes*
knowledgeable   *Apollo, Athene, Helius, Muses, Zeus*

lacking in vision   *Epimetheus, Hades, Oedipus, Polyphemus*
lack of support and understanding from family   *Pelops, Tyro*
lame   *Dionysus, Hephaestus, Odysseus*
languorous   *Narcissus*
late developer   *Adonis, Artemis, Ariadne, Eros, Theseus*
lateral thinker   *Daedalus, Hermes, Odysseus, Perseus*
lawyer   *Athene, Hermes, Minos*
lazy   *Pan, Silenus*
leader   *Achilles, Apollo, Aristaeus, Athene, Atlas, Caenis, Hecate,*
     Hera, Odysseus, Perseus, Zeus
learner from experience   *Orion*
'leave me alone'   *Actaeon, Daphne, Narcissus, Selene, Thetis, Tyro*
left-handed   *Cronus*
lesbian   *Amazons, Artemis, Daphne*
lethargic   *Narcissus, Silenus*
lets his/her hair down   *Aphrodite, Ariadne, Dionysus, Pan*
'let's you and him fight'   *Ares, Eris*
liable to abduction   *Persephone*
liable to be kidnapped   *Ganymedes*
liable to be raped   *Ganymedes, Persephone, Tyro*
liable to be seduced   *Adonis, Aphrodite, Ganymedes, Tyro*
liable to 'blow his top'   *Achilles, Ares, Poseidon, Typhon*
liar   *Atreus, Hera, Hermes, Muses, Pan*
liberal   *Apollo, Athene, Prometheus*
licentious   *Dionysus, Heracles, Pan, Silenus*
light-fingered   *Hermes*
'like hell I will!'   *Artemis, Atlas, Poseidon, Prometheus, Zeus*
limelight-hogger   *Achilles, Apollo, Narcissus, Niobe, Tantalus*
linguist   *Hermes, Muses*
literary   *Cronus, Heracles, Muses*
lively   *Adonis, Cyrene, Dionysus, Hermes, Pan*
'local boy makes good'   *Hephaestus, Midas, Perseus*
logical   *Apollo, Athene, Prometheus*
lonely   *Actaeon, Demeter, Erigone, Narcissus, Niobe, Orion, Tyro*
loner   *Actaeon, Artemis, Hippolytus, Narcissus, Pan*
long-haired   *Aphrodite, Apollo, Pan*
long illness in old age   *Centaurs*

'look at *me*'   *Apollo, Atreus, Caenis, Medea, Niobe, Tantalus,
   Theseus*
loose-tongued   *Actaeon, Athene, Eris, Helius, Rhea*
loss of children   *Demeter, Niobe*
loss of former skills   *Polyphemus*
loss of self-esteem   *Niobe, Oedipus*
loud voice   *Achilles, Ares, Athene, Atlas, Caenis, Eris, Helius,
   Narcissus, Pan, Poseidon, Uranus, Sirens, Zeus*
'love me, love my dog'   *Actaeon, Artemis, Orion*
love of caving   *Earth Mother, Hades, Hecate, Pan, Persephone, Zeus*
love of change   *Adonis, Heracles, Hermes, Pan*
love of children   *Artemis, Demeter, Earth Mother, Great Mother*
love of darkness   *Aphrodite, Dionysus, Hades, Hecate, Pan,
   Persephone*
love of flying   *Artemis, Daedalus, Eros, Ganymedes, Perseus*
love of good living   *Cyrene, Midas, Zeus*
love of high society   *Niobe, Tantalus*
love of hunting   *Actaeon, Amazons, Artemis, Hippolytus, Orion*
love of isolation   *Actaeon, Apollo, Ariadne, Artemis, Circe, Midas,
   Sirens*
love of sailing   *Aphrodite, Ganymedes, Orion, Thetis*
love of self   *Aphrodite, Narcissus*
love of sport   *Achilles, Cyrene, Heracles, Hippolytus, Perseus,
   Theseus*
love of the new   *Adonis, Hermes*
love of the sea   *Aphrodite, Odysseus, Orion, Poseidon, Thetis*
love of virginity   *Artemis, Athene, Hestia, Hippolytus, Selene*
love-shy   *Actaeon, Amazons, Artemis, Cyrene, Hippolytus,
   Narcissus, Selene, Thetis*
loving   *Aphrodite, Demeter, Earth Mother, Great Mother, Orion,
   Orpheus, Rhea*
loyal   *Aphrodite, Dioscuri, Hera, Orion, Orpheus, Perseus*
lucky   *Atreus, Hecate, Hermes, Midas, Minos, Perseus*
lustful   *Aphrodite, Dionysus, Eros, Pan, Silenus, Zeus*

macho   *Achilles, Apollo, Ares, Heracles, Odysseus, Perseus, Theseus,
   Zeus*
'made of money'   *Hades, Midas*
madness   *Artemis, Dionysus, Epimetheus, Furies, Orestes, Pan*
magician   *Eros, Hecate, Hephaestus, Hermes, Medea*
magnanimous   *Athene, Pelops, Zeus*
maiden aunt   *Hestia*
'makes an ass of himself'   *Midas*
male chauvinist   *Achilles, Apollo, Heracles, Odysseus, Theseus, Zeus*
male sex-object   *Adonis, Dionysus, Eros, Orpheus*

maltreater of elderly husband   *Aphrodite*
man-hater   *Amazons, Daphne, Great Mother*
man-hunter   *Aphrodite, Artemis*
manic depressive   *Adonis, Artemis, Persephone*
manipulative   *Apollo, Athene, Atreus, Perseus, Theseus*
manly   *Achilles, Ares, Dioscuri, Heracles, Odysseus, Perseus, Theseus*
man of action   *Achilles, Ares, Aristaeus, Atlas, Dioscuri, Heracles, Odysseus, Perseus, Theseus*
man of few words   *Aristaeus, Polyphemus*
manual worker   *Athene, Hephaestus, Polyphemus*
marriage as an escape   *Ariadne, Epimetheus*
martinet   *Athene, Medusa, Uranus*
martyr to conscience   *Eumolpus, Furies, Orestes*
masculine woman   *Artemis, Athene, Caenis, Medusa*
masochistic   *Odysseus, Oedipus, Orestes, Prometheus*
mass hysteria   *Centaurs, Dionysus*
mass militancy   *Amazons, Centaurs*
mass orgies   *Centaurs, Dionysus*
masturbation   *Aphrodite, Dionysus, Eros, Narcissus, Pan*
materialist   *Atlas, Earth Mother, Epimetheus, Great Mother, Midas, Orion, Polyphemus, Poseidon, Prometheus*
mathematician   *Apollo, Athene*
matriarch   *Amazons, Aphrodite, Athene, Great Mother, Hestia, Rhea*
matricidal   *Orestes*
meddler   *Hephaestus, Hera*
mediator   *Ares, Apollo, Athene, Hestia*
medically knowledgeable   *Apollo, Asclepius, Athene, Centaurs, Medea*
'medicine-woman'   *Rhea*
medium   *Hecate, Hermes, Rhea*
megalomaniac   *Amazons, Atreus, Caenis, Minos, Pelops, Poseidon, Zeus*
melancholic   *Artemis, Cronus, Demeter, Narcissus, Tyro*
member of female musical group   *Muses, Sirens*
member of women's group   *Amazons*
menstrual problems   *Furies, Selene*
mental torments   *Epimetheus, Orion, Prometheus, Tantalus, Tyro*
mentally disturbed   *Artemis, Dionysus, Epimetheus, Furies, Orestes, Pan*
mentally ill   *Artemis, Dionysus, Orion, Rhea*
mercurial   *Apollo, Hermes, Perseus*
metal-worker   *Athene, Hephaestus, Polyphemus*
methodical   *Apollo, Athene, Hephaestus, Medea, Prometheus*

middle-of-the-roader   *Athene, Hestia*
migraine   *Dionysus, Pan, Tantalus*
militant   *Amazons, Ares, Caenis, Centaurs, Eris, Prometheus*
military   *Achilles, Ares, Caenis, Centaurs, Dioscuri, Eris*
military instructor   *Centaurs*
military 'special operations'   *Odysseus, Perseus*
misanthrope   *Circe, Cronus*
miser   *Hades*
misplaced trust   *Orion*
mistrustful of help   *Pan, Tyro*
mistrustful of women   *Actaeon, Zeus*
misunderstood by family   *Tyro*
money-grabbing   *Midas, Pelops*
moods of negativity   *Aphrodite, Artemis, Cronus, Hermes*
moody   *Achilles, Demeter, Poseidon, Typhon*
moralistic   *Aristaeus, Furies, Hestia, Orion, Orpheus*
morally upright   *Aristaeus, Athene, Hestia, Hippolytus, Orestes,*
    Orpheus
morbid   *Cronus, Epimetheus, Hades*
morose   *Cronus, Epimetheus, Hades, Nemesis, Polyphemus*
mother-dominated   *Helius, Orestes, Thetis*
mother-figure   *Aphrodite, Ariadne, Artemis, Athene, Demeter, Earth*
    Mother, Erigone, Great Mother, Hera, Hestia, Niobe, Rhea,
    Selene
mother-fixated   *Hephaestus, Perseus, Thetis*
mother-hater   *Ares, Hephaestus, Orestes*
mother-haunted   *Orestes*
mother-lover   *Oedipus, Perseus, Thetis*
mother's boy   *Achilles, Dionysus, Oedipus*
murderous   *Achilles, Ares, Daedalus, Dionysus, Eris, Heracles,*
    Medea, Perseus, Theseus, Typhon, Zeus
muscular   *Achilles, Artemis, Caenis, Hephaestus, Heracles,*
    Polyphemus, Theseus
musical   *Apollo, Athene, Eumolpus, Hermes, Muses, Orpheus, Pan,*
    Silenus, Sirens
music as a sex-substitute   *Pan*

nail biter   *Orestes*
naïve   *Apollo, Ares, Artemis, Centaurs, Eris, Polyphemus, Selene*
naive in personal relationships   *Adonis, Orion*
narcissistic   *Aphrodite, Narcissus*
narrow-minded   *Polyphemus*
nasty attitude at times   *Ares, Eris, Furies, Hecate, Nemesis*
natural   *Aphrodite, Daphne, Dionysus, Pan*
natural leader   *Achilles, Apollo, Aristaeus, Caenis, Heracles, Minos,*

   Odysseus, Pelops, Perseus, Theseus
naturist   *Aphrodite, Daphne, Hermes, Pan, Thetis*
nearly killed in accident   *Hippolytus*
need for catalytic sexual relationship   *Adonis, Ariadne, Perseus,
      Theseus*
need for entertainment   *Cyrene, Midas, Polyphemus*
negative   *Artemis, Erigone, Furies, Great Mother, Nemesis*
negative towards all initiatives   *Furies, Nemesis*
negative when provoked   *Achilles, Amazons, Dionysus, Heracles*
neophobic   *Cronus, furies, Nemesis*
nepotist   *Medea, Niobe, Tantalus*
nightmares   *Actaeon, Pan, Typhon*
'nobody loves me'   *Narcissus, Tyro*
nocturnal   *Dionysus, Hecate, Hermes, Hades*
noisy   *Ares, Caenis, Dionysus, Eris, Pan*
nomad   *Daphne, Hermes, Odysseus, Oedipus, Orestes, Orion, Pan,
      Perseus*
nostalgic   *Cronus, Epimetheus, Hades, Orpheus*
nostalgic for virginity   *Aphrodite, Hera*
'not a sex-object'   *Amazons, Artemis, Orpheus*
'nothing to excess'   *Athene, Hestia*
nouveau riche   *Midas*
nubile   *Artemis, Selene*
nudist   *Aphrodite, Daphne, Hermes, Pan, Thetis*
nun   *Hestia, Sirens*
nymphomaniac   *Aphrodite, Demeter*

obdurate   *Apollo, Atlas, Cronus*
oblivious to effect on others   *Athene*
obscene   *Dionysus, Eros, Pan, Silenus*
obsessed with appearance   *Aphrodite, Midas, Narcissus*
obsessed with death   *Hades, Persephone*
obsessed with family rights and duties   *Furies, Orestes, Perseus*
obsessed with fighting and war   *Achilles, Ares, Caenis, Centaurs,
      Dioscuri, Eris*
obstinate   *Achilles, Athene, Cronus, Hades, Nemesis, Prometheus*
occasional madness   *Artemis, Pan*
occasionally lustful   *Hades*
occasional pederast   *Apollo, Poseidon, Zeus*
occultist   *Circe, Hecate, Hermes, Medea*
old   *Cronus, Furies, Hades, Rhea*
'old is good; new is bad'   *Cronus*
old, ragged clothes   *Demeter, Odysseus*
Olympian detachment   *Hestia*
open to challenges   *Achilles, Cyrene, Heracles, Perseus, Theseus*

opportunist   *Atreus, Hermes, Medea, Odysseus, Perseus*
opposed by intended's father   *Pelops*
opposed by women   *Heracles, Perseus, Theseus*
opposed to grandfather   *Perseus*
opposed to male aggression   *Amazons, Hera, Thetis*
optimist   *Daedalus, Dionysus, Fates, Heracles, Orpheus, Theseus*
orchestral conductor   *Hermes, Muses*
organiser   *Apollo, Aristaeus, Athene, Cronus, Hecate, Minos,*
        Theseus, Zeus
orgies   *Aphrodite, Dionysus, Eros, Muses, Silenus*
original   *Daedalus, Hephaestus, Heracles, Hermes, Muses, Odysseus,*
        Orpheus, Perseus
ostracised   *Medusa*
outcast   *Hephaestus, Orestes, Orpheus, Perseus*
outdoor activities   *Achilles, Artemis, Cyrene, Daphne, Earth Mother,*
        Heracles, Hippolytus, Pan, Perseus, Theseus, Thetis
outwardly negative   *Athene, Cronus, Medusa*
over-achiever   *Achilles, Atreus, Caenis, Hephaestus, Pelops*
over-attachment to daughter   *Demeter*
over-confident   *Achilles, Daedalus, Dionysus, Heracles, Helius,*
        Odysseus, Theseus
over-conscientious   *Furies, Helius, Orestes, Orion, Orpheus*
over-developed upper body   *Hephaestus*
over-eager   *Helius, Heracles, Orion, Perseus, Theseus*
over-dressed   *Niobe, Tantalus*
over-heroic   *Achilles, Amazons, Caenis, Odysseus, Theseus*
over-loving as mother   *Artemis, Demeter, Niobe, Rhea*
'over my dead body'   *Athene, Atlas, Orpheus, Prometheus*
over-protected by father   *Selene*
over-protective of offspring   *Demeter, Niobe, Rhea*
over-reactive   *Achilles, Apollo, Ares, Eris, Orion, Perseus, Poseidon,*
        Typhon
over-ready with answers   *Apollo, Athene*
over-responsive to sexual advances   *Adonis, Aphrodite, Eros*
over-responsible   *Aristaeus, Athene, Atlas, Orion*
over-sensitive to women's wishes   *Orion, Orpheus*
over-sexed   *Aphrodite, Eros, Pan, Silenus, Uranus, Zeus*
over-talkative about spiritual matters   *Hecate, Hermes, Rhea*
over-vengeful   *Achilles, Ariadne, Atreus, Furies, Hera, Orestes,*
        Orion, Perseus

pacifier   *Athene, Hephaestus, Hestia, Orpheus, Thetis*
panic-stricken   *Actaeon, Daphne, Pan, Selene*
paradoxical   *Amazons, Artemis, Dionysus, Great Mother, Hermes*
paralysed   *Prometheus, Tantalus, Typhon, Zeus*

paralysed in the face of events   *Asclepius, Hermes, Pan*
paranoid   *Actaeon, Daedalus, Daphne*
passionate   *Amazons, Artemis, Dionysus, Eros, Hephaestus, Pan, Thetis*
passion for the sea   *Aphrodite, Orion, Poseidon, Thetis*
passive   *Ganymedes, Hestia*
paternalist   *Helius, Uranus, Zeus*
patriarch   *Cronus, Uranus, Zeus*
patricidal   *Oedipus, Zeus*
pederast   *Apollo, Minos, Poseidon, Zeus*
periodic madness   *Adonis, Artemis, Persephone*
perjurer   *Atreus, Cronus, Hermes, Tantalus*
persistent   *Athene, Atlas, Helius, Hercules, Perseus; Prometheus*
personal drive   *Achilles, Artemis, Athene, Atlas, Atreus, Caenis, Heracles, Odysseus, Pelops, Perseus, Theseus*
perspicacious   *Apollo, Asclepius, Helius, Hermes, Hestia, Minos, Rhea*
persuasive   *Athene, Hermes, Orpheus, Perseus*
pessimist   *Cronus, Fates, Nemesis*
Peter Pan   *Adonis, Artemis, Eros, Ganymedes, Narcissus*
petrifying   *Athene, Medusa, Zeus*
petty tyrant   *Uranus*
petulant   *Achilles, Uranus, Zeus*
philanthropist   *Athene, Great Mother, Hades, Hephaestus, Orpheus, Pelops, Prometheus*
philistine   *Atreus, Midas, Polyphemus*
physical infant-prodigy   *Heracles, Hermes*
physically ill   *Prometheus, Rhea, Tantalus*
pillar of society   *Aristaeus, Athene, Atlas, Heracles*
pioneer   *Amazons, Aristaeus, Athene, Heracles*
pious   *Daphne, Eumolpus, Hestia, Hippolytus, Orpheus*
plagued by riches   *Hades, Midas, Niobe*
plaited or braided hair   *Circe*
planner   *Aristaeus, Athene, Odysseus, Orestes, Prometheus, Theseus*
playful   *Dionysus, Hermes, Pan*
pleasure-loving   *Cyrene, Midas, Silenus, Sirens, Zeus*
plotter   *Atlas, Atreus, Dioscuri, Eumolpus, Hera, Medea, Odysseus*
poet   *Hermes, Muses, Orpheus*
poisoner   *Medea*
politician   *Apollo, Athene, Atreus, Eumolpus, Minos, Perseus, Zeus*
poor at personal relationships   *Orion, Narcissus, Selene, Theseus, Tyro*
poor self-expression   *Aristaeus, Tyro*
possessive   *Ares, Eris, Great Mother, Hades, Persephone, Rhea,*

Uranus

possessive of family   *Demeter, Uranus*

powerful personality   *Athene, Atlas, Caenis, Hecate, Minos, Pelops, Perseus, Uranus, Zeus*

power-mad   *Atreus, Asclepius, Caenis, Poseidon, Zeus*

practical   *Athene, Earth Mother, Hephaestus, Heracles, Perseus*

pragmatist   *Athene, Atreus, Hermes, Perseus*

predator   *Artemis, Atreus, Eros, Furies, Sirens, Typhon*

predictable   *Cronus, Hades*

prepared to kill or cure   *Asclepius, Hermes*

prey to mother's taboos   *Furies, Orestes, Sirens*

prey to older women   *Adonis*

priest/priestess   *Daphne, Eumolpus, Hermes, Hestia, Hippolytus, Orpheus*

prima donna   *Achilles, Caenis, Hera, Narcissus, Niobe*

primitive   *Hephaestus, Pan, Polyphemus*

problem-solver   *Athene, Oedipus, Perseus, Theseus*

profane   *Minos, Polyphemus, Tantalus*

professionally jealous   *Daedalus*

promiscuous   *Amazons, Aphrodite, Demeter, Dionysus, Eros, Heracles, Muses, Poseidon, Zeus*

promoted to power   *Ariadne, Athene, Eumolpus, Minos, Pelops*

prone to seek exile   *Aristaeus, Furies, Orestes*

prone to self-disguise   *Furies, Orestes, Perseus, Selene*

prone to sudden urges   *Artemis, Dionysus, Great Mother, Pan, Poseidon, Typhon*

prone to vice   *Aphrodite, Epimetheus, Eros*

prophetic   *Apollo, Aristaeus, Circe, Earth Mother, Hermes, Muses, Orpheus, Silenus, Sirens, Thetis, Zeus*

protector   *Athene, Earth Mother, Great Mother, Perseus, Zeus*

protector of mother   *Perseus*

proud   *Achilles, Caenis, Niobe, Odysseus, Pelops, Zeus*

proud of own children   *Niobe*

providence-tempter   *Achilles, Dioscuri, Heracles, Perseus*

provider   *Artemis, Demeter, Great Mother, Uranus, Zeus*

provocative   *Achilles, Aphrodite, Athene, Ares, Dionysus, Eris, Eros*

provocative to men   *Aphrodite, Circe, Selene*

provocative to women   *Poseidon, Theseus*

prude   *Actaeon, Artemis, Athene, Hera, Hestia, Selene*

psychic   *Circe, Hecate, Hermes, Medea*

psychological disorders   *Artemis, Dionysus, Heracles, Hermes, Pan, Tantalus*

psychologically complex   *Ariadne, Minos*

psychologically well-balanced   *Amazons, Ariadne, Aristaeus,*

Dionysus, Hestia, Orpheus, Rhea
psychologically wounded   Hephaestus, Nemesis, Niobe
psychosomatic illness   Epimetheus, Hephaestus, Prometheus,
    Tantalus
psychotherapist   Ariadne, Asclepius, Heracles, Hermes, Orpheus,
    Rhea
public speaker   Athene, Eumolpus, Narcissus, Orpheus
pure   Athene, Helius, Hestia, Hippolytus, Orpheus, Selene
puritanical   Aristaeus, Daphne, Furies, Hades, Hestia, Odysseus,
    Orestes, Sirens
pursued by men   Aphrodite, Daphne, Ganymedes, Selene
pursued by mother's taboos   Orestes, Sirens
pursued by women   Adonis, Dionysus, Orpheus
pushed by parents   Achilles, Atreus, Tyro
pushy   Atreus, Caenis, Hecate, Niobe, Pelops, Tantalus
puts women off   Aristaeus, Theseus
pyromaniac   Eros, Hephaestus, Typhon

quarrelsome   Achilles, Ares, Eris, Hera, Poseidon, Zeus
quarrelsome children   Tyro
quick learner   Apollo, Hermes, Muses
quick-witted   Apollo, Athene, Hermes, Perseus

racing driver   Hippolytus
raconteur   Cronus, Orpheus, Silenus
ragged clothes   Demeter, Odysseus
raging   Atlas, Prometheus, Typhon
randy   Eros, Dionysus, Heracles, Hermes, Pan, Silenus
rank-puller   Niobe, Tantalus, Zeus
raped by son   Rhea
rapid mood-swings   Achilles, Adonis, Amazons, Artemis, Great
    Mother, Pan
rapist   Actaeon, Pan, Poseidon, Zeus
reassuring   Earth Mother, Great Mother, Hestia, Zeus
rebellious   Amazons, Apollo, Atlas, Cyrene, Dionysus, Eumolpus,
    Heracles, Poseidon, Prometheus, Zeus
recluse   Circe, Hades, Midas, Minos, Polyphemus, Sirens
red hair   Odysseus
reflective   Asclepius, Athene, Cronus, Epimetheus, Prometheus
reformer   Aristaeus, Athene, Nemesis, Orpheus
refugee   Daphne, Hippolytus, Odysseus, Perseus
refusal to let go   Cronus, Prometheus, Selene, Thetis
regretful   Epimetheus, Cronus, Demeter, Niobe, Orpheus
rejected by mother   Hephaestus
rejected by others   Medusa, Orestes, Orpheus, Theseus

reliable   *Aristaeus, Athene, Atlas, Hestia, Orion*
reliant on wits   *Apollo, Hermes, Odysseus, Perseus*
religious   *Daphne, Eumolpus, Hestia, Hippolytus, Orpheus, Sirens*
reneger on agreements   *Atreus, Eros, Hermes, Pelops*
repellent to men   *Athene, Medusa*
repressed   *Aristaeus, Eumolpus, Furies, Hippolytus, Orestes, Selene,
    Thetis*
repressed rage   *Atreus, Poseidon, Sirens, Typhon*
repressive   *Cronus, Uranus, Zeus*
repulsive-looking   *Athene, Hephaestus, Medusa*
resentful   *Achilles, Ariadne, Cronus, Demeter, Epimetheus, Minos,
    Pelops, Prometheus*
resentful of marriage   *Demeter, Thetis*
resistance to daughter's marriage   *Demeter*
resolute   *Achilles, Aristaeus, Athene, Atlas, Heracles, Orestes,
    Perseus, Prometheus, Zeus*
resourceful   *Aristaeus, Athene, Heracles, Odysseus, Orestes, Perseus,
    Theseus*
responsive to unconscious   *Aphrodite, Earth Mother, Great Mother,
    Hephaestus, Hermes, Orpheus, Poseidon, Typhon*
restless   *Adonis, Eros, Heracles, Hermes, Odysseus, Perseus, Pan,
    Theseus*
restorer and regenerator   *Athene, Great Mother, Hecate, Orpheus,
    Persephone, Rhea*
restrained   *Aristaeus, Athene, Eumolpus, Hestia, Selene*
restrictive   *Cronus, Uranus, Zeus*
retailer of others' ideas   *Athene, Helius*
retrospective   *Cronus, Epimetheus, Hades, Niobe, Orpheus*
revolutionary   *Amazons, Atlas, Nemesis, Orpheus, Prometheus*
rich   *Hades, Hecate, Midas, Niobe*
rich recluse   *Hades, Midas*
righteous anger   *Furies, Orestes, Perseus, Sirens, Zeus*
rigid   *Cronus, Hades, Uranus*
riotous   *Dionysus, Eros, Pan*
robotics   *Hephaestus*
rogue   *Atreus, Dioscuri, Hermes, Odysseus*
romancer   *Hermes, Silenus*
routine-bound   *Daphne, Hades, Orestes*
rumour-monger   *Apollo, Athene, Eris, Helius, Tantalus*
running away when depressed   *Demeter*
ruthless   *Achilles, Athene, Atlas, Atreus, Caenis, Hera, Medea,
    Odysseus, Pelops, Perseus, Zeus*

sacrificer of own children   *Medea, Tantalus*
sacrilegious   *Medea, Minos*

sad *Adonis, Demeter, Narcissus, Persephone, Niobe*
sadistic *Achilles, Apollo, Ares, Artemis, Eris, Medea, Minos, Tantalus*
sado-masochistic *Artemis, Dionysus, Odysseus*
safety-minded *Athene, Hestia*
sailor *Aphrodite, Dionysus, Odysseus, Orion, Thetis*
savage to men *Achilles, Amazons, Artemis, Sirens*
savage to women *Artemis, Hephaestus, Heracles, Perseus, Theseus*
saviour *Athene, Hermes, Orpheus, Perseus, Theseus, Zeus*
schemer *Atreus, Hera, Medea, Odysseus, Perseus, Prometheus*
scientist *Apollo, Athene, Daedalus, Hephaestus*
scolder *Demeter, Earth Mother, Furies, Nemesis, Sirens*
scorned for physical reasons *Hephaestus*
sculptor *Athene, Daedalus*
second thoughts *Athene, Epimetheus, Great Mother*
secretive *Atreus, Daedalus, Hermes, Midas, Pan*
secret worrier *Daphne, Odysseus, Prometheus, Selene, Thetis*
seditious *Atlas, Atreus, Eumolpus, Prometheus*
seduced by glitter *Eros, Tantalus*
seducer *Aphrodite, Dionysus, Eros, Hermes, Pan, Poseidon, Zeus*
seductive *Aphrodite, Circe, Eros, Selene*
seething *Achilles, Ares, Atlas, Eris, Poseidon, Typhon*
selectively attractive and charming *Hecate*
self-admirer *Aphrodite, Narcissus, Niobe, Tantalus*
self-assertive *Achilles, Aristaeus, Artemis, Athene, Atlas, Atreus, Caenis, Hera, Heracles, Medusa, Minos, Odysseus, Pan, Pelops, Perseus, Poseidon, Tantalus, Theseus, Uranus, Zeus*
self-condemned *Oedipus, Orestes, Tyro*
self-confident *Achilles, Athene, Caenis, Daedalus, Dionysus, Earth Mother, Great Mother, Heracles, Narcissus, Pelops, Perseus, Theseus, Zeus*
self-contradictory *Artemis, Dionysus, Great Mother, Hermes*
self-crucified *Ariadne, Great Mother, Minos, Orestes, Orpheus, Tantalus, Tyro*
self-destructive *Actaeon, Erigone, Hephaestus, Narcissus, Orestes, Tantalus*
self-destructive if scorned *Sirens*
self-doubter *Asclepius, Hermes*
self-effacing *Hestia, Tyro*
self-glorifier *Achilles, Atreus, Caenis, Hecate, Pelops, Zeus*
self-improver *Aristaeus, Eumolpus, Hephaestus, Hippolytus, Muses*
selfish *Aphrodite, Apollo, Caenis, Theseus*
self-justifier *Cronus*
self-made man *Hephaestus, Odysseus, Perseus*

self-mutilation   *Amazons, Orestes*
self-neglecting   *Demeter, Furies, Niobe, Odysseus*
self-obsessed   *Hecate, Medea, Narcissus*
self-pitying   *Demeter, Narcissus, Niobe, Polyphemus*
self-punisher   *Medusa, Oedipus, Orestes*
self-rejector   *Hephaestus, Medusa, Orestes, Thetis*
self-sacrificial   *Achilles, Ariadne, Centaurs, Eros, Heracles, Orpheus*
self-seeker   *Achilles, Aphrodite, Atreus, Tantalus, Theseus*
self-sufficient   *Ariadne, Artemis, Dionysus, Odysseus, Pan*
self-willed   *Achilles, Amazons, Artemis, Caenis, Pelops, Zeus*
senile   *Cronus, Hades, Oedipus*
sense of challenge   *Achilles, Cyrene, Heracles, Odysseus, Orpheus,*
   Perseus, Theseus
sense of destiny   *Atlas, Fates*
sense of fair play   *Achilles, Minos, Nemesis, Zeus*
sense of family   *Fates, Earth Mother, Great Mother, Hestia*
sense of honour   *Achilles, Athene, Odysseus, Orestes, Perseus*
sense of justice   *Aristaeus, Athene, Fates, Minos, Nemesis, Orestes,*
   Perseus, Zeus
sense of place   *Hestia*
sense of propriety   *Fates, Hera, Hestia, Orestes, Pelops, Selene*
sense of ridiculous   *Heracles, Pan*
sense of security   *Cronus, Hades, Hestia*
sensitive   *Daphne, Heracles, Medusa, Muses, Orpheus, Selene*
sensitive to nature   *Artemis, Daphne, Pan*
sensual   *Actaeon, Aphrodite, Dionysus, Eros, Pan*
serendipitous   *Hermes*
setting affairs in order   *Athene, Hades, Hestia, Minos*
severe   *Artemis, Athene, Cronus, Hades, Hippolytus, Medusa,*
   Minos, Perseus
sex-exploiter   *Aphrodite, Circe, Demeter, Eros, Hera*
sex-mad   *Actaeon, Aphrodite, Circe, Dionysus, Eros, Muses, Pan*
sexual abstinence   *Actaeon, Amazons, Artemis, Athene, Daphne,*
   Eumolpus, Hestia, Hippolytus
sexual boaster   *Actaeon*
sexual greed   *Aphrodite, Eros*
sexual manipulator   *Aphrodite, Circe, Demeter, Eros, Hera*
sexual nightmares   *Eros, Muses, Pan*
sexual turn-off to men   *Athene, Medusa*
sexual victim of malicious uncle   *Tyro*
sexually balanced   *Amazons, Ariadne, Artemis, Dionysus,*
   Hephaestus, Poseidon
sexually immature   *Actaeon, Adonis, Daphne, Eros, Dionysus,*
   Ganymedes, Narcissus, Pan, Selene, Thetis

sexually indiscriminate   *Aphrodite, Ariadne, Centaurs, Dionysus,*
   Eros, Pan
sexually inexperienced   *Actaeon, Adonis, Artemis, Daphne,*
   Narcissus, Selene, Thetis
sexually naive   *Actaeon, Adonis, Orion, Selene*
sexually repressed   *Actaeon, Adonis, Artemis, Athene, Daphne,*
   Hestia, Orpheus, Selene, Thetis
sexually self-sufficient   *Amazons, Ariadne, Artemis, Dionysus, Pan*
sexually uncontrolled   *Aphrodite, Dionysus, Eros, Hephaestus, Pan*
sexy   *Adonis, Aphrodite, Circe, Dionysus, Eros, Hecate*
'shall I, shan't I?'   *Asclepius, Hermes, Selene*
shaman   *Hecate, Hermes, Orpheus, Rhea*
sharp-sighted   *Helius, Hermes, Pan*
shaven-headed   *Dioscuri*
shingles   *Heracles*
short   *Hephaestus*
short hair   *Ares, Dioscuri*
short legs   *Odysseus*
short-term relationships only   *Adonis, Dionysus, Pan, Sirens*
short-term severe illnesses   *Hera*
shy   *Actaeon, Amazons, Aristaeus, Artemis, Daphne, Selene*
shy of exposing face   *Furies, Orestes, Selene*
simple and straightforward   *Heracles, Hestia, Polyphemus*
simple-minded   *Polyphemus*
simplistic   *Atlas, Hestia, Nemesis, Polyphemus*
singer   *Circe, Eumolpus, Muses, Orpheus, Sirens*
single-minded   *Ariadne, Aristaeus, Athene, Heracles, Medea, Pelops,*
   Theseus
sixth sense   *Circe, Hecate, Hermes, Medea, Pan*
skilled fighter   *Achilles, Ares, Athene, Caenis, Dioscuri, Eris,*
   Heracles, Odysseus, Perseus, Theseus
skilled worker   *Daedalus, Hephaestus*
skin-problems   *Dionysus, Heracles, Orestes, Pelops*
sleepy   *Hermes, Silenus*
slippery   *Hermes, Pan, Perseus, Thetis*
slow adjuster to marriage   *Ariadne, Thetis*
slow-witted   *Polyphemus*
smelly   *Pan*
smothered by mother   *Hippolytus, Orestes, Persephone*
snake-hater   *Apollo*
snob   *Niobe, Tantalus*
sociable with other women   *Amazons, Artemis, Daphne, Great*
   Mother, Sirens
socially naive   *Orion, Tyro*

soft inside   *Aristaeus, Asclepius, Athene, Medusa*
soldier   *Achilles, Amazons, Ares, Athene, Dioscuri, Eris*
solid   *Athene, Atlas, Hephaestus, Hercules, Prometheus*
son of remote or indifferent father   *Ares, Hephaestus*
soothing effect on men   *Orpheus, Selene, Sirens*
soothing presence   *Asclepius, Orpheus*
speech-difficulties   *Aristaeus*
spell-binder   *Circe, Hermes, Rhea, Selene*
spiritual guru   *Hecate, Hermes, Orpheus, Rhea*
spiritually aware   *Aristaeus, Daphne, Dionysus, Eumolpus, Hermes,*
     Hippolytus, Orpheus, Rhea
spiritual reformer or pioneer   *Aristaeus, Demeter, Orpheus*
spiritual torments   *Asclepius, Prometheus, Orpheus*
spoiler of children   *Niobe, Rhea*
spoilt   *Achilles, Ares, Atreus, Eris*
spontaneous   *Aphrodite, Dionysus, Hermes, Pan, Zeus*
sports-orientated   *Achilles, Cyrene, Dioscuri, Heracles, Hippolytus,*
     Odysseus, Perseus, Theseus
spy   *Helius, Hermes, Odysseus*
stable and reliable   *Aristaeus, Athene, Hestia, Orion*
stable marriage   *Ariadne, Dionysus, Hestia*
stay-at-home   *Hestia*
stern face   *Athene, Hades, Hippolytus, Medusa, Minos*
stirrer   *Aphrodite, Ares, Atlas, Eris, Eros, Hera, Prometheus*
stormy marriage   *Ariadne, Hera, Theseus, Thetis, Uranus, Zeus*
straggly hair   *Medusa*
stroke   *Cronus*
strong   *Achilles, Artemis, Athene, Atlas, Hephaestus, Heracles,*
     Odysseus, Perseus, Polyphemus, Theseus, Typhon, Zeus
strong hidden urges   *Dionysus, Eros, Great Mother, Hephaestus,*
     Hermes, Pan, Persephone, Poseidon, Typhon
strong on the surface   *Medusa*
strong-willed   *Achilles, Aristaeus, Artemis, Athene, Caenis, Hera,*
     Heracles, Odysseus, Perseus, Prometheus, Theseus, Thetis, Zeus
subject to despair   *Artemis, Demeter, Erigone, Narcissus, Niobe,*
     Persephone, Selene
subject to fevers   *Pelops, Sirens*
subject to homosexual advances   *Ganymedes*
subject to road-accidents   *Hippolytus*
subjugator of women   *Heracles, Theseus, Uranus, Zeus*
sublimator of sex-drive   *Eumolpus, Hippolytus, Orpheus, Muses,*
     Sirens
subversive   *Hermes, Pan, Prometheus*
success-orientated   *Achilles, Atreus, Hephaestus, Medea, Pelops,*
     Tantalus

sudden insights   *Earth Mother, Great Mother, Hecate, Hermes, Zeus*
suicidal   *Epimetheus, Erigone, Furies, Narcissus, Orestes, Sirens*
suicide of mother   *Oedipus*
sulky   *Achilles, Demeter*
sullen   *Cronus, Polyphemus*
supporter of military action   *Achilles, Amazons, Ares, Athene, Atlas,
     Caenis, Dioscuri, Eris, Zeus*
supporter of own children   *Artemis, Demeter, Great Mother, Medea,
     Niobe, Zeus*
supporter of underdog   *Prometheus*
supporter of women's groups and rights   *Amazons*
surly   *Polyphemus, Poseidon*
survivor   *Atreus, Odysseus, Pan, Perseus*
suspicious   *Daedalus, Pan, Selene*
sweet tooth   *Dionysus*
swift-footed   *Ares, Artemis, Eris, Hermes, Perseus*
swollen feet or legs   *Oedipus*
sympathetic   *Circe, Demeter, Hestia, Orpheus, Rhea*

'take it or leave it'   *Odysseus*
take-over of female role   *Ganymedes*
take-over of male privileges   *Caenis, Great Mother*
taking others at their word   *Orion, Selene*
tale-bearer   *Athene, Helius, Tantalus*
tall   *Ares, Atlas, Dionysus, Epimetheus, Orion, Polyphemus*
tantalised by status   *Achilles, Medea, Niobe, Tantalus*
tasteless   *Midas*
tattered clothes   *Demeter, Odysseus*
teacher   *Athene, Centaurs, Eumolpus, Hermes, Orpheus, Silenus*
tearaway   *Cyrene, Dionysus*
tearful   *Niobe, Tyro*
teasing   *Aphrodite, Hermes, Pan*
technically-minded   *Apollo, Athene, Daedalus, Hephaestus*
teenager   *Actaeon, Adonis, Aphrodite, Artemis, Dionysus, Dioscuri,
     Eros, Ganymedes, Narcissus, Pan*
teetotal   *Demeter, Orpheus*
temper   *Achilles, Aphrodite, Ares, Demeter, Hephaestus, Hera,
     Oedipus, Orion, Prometheus, Thetis, Typhon, Zeus*
tempted to kill patients   *Asclepius*
tempted to rape   *Hephaestus, Typhon*
tempting providence   *Achilles, Dioscuri, Heracles, Perseus, Theseus*
tender   *Demeter, Dionysus, Earth Mother, Great Mother, Hera,
     Orpheus, Rhea*
territorial disputes   *Amazons, Ares, Eris, Poseidon*

terror-monger   *Dionysus, Earth Mother, Typhon*
terrorist   *Dioscuri, Odysseus*
'there's nothing you can do to help me'   *Artemis, Demeter, Pan, Tyro*
thick-skinned   *Atlas, Caenis, Polyphemus*
thief   *Hermes, Tantalus*
thinker   *Apollo, Athene, Epimetheus, Orpheus, Prometheus*
thorough   *Achilles, Aristaeus, Athene, Orion, Perseus*
thoughtless   *Athene, Theseus*
threatener   *Achilles, Apollo, Ares, Eris*
throat-problems   *Medusa, Midas, Orpheus, Tantalus*
tidy   *Apollo, Hestia*
tight-lipped   *Tyro*
tinnitus (ringing in the ears)   *Odysseus*
tomboy   *Artemis, Caenis, Cyrene*
tongue-tied   *Aristaeus, Tyro*
too anxious to please   *Orion*
too loving   *Orion, Rhea*
top dog   *Achilles, Atreus, Caenis, Zeus*
tough   *Achilles, Amazons, Artemis, Athene, Atlas, Polyphemus,
     Poseidon, Prometheus, Zeus*
tower of strength   *Achilles, Athene, Atlas, Caenis, Heracles, Zeus*
tradesman   *Hermes*
traitor   *Atreus, Hermes, Odysseus*
tramp   *Demeter, Hermes, Oedipus, Pan*
transcender   *Ariadne, Daedalus, Orpheus, Perseus*
transexual   *Aphrodite, Eros, Narcissus*
transvestite   *Caenis, Heracles*
traveller   *Aristaeus, Artemis, Heracles, Hermes, Odysseus, Oedipus,
     Orion, Perseus, Theseus*
trickster   *Eros, Hermes, Medea*
tricky   *Atreus, Medea, Pelops*
trouble-maker   *Achilles, Aphrodite, Ares, Athene, Atlas, Dionysus,
     Eris, Eros, Medea, Poseidon, Typhon*
trouble-shooter   *Athene, Oedipus, Theseus*
'turning out rubbish'   *Hades*
two-faced   *Atreus, Epimetheus, Hecate, Hermes, Prometheus*

ugly   *Athene, Demeter, Hephaestus, Medusa, Polyphemus*
unable to accept love   *Actaeon, Narcissus, Selene, Sirens, Thetis,
     Tyro*
unable to control children   *Helius, Rhea*
unable to cope with unconscious   *Apollo, Ares, Eris, Heracles, Zeus*
unable to express inner problems at home   *Tyro*
unable to hold alcohol   *Centaurs, Hephaestus, Polyphemus*
unable to maintain long-term relationships   *Adonis, Hephaestus,
     Sirens*

unable to settle down   *Adonis, Centaurs, Cyrene, Dionysus, Eros,*
   Heracles, Odysseus, Pan
unable to tell truth from falsehood   *Athene, Silenus*
unattractive   *Athene, Hephaestus, Medusa*
unbridled passions   *Achilles, Amazons, Artemis, Dionysus, Pan,*
   Poseidon, Typhon
uncompassionate   *Achilles, Amazons, Atreus, Hades, Tantalus*
unconscious urges   *Great Mother, Muses, Poseidon, Typhon, Tyro*
uncontrollable temper   *Achilles, Aphrodite, Ares, Eris, Typhon, Zeus*
unconventional   *Amazons, Artemis, Daedalus, Daphne, Dionysus,*
   Hecate, Heracles, Hermes, Pan, Sirens
uncreative   *Nemesis, Polyphemus*
uncultured   *Midas, Polyphemus*
underground worker   *Hades, Hecate, Hephaestus, Persephone*
undervaluer of feminine   *Apollo, Caenis, Heracles, Prometheus,*
   Theseus
unexpected promotion   *Ariadne, Atreus, Minos*
unfaithful   *Aphrodite, Heracles, Minos, Poseidon, Zeus*
ungovernable   *Artemis, Atlas, Dionysus, Eros, Eumolpus, Great*
   Mother, Pan, Prometheus, Thetis, Typhon, Uranus, Zeus
ungrateful sons   *Niobe, Oedipus, Rhea*
unhappy with own femininity   *Artemis, Caenis*
unifier   *Athene, Hestia, Zeus*
uniformed   *Ares, Dioscuri, Eris*
uninhibited   *Aphrodite, Ariadne, Dionysus, Eros, Pan, Silenus*
unkind to suitors   *Artemis, Thetis*
unlucky as mother   *Demeter, Niobe*
unobservant   *Athene, Hecate, Helius, Oedipus, Polyphemus*
unpredictable   *Adonis, Artemis, Atreus, Dionysus, Eros, Great*
   Mother, Persephone, Zeus
unreliable   *Atreus, Dionysus, Eros, Hermes, Medea, Pan*
unrequired love   *Narcissus, Orion, Tyro*
unselfish   *Aristaeus, Athene, Hestia, Prometheus*
unskilled worker   *Polyphemus*
unsociable   *Atlas, Hades, Midas, Minos, Narcissus, Orpheus,*
   Polyphemus
unsophisticated   *Hestia, Midas, Polyphemus*
unsuccessful lover   *Actaeon, Apollo, Hephaestus, Orion, Sirens*
untamable   *Amazons, Artemis, Atlas, Caenis, Cyrene, Dionysus,*
   Eros, Great Mother, Pan, Prometheus
untidy   *Dionysus, Pan*
untrustworthy   *Atreus, Dionysus, Eros, Hermes, Medea*
unwilling avenger   *Orestes*
urban planner   *Apollo, Aristaeus, Athene, Dionysus, Poseidon*

vandal *Dionysus*
vegetarian *Orpheus*
venereal disease *Aphrodite, Dionysus, Eros, Ganymedes, Heracles,
    Minos, Pan, Poseidon, Zeus*
venomous *Medea*
vengeful *Achilles, Apollo, Ares, Ariadne, Atlas, Atreus, Centaurs,
    Earth Mother, Eris, Furies, Great Mother, Hephaestus, Hera,
    Heracles, Minos, Orestes, Orion, Polyphemus, Poseidon, Zeus*
versatile *Apollo, Athene, Daedalus, Hephaestus, Hermes, Odysseus*
victimised by rivals *Daedalus, Hephaestus*
victim of grandfather's fears *Perseus*
victim of own success *Achilles, Midas, Odysseus, Theseus*
victim of pederasty or sodomy *Dionysus, Ganymedes, Narcissus,
    Pelops*
victim of philistines *Muses, Orpheus*
vindictive to men *Achilles, Amazons, Artemis, Circe, Great Mother,
    Persephone, Sirens*
violator of mother *Orion, Zeus*
violent *Achilles, Amazons, Ares, Artemis, Athene, Atlas, Caenis,
    Eris, Hephaestus, Heracles, Odysseus, Perseus, Thetis, Poseidon,
    Typhon, Zeus*
virgin *Amazons, Artemis, Athene, Daphne, Hestia, Selene, Sirens*
virile *Apollo, Ares, Heracles, Odysseus, Theseus, Zeus*
'vote for me' *Athene, Atreus*
voyeur *Actaeon*
vulnerable *Achilles, Adonis, Daphne, Medusa, Orion, Orpheus,
    Selene, Sirens*
vulnerable to outside influences *Dionysus*

'walking disaster-area' *Helius, Hera, Rhea*
wall of silence *Aristaeus, Tyro*
warlike *Achilles, Amazons, Ares, Athene, Atlas, Caenis, Dioscuri,
    Eris, Great Mother, Zeus*
warm emotions *Hera, Hestia, Orpheus*
wary *Actaeon, Daphne, Odysseus, Prometheus, Selene*
wary of men *Amazons, Daphne, Hestia, Medusa, Selene*
wealthy *Athene, Hades, Midas*
wearing men's clothes *Amazons, Artemis, Caenis*
weaver *Athene, Circe, Fates, Hecates*
weeping *Niobe, Tyro*
well-balanced *Ariadne, Aristaeus, Athene, Centaurs, Dionysus,
    Hephaestus, Heracles, Orpheus, Pan, Silenus*
well-educated *Apollo, Athene, Fates, Orpheus, Muses, Silenus*
well-integrated *Ariadne, Athene, Hephaestus, Hestia, Rhea, Silenus*
wet blanket *Cronus, Erigone, Fates, Furies, Nemesis*

'what a good boy am I!'   *Achilles, Atreus, Helius, Orion*
'what did I do to deserve this?'   *Demeter, Niobe, Orion*
'what's next?'   *Adonis, Artemis, Dionysus, Heracles, Hermes*
'when I was your age . . .'   *Cronus*
'where were you last night?'   *Hephaestus, Hera*
wife-neglecter   *Hephaestus, Odysseus, Theseus, Zeus*
wild   *Artemis, Centaurs, Cyrene, Dionysus, Eros, Pan*
wild driver   *Hippolytus*
wilful   *Aphrodite, Ares, Artemis, Atlas, Caenis, Cyrene, Eros,
    Prometheus*
wilful blindness   *Hades, Oedipus*
winter depression   *Adonis, Artemis, Demeter, Persephone*
witchcraft   *Artemis, Circe, Hecate, Hermes, Medea, Rhea*
woman-dominated   *Hephaestus, Heracles*
worldly-wise   *Atreus, Rhea, Silenus*
worried by time   *Cronus, Fates, Hades, Prometheus*
worrier   *Actaeon, Asclepius, Demeter, Epimetheus, Erigone, Furies,
    Orestes, Prometheus, Selene*
'wounded healer'   *Centaurs*
wounded lover   *Adonis, Orion, Sirens*
wounded pride   *Achilles, Niobe*
wounder of mother   *Heracles, Orestes*
wrestler   *Artemis, Heracles, Theseus*

yearner for unattainable   *Narcissus, Orpheus, Tyro*
'you ought to . . .'   *Furies, Nemesis, Orestes, Sirens*
young man   *Achilles, Actaeon, Adonis, Apollo, Dionysus, Dioscuri,
    Eros, Heracles, Ganymedes, Hippolytus, Narcissus, Perseus*

THEOTHERAPY: REPERTORY OF TREATMENTS

NOTE: The non-Greek alternative names listed are approximate equivalents only. See pages 71 to 85 for instructions.

ACHILLES

A. Adolescence spent among girls; tendency to treat women as chattels; savagery towards self-assertive women; glory-seeking; 'champion' or 'prima donna' mentality; jealousy; sulks; wounded pride; stubbornness; violent mood-swings; over-reaction; temper; overwhelming fury; exaggerated vengefulness; sadistic cruelty; tendency to add insult to injury; loud voice; proneness to gloating; providence-tempting; *hubris*; disregard of warnings of impending disaster; delusions of invulnerability; calamitous downfall at moment of supreme triumph.

B. Bravery; spirit of self-sacrifice; deep sense of honour; strength; competitiveness; tight-lipped determination; ruthlessness; outstanding physical competence; good leadership qualities; charisma; powerful voice; popularity.

THERAPIES Name, imagine and invoke the legendary hero of the Trojan War, the swashbuckling, if somewhat overbearing son of the sea-nymph THETIS; competitive activities of all kinds; military service; martial arts; sports; limelight of whatever sort; media exposure; alcohol (WARNING: beware of addiction).

SYMBOLS Possibly sword, spear and shield.

Notes Achilles is in many respects a spoilt child who has never really grown up. Perhaps because he is too used to being treated as mother's golden boy whom she will protect against all comers, he has somehow become convinced that he has an absolute right to everything he desires, whatever the cost may be to others, including his closest friends. At the same time he also feels driven to excel at all costs — mainly as a result of pressure from his father, who is keen to see him achieve all the things that he himself failed to do. Fortunately, however, this very trait can prove something of a saving grace for him, since the competitive streak is highly prized in modern Western society at least. What he would do well to beware of, however, is a tendency to petulant sulks and violent mood-swings, since these can undermine his competitive position at any given moment, so leading to a tendency to *over*-competitiveness at the next. It is this latter characteristic that threatens to be the real killer, since it lays him open to attack by exposing various personal weaknesses based in paternal conditioning — imbalances which, in a more controlled context, he would never have needed to express in the first place. It is the tendency to 'go over the top', together with a refusal to take warnings seriously, that continually threatens to bare his 'Achilles' heel' to more canny competitors, to the barbs of affronted intellectuals of the APOLLO type (q.v.), or possibly just of over-tempted Providence — whether the threats arise in the political, professional, military, sporting or even medical spheres.

All of which suggests that Achilles would do well to engage himself in some kind of regulated *group*-endeavour — team games, for example, in preference to individual sports — which will give ample scope for his go-getting spirit of competition in a relatively controlled context, rather than risk placing himself alone on the sidelines, where it is all too easy for him to get his personal position fatally out of perspective. In the long run Achilles has the choice between simple survival and glorious immortality, and it is unlikely that he will ever be granted both.

ACTAEON
See also SELENE

A. Voyeurism; would-be rape; sexual boasting; gossip; fear of women; irrational fears; paranoia; nightmares; psychological disintegration; accident-proneness; self-destruction.

B. Love of wilderness; attraction to female beauty.

THERAPIES Name, imagine and welcome the ill-fated young hunter, and son of Aristaeus, killed by ARTEMIS for peeping; dogs; wilderness; hunting (in whatever form — see page 79); living by the sea.

SYMBOLS Stag; stag's horns.

Notes Actaeon's myth is sparse, but he comes across as a shy young man who loves solitude but is troubled by unsatisfied sexual desires which too easily drive him to madness and even to self-destruction. Obsessed with sex, he adores women, yet is scared to death of being taken seriously by them. Among his friends he therefore tries to make up for this failing with brave talk. The wilderness, it seems, can be his salvation, provided that he can avoid human company, and especially the predatory type of female (the reflection, perhaps, of his own over-possessive mother) whose excitation of his animal instincts is likely to prove his chief danger. The syndrome seems likely to weaken progressively with age.

ADONIS
See also GANYMEDES, NARCISSUS

A. Retarded or long-unexpressed sexuality; sexual naïveté; over-susceptibility to erotic advances (especially by older women or mother-figures); resulting proneness to emotional wounding; immaturity; inability to develop lasting relationships; hyperactivity; manic depression; unwillingness to grow up (the 'Peter Pan' or *puer aeternus* syndrome); vulnerability to the predatory female (see ARTEMIS) and to the lure of combat (see ARES).

B. Adolescent beauty; sexual innocence; prolonged youthfulness; capacity for constant change; taste for activity; enthusiasm for the new; refusal to accept old, rigid dogmas.

THERAPIES Name, imagine and welcome the exquisitely-proportioned young god who so symbolises male beauty and desirability in the eyes of women that they feel driven to sacrifice their feminity to him, yet who at the same time is all too liable to fall foul both of the predatory type of woman and of the martial instinct; self-involvement in a variety of sexual relationships involving both extraverted and introverted (and possibly older) women; non-sexual interests, and especially aggressively masculine activities; myrrh (consult a reputable herbalist).

SYMBOLS Dove; fish; myrrh tree; red anemone; red rose; pomegranate; ephemeral pot-gardens containing seed that is watered once only.

Notes The young and beautiful Adonis — one of a number of Middle Eastern corn-gods who die and rise again each Easter — comes to most males at about the age of puberty. Possibly he has his female equivalent in ARTEMIS or APHRODITE. Whether he is to be welcomed or helped on his way is a matter for personal choice. Society needs its share of Adonis-types. Yet maturity is the natural aim of each individual, and it cannot be achieved while Adonis remains in control. Provided that he is kept in balance, the normal maturing process will eventually leave him behind.
    Normally speaking, the seductive APHRODITE (q.v.) can be trusted

to spark this process off — though the initial relationship is likely to be a dark and secret one. It is a truly initiatory encounter with PERSE-PHONE, however, that is most likely finally to take the lid off Adonis's adolescent sexuality. True, his subsequent path is unlikely to be a smooth one. It is almost bound to be marked by emotional ups and downs, rivalries, conflicts and even mortal hatreds. Taken too seriously, these could even destroy him. If, consequently, he is to attain full maturity, he will need to learn to take the rough with the smooth, and to realise that adult married life can never be all sweetness and light. Nevertheless, all the while the archetype remains prominent, spring and summer will tend to be joyful, heady times, full of warmth and passionate love.

AMAZONS
See also ARES, ARTEMIS, CYRENE, ERIS

A. Feminism; initial love-shyness; violent rage when treated as a sex-object; anti-male feelings; opposition to male chauvinism (see HERA-CLES); warlike attitudes, possibly leading to violence; anti-domesticity; anti-monogamy; promiscuity; all-devouring love; emotional ups and downs; violent swings of mood; child-cruelty; self-mutilation; unconventional attitudes and behaviour; possible tendency to breast-cancer.

B. Fair dealing; basic human friendliness; independent-mindedness; psychological balance; matriarchy.

THERAPIES Name, imagine and invoke the marauding army of determined, bare-breasted Amazons, bows and arrows in hands; horses; hunting; music (especially pipes, flute, woodwinds); matriarchal societies; women's groups; reversal of traditional sex-roles; colonisation; city-founding.

SYMBOLS Bull; date-palm; bow and arrow; double axe; the moon.

Notes The Amazons, champions of femininity, are present whenever women combine to assert their collective rights in the face of male domination and exploitation. Perfectly feminine when allowed to be themselves, but highly negative when provoked or treated as mere sex-objects, they represent the natural spirit of female aggression in combination with the spirit of comradeship — ARTEMIS and/or ERIS (q.v.) in collectivity. Their natural milieu is always on the fringes of society. Yet it is also in the nature of the Amazons eventually to over-reach themselves. They would therefore be well-advised to seek moderation and constantly to ask themselves what their real purpose is. In view of their roots in revolutionary protest, any attempt to hijack the establishment is almost bound to lead to their own self-destruction.

APHRODITE
= Eos, Cybele, Ishtar, Astarte, Ashtaroth, Venus,
Isis, Freyja, Yemanjá, Oshoun

A. Initial shyness; eroticism; promiscuity; nymphomania; exploitation of sexuality for personal gain; possible transexuality; auto-eroticism; narcissism; nostalgia for virginity; jealousy; sexual greed; perverse love of strife for its own sake; horror at own perversity; centre of male rivalries; unfaithfulness to husband when presented with a more attractive lover; irrationality; uncontrollable temper (see FURIES); possible maltreatment or even imprisonment of increasingly impotent partner in old age; moods of black negativity; love of darkness; depression; anorexia; lack of favour with women of the ATHENE, ARTEMIS and HECATE types (q.v.).

B. Lovingness; passionate, long-term devotion to eventual chosen partner; lovableness; beauty; attractiveness; sexual allure; fertility; motherhood; child-care skills; tender, mother-like care of partner in middle age.

THERAPIES Name, imagine and welcome the archetypal blonde sex-goddess, the ultimate in female beauty and allure, who brings peace, laughter and universal love in her train; motherhood; self-beautification; red clothes; expensive jewellery; contemplation of own beauty; nudity; naturism; teasing and hoaxes; sex at midsummer; aphrodisiacs; eventual marriage; gardening, and especially flower-growing; pets and animal husbandry; wild beasts; sea-bathing; seafood, myrtle (consult a reputable herbalist).

SYMBOLS Dove; sparrow; swan; frog; buck; fish; dolphin; scallop-shell; mussel; rose; oak; myrtle; cypress; pomegranate; decorated, many-coloured girdle; the planet Venus.

Notes The golden Aphrodite, goddess of the sea, of animals, of gardens and of death-in-life, is also both the quintessential spirit of female sexual desire and an expression of the mother-archetype. Sea-born from the severed genitals of URANUS, she arrives ashore standing naked on a scallop-shell, thus representing the natural female antithesis and complement of male dominance and fatherhood. Fashioned from the foam of the sea, she is bubbly, even sparkling, but at the same time evanescent, and for obvious reasons her charms cut little ice with more conventionally-minded women — especially older ones — who generally affect to despise her.

Aphrodite comes to the fore most noticeably in early adulthood, while her negative characteristics are most prominent when the sex-drive is frustrated by middle age or by uncaring male attitudes. As the astrological Venus, she seems particularly prone to make her presence felt in the spring and autumn. The associated word 'venereal' serves as an apt warning of the risks of sexually-transmitted disease that tend to go with an over-free expression of her archetype in the context of present-day society.

APOLLO
= Horus. Brother and male counterpart of ARTEMIS
See also ASCLEPIUS, MUSES

A. Male chauvinism; naïveté; hatred of snakes; infectious disease; self-seeking; arrogance; shameless behaviour; independent-mindedness; inability to get on with brothers or half-brothers of the HERACLES type; manipulation of others; obsessive reductionism; over-reaction; jealousy; hot-headedness; threatening talk; rebelliousness; need to learn the hard way; unforgiving nature; vengefulness; sadism; bisexuality; homosexuality, perhaps with special attraction to adolescent Dionysians (see DIONYSUS); possible taste for witchcraft and the occult; long hair; failure in love.

B. Youthful attraction to boys of similar age or type; virility; clean living; intellectual brilliance; clear-headedness; analytical mind; methodicalness; tidiness; symmetry; classicism; moderation; rapid learning; musical ability; adaptability; persistence; determination; sense of justice; protection of the oppressed and disadvantaged; oracular or prophetic insight; healing powers; conventional medical knowledge.

THERAPIES Name, imagine and welcome the resplendent solar god and initiator of adolescent boys, with his long, golden locks, his lyre and his bow and arrow; early contact with nature; sunbathing; companionship of boys of similar age and type; adolescent life in single-sex groups or institutions (e.g. Scouts, camps, boys' boarding schools); homosexual and heterosexual affairs; bachelordom; travel; moderate living; specialised technology of all kinds; military work; archery; ballistics; medicine; healing generally; science; mathematics; astronomy; music (especially plucked instruments and flute) and the other arts; vowel-based music therapy;[11] formal dancing; discus-throwing; divination; dream-interpretation; reflection; philosophy; scented clothes; early rising; hunting (in whatever form, see page 79; animal taming and husbandry; youth work;

architecture; construction work; city-planning; law-making; politics; social exile; laurel or bayleaves (consult a reputable herbalist).

SYMBOLS Sun; lyre; bow and arrow; stag; mouse; ass; goat; ram; wolf; tortoise; dolphin; serpent; quail; crow; kite; white raven; vulture; swan; goose; apple; palm tree; olive; laurel (or bay tree).

Notes Apollo, the young and brilliant Sun God, embodies many of the most typically male aspects of the psyche, and can be observed in many a bright adolescent or flamboyant young leader. Though deriving initially from the depths of the unconscious (as does all human consciousness), the spirit of Apollo now has difficulty in recognising the role of the deeper psyche: or possibly his hatred of snakes merely indicates a total rejection of death. Life — and specifically the life of the head — is all, a point which underlies the importance (rarely recognised in the West) of having done with this god before the second half of life sets in, if arrested development is not to result. The point is reflected in Apollo's traditional youthfulness and love of youthful companions. Even — and perhaps especially — if you are currently acting out the role of Apollo, there comes a time to rest on your laurels.
    All this having been said, however, Apollo lies at the basis of most of the secular values currently most cherished by Western civilisation, and is therefore to be welcomed and nurtured in his due time.

ARES
= Mars, Ogoun. Male version of ERIS

A. Conflict for its own sake; combativeness; belligerence; revenge; jealousy; possessiveness; irrationality; unconscious rage; impetuousity; insensitivity; violence; contempt for process of law; mistreatment or betrayal of mother; tendency to scream when hurt; drunkenness.

B. Fertility; competitiveness, growth; expansion; tallness; fleetness of foot; masculinity; strict control.

THERAPIES Name, imagine and welcome this fearsome and brutal martial god, who is both armoured and armed to the teeth; love; self-sacrifice in some idealistic cause; approved military activities; martial arts; military administration; team challenges; justice; civilised arts and sciences; peacemaking and mediation; dancing; female company.

SYMBOLS Spear and shield; horse; wild boar; blackthorn; violet; and, latterly, the sword, bugle, rifle and rocket-missile.

Notes Ares (who has a twin and exact female counterpart in ERIS) is the

Greeks' young, straight-limbed, impetuous God of War — and for that very reason not the easiest of customers to deal with. His difficult nature seems to spring mainly from the absence of a father in his early years, together with the malign influence of desperately violent young companions. Female company may help, but by and large the safest course appears to be simply to give him suitable outlets for his aggression, appropriate situations for him to control, and safe areas in which to indulge his passion for trouble-making — at least until the youthful, martial impulse starts to mellow with age. The use of 'team challenges' as therapy seems not to be without its dangers; the story of the Argonauts' theft of the Golden Fleece from Ares' temple at Colchis suggests that it could merely serve to stir up subterranean passions which only drugs (in the form of MEDEA) can then hope to calm.

Astrologically, as the Roman Mars, Ares seems most likely to make his presence felt in spring and late autumn.

ARIADNE
See also APHRODITE, PERSEPHONE, THESEUS, DIONYSUS

A. Hatred of brother; fratricidal feelings; disproportionate vengeance; desertion of roots for love; difficult or impossible childbirth; difficulty in adjusting to marital status; stormy marital relationship; unfaithfulness; abandonment; subsequent tendency to alcoholism and hysteria; late development; bisexuality; suffering at hands of own children (on account of ARTEMIS); obsession with death; self-crucifixion.

B. Fertility; initiative; ingenuity; self-sacrifice; administrative ability; psychological and sexual self-sufficiency; late dropping of inhibitions; inner wisdom; eventual transcendence of problems; transformation and metamorphosis; beautiful hair.

THERAPIES Name, imagine and invoke the intelligent, if somewhat complicated, fugitive daughter of MINOS, mistress of the labyrinth, lover of the hero THESEUS and eventual wife of DIONYSUS; careful pursuing of a single thread or life-theme through all difficulties; single-mindedness; transformative, even if difficult, relationship with a strong-willed man; separation; divorce; second partnership or marriage; administration; counselling; psychotherapy; work as a psychotherapist; embroidery; moonlight; wine (WARNING: beware of addiction); child-bearing; motherhood.

SYMBOLS Labyrinth; snakes; ball of thread; sword; fruit-laden bough;

rose-wreath crown made of gold and Indian jewels; wind-swung female dolls; the moon; the star-group known as Ariadne's Crown.

Notes The complex Ariadne brings with her bright hopes and much energy in the early stages, but disillusionment and sadness follow as a result of temporarily ignoring her own inner strengths and committing herself to an unsatisfactory sexual relationship. The best way of appeasing her daemon initially is likely to be to find a long-term interest or occupation to take the mind off current difficulties. Nevertheless her experience of failed sexual relationship is likely to help in the discovery of her true self, and a better, more fulfilling and long-lasting marital opportunity may well arise eventually, if from an unexpected quarter and far from home. This is likely to coincide with a new taste for relaxation and enjoyment and a new ability to express herself emotionally — which in turn should lead to a rediscovery of inner balance and completeness, together with a gift for helping others to find theirs.

ARISTAEUS
See also APOLLO, ZEUS

A. Difficulty in self-expression; stutter or other speech-impediment; negative effects on women; drunkenness.

B. Dynamic leadership; initiative; single-mindedness; reliability; clean living; sense of justice; reforming spirit; enthusiasm for spiritual renewal; love; healing; prophecy.

THERAPIES Name, imagine and welcome this thoroughly good-hearted and competent, but socially gauche stutterer, the son of APOLLO and CYRENE, who is always full of energy and idealism; agriculture; cheese-making; beekeeping; olive-growing and pressing; animal husbandry; trapping; hunting (in whatever form — see page 79); public health; emigration; colonisation; city-founding; swimming and subaqua diving.

SYMBOLS Sheep; fish; myrtle; Sirius, the Dog Star.

Notes Aristaeus is perforce a man of action rather than words. Perhaps as a result of early parental (and especially maternal) neglect or lack of attention — or merely as a result of having been sent away to school and subjected to a somewhat stern and military form of discipline — he sometimes appears sheepish, and quite often comes across socially as a fish out of water. But beneath his unprepossessing exterior he has a heart of gold, a will of iron and all the outgoing practical effectiveness of his father APOLLO. Since there is little to be done about the way he comes across to others, the obvious course of action for him to take is simply to get on with what he does best — preferably well away from the parental home. Possibly, indeed, he could take a leaf out of the book of Moses — very much his spiritual kinsman — and get himself a good public-relations officer.

ARTEMIS
= Diana, Iphigenia, Cybele, Kali
See also AMAZONS, APOLLO

A. Suppressed sexuality; love-shyness; coyness; difficult childbirth; pursuit and destruction of the untamed (and possibly untamable) young male — especially when PAN is in control (q.v.); savagery towards, and emasculation of, men — except, possibly, the 'muscular religious' type (see HIPPOLYTUS); feminism; possible lesbianism; masculine — possibly even tomboyish — characteristics; cattiness, or even cruelty, to other women, especially pregnant ones; wildness; aggression; goal-orientation; unattractive 'mask' (compare MEDUSA); strong feelings of modesty; disapproval of others' sexuality; overwhelming love of own children; naïveté; paradoxical nature; rapid mood-swings; witchcraft; intervals of madness; proneness to infectious disease, depression and/or sudden death; possible anorexia.

B. Tomboyishness; love of virginity; sexual abstinence; emotional self-sufficiency; childbirth; loving motherhood; healing powers; sexual and personal independence; love of solitude; initiative; enthusiasm; love of wild creatures; love of dance.

THERAPIES Name, imagine and invoke the fierce and demanding Goddess of the Moon and of Fertility, the patroness of female adolescent initation and the shadowy, winged protectress of animals and of all wild things, accompanied by her hunting-hounds; youthful companionships of girls of similar age or type; adolescent life in single-sex groups or institutions (e.g. Girl Scouts, Guides, girls' boarding schools, camps and expeditions); lesbian affairs; motherhood; childbirth; midwifery; healing; casual affairs; young female friends; child-care; youth-work; teaching; dogs; wild animals (especially young ones); highly physical activities; ritual baths or showers; archery; hunting (in whatever form — see page 79); wilderness; mountains; light; city-life (preferably in one particular city); travel and commerce; music (especially singing); dancing; moonlight; deep sleep; the colour saffron.

SYMBOLS She-bear; lioness; stag; wild goat; dog; horned bitch; gryphon; guinea-fowl; amputated bull's testicles; dolphin; fish; bee; corn;

THE HEALING OF THE GODS

date-palm; cedar; oak; laurel or bay tree; hazel; myrtle; willow; oak; moon; flaming torch; bow and arrow; swastika.

Notes Artemis is, at heart, an adolescent girl with an inbuilt resistance to growing up and a pronounced tomboyish streak. As she grows older, she shows herself to be a self-sufficient, strong-willed and even predatory character. Once installed, she is not easily driven out. At best she can be distracted. As the quintessential Moon Goddess, she has a good deal of black night, i.e. death-in-life, about her. For her, sex is something deadly serious, and not to be undertaken lightly. She can be friendly, yet is quite liable to put her dogs and other pets, or her private and professional pursuits, before her human relationships. If her influence remains dominant in later life, she can turn into a particularly destructive version of the mother-archetype, apparently resentful of the burdens and responsibilities of mature womanhood. In this role particularly, she is maddeningly inconsistent and unpredictable, forever moving amid a fathomless sea of unconscious urges and instincts. Rarely understood by men, and a particular danger to men of the ACTAEON and ORION types (q.v.), she is (for obvious reasons) especially prominent in professional women and divorcees. For equally obvious reasons, her salvation may well lie in work with animals, or with adolescent girls and young children generally. In this latter way particularly, she can combine her much-prized independence with a social role that is capable of bringing her considerable human fulfilment.

In her astrological persona as the moon, Artemis's prime time is midsummer.

ASCLEPIUS
= Aesculapius, Imhotep, Omolu
See also APOLLO, CENTAURS, HERMES

A. Ambivalent attitude to healing powers; awareness that any cure can also have harmful side-effects; preparedness to kill; attraction to godlike power over others, whether for life or death; tendency to philosophical paralysis in the face of events; periodic 'seasons in hell'.

B. Healing powers generally; medicinal knowledge; awareness that even poisons can have curative effects; restoration of fertility; constant gentleness; philosophical holism; support from APOLLO (i.e. civilisation and technology).

THERAPIES Name, imagine and welcome the Divine Healer with his gentle hands, the beloved son of APOLLO; lifesaving; healing or medical practice; first aid; dreams, and dream-interpretation (after fasting); mistletoe (consult a reputable herbalist); hunting; light.

SYMBOLS Snake on staff; bitch; mistletoe; willow; pine-cone.

Notes Right from birth, there seems to be something special about those who are taken over by Asclepius. Perhaps that birth was especially traumatic. Possibly they were exposed to the natural world at an unusually early age. At all events, the ever-helpful Asclepius turns out to be a natural healer. And because he is a true healer, and not merely a dispensing chemist, he has his share of worries and self-doubts, which are duly shared at various times both by conventional practitioners and by alternative healers. All of us, for that matter, act as healers and helpers at some time or other, and his myth speaks to us in our consequent dilemmas. The ever-present temptation to use healing as a tool for personal power is an obvious case in point. But Asclepius's particular problem is that he is only too aware that there can be no mountains without valleys, no light without darkness. He realises that organic diseases can be psychologically beneficial as well as physically harmful, that supposed 'cures' can be harmful as well as beneficial. He is fully aware that anything he does for his patients is likely to hinder them just as much as it helps them, even if this hindering may manifest itself in more subtle and less obvious ways. 'You don't,' in the popular phrase, 'get something for nothing.' And so Asclepius hovers, HERMES-like, perpetually between action and non-action, between intervention and non-intervention, knowing full well that the (literally) godlike powers with which he is popularly credited are largely illusory, and that the only person who can help the patient is ultimately the patient himself, guided by the symbolic intuitions and dream-insights of his own psyche. Perhaps it is appropriate, then, that his prime symbol has been transformed over the centuries into a staff which, like the *caduceus* of HERMES, bears *two* snakes instead of the original one — each opposing the other and so seeming to cancel out the power for 'masculine' action represented by the phallic staff itself.

ATHENE
= Hephaestia, Hygieia, Pallas, Minerva, Inanna
See also ARTEMIS, MEDUSA, PERSEPHONE, SELENE

A. Jealously guarded virginity; excessive modesty; impulsive destructiveness; trouble-making; belligerence; confrontationalism; gossip; unawareness of impression made on others; flattery; diplomatic trickery; inner conflict; deliberate mask of unattractiveness; masculinity; horsiness; fear of spiders; tendency to take on and thus suffer from, others' problems; tendency to be fooled by own arguments; over-hasty responses.

B. Fertility; hygiene; generosity; respect for father; reason; logic; inner balance; restraint; caution; reflection; wisdom; conventionality; pacification and mediation; championing of just causes; invincible determination in war and conflict; courage; persuasiveness; liberalism; tactical efficiency; good judgement; ready intellect; craftsmanship; maternal qualities; healing gifts; counselling; clairvoyance; divination; foresight.

THERAPIES Name, imagine and welcome the powerful, owl-eyed Queen of Heaven and former winged, orgiastic Moon Goddess, resplendently decked out with golden armour, spear and shield; civilised arts and sciences; mathematics; peacemaking and mediation; justice; campaigning for just causes; support of hero-figures (see PERSEUS, ODYSSEUS); civics; politics; diplomacy; teaching; planning; medicine; obstetrics and midwifery; oracular guidance; tree planting; crafts, especially metalwork, spinning, weaving and pottery; silver; flute music.

SYMBOLS Owl; eagle; vulture; gannet; grey puffin; shearwater; swallow; dove; lark; lion; horse; dolphin; goat; serpent; willow; mistletoe; olive-branch; moon; parasol; helmet; spear; shield; flute; clay bowl; *aegis* (goatskin breastplate) with head of MEDUSA attached; swastika.

Notes Athene (who has, in Pallas, a masculine counterpart) is literally the brainchild of ZEUS, and is thus the direct heir to many of his more forceful qualities (q.v.). Since she is also born with the aid of PROMETHEUS and/or HEPHAESTUS, her endeavours are seen to be the direct gift of human consciousness and technology.

In her right niche, Athene is a pillar of society, representing all the most creative gifts of woman, even though she may not express them in sexual terms. As such, her potential is virtually unlimited, her patronage widely sought and freely granted. A born administrator, she nevertheless has a strong negative side to her nature — most clearly seen in the 'battle-axe' syndrome –- which can get her into deep trouble. It is at this point that she starts to become a problem and needs to be treated as such, lest depression and loss of confidence should take a hold and transform her into a PERSEPHONE or SELENE. Given appropriate therapy, however, she is likely to remain the personification of all that is best in a well-ordered and beneficient state, and the very embodiment of the founding ideals of civilisation.

ATLAS

A. Rebelliousness; sedition; implacable fury; aggression; tendency to 'bear the world on his shoulders'; proneness to accept over-heavy responsibilities; hunched shoulders; possible hypertension; back or heart problems; possible hernia; gullibility; simplistic outlook; dangerous intuitive wisdom; inhospitality.

B. Marine knowledge; strength; rock-like resolve; solid presence; leadership.

THERAPIES Name, imagine and welcome the mighty leader of the Titans and elder brother of PROMETHEUS, condemned forever to hold up the sky; diving; submarine activities; revolutionary activities; government; large-scale administration; positions of responsibility; leadership; especially in war; gardening; sunset.

SYMBOLS Moon, oak.

Notes Atlas is a tower of strength. Terrible when thwarted, and an insufferable subordinate, he flourishes when given responsibility, and turns out to be a magnificent leader, especially in times of crisis. He has broad shoulders, a massive, solid presence and an earthy, simplistic nature which sometimes translates itself into a lack of insight and finesse. His main problem is that other people tend too readily to saddle him with theirs: indeed, once he has taken up a given burden, they will not allow him to put it down again. Management and administration therefore beckon, but for his own health he would do well to delegate, and to surround himself with good advisers. Perhaps his major task is to make up his mind just when is the best moment for him to resign and finally call a halt. By and large, the answer is likely to be sooner rather than later.

ATREUS

A. Fratricidal tendencies; deviousness; falseness; profanity; greed; attempt to eat cake and have it too; boasting about ill-gotten gains; undermined by own strategems; misfiring dirty tricks; feigned forgiveness; repressed rage; ruthless vengeance; loss of wife in childbirth; destruction of successive wives; final calamitous downfall; family curse.

B. Good luck; unexpected power and responsibility; riches; fortuitous survival of severe setbacks.

THERAPIES Name, imagine and invoke this shifty, ill-omened, semi-mythical founder of the royal house of Mycenae; administration; government; sheep-farming; astronomy.

SYMBOLS Golden lamb.

Notes Atreus is the archetypal go-getting politician, pathologically deficient in principles or scruples. His 'golden lamb' symbolism suggests that his problem lies in having been treated by his parents as their 'golden boy' who can do no wrong. In order to continue to feel inwardly approved, he has a compulsion to excel at whatever cost — and with such motivation he has an almost irrepressible ability to bounce back after setbacks. Yet this over-achiever always risks over-reaching himself, with catastrophic results both for himself and for his family. And so, while government and administration beckon almost irresistibly, he would do well to lower his sights to some profession without prospects of power or promotion, and to remind himself occasionally of his own relative insignificance. Tempting as it may be for him to say (like the proverbial man jumping over a cliff), 'I seem to have survived all right so far', failure to recognise and treat his syndrome is almost bound to lead to disaster in the end, few though the specifically recommended therapies unfortunately are.

CAENIS
= Caeneus

A. Hatred of own femininity; usurpation of male role; aggression; forceful dominance; militancy; greed for power; overwhelming ambition and pride; thick skin; self-glorification; suppression by CENTAURS; smothered by force of male numbers.

B. Adventurousness; self-confidence; tomboyish behaviour; self-assertion; leadership; rediscovery of own femininity at death.

THERAPIES Name, imagine and invoke the ambitious nymph who lies with POSEIDON and invokes masculinity as her love-gift; masculine activities; armed services; leadership of expeditions; administration.

SYMBOLS Men's clothes; spear; cuckoo.

Notes Caenis's association with POSEIDON reveals that her need to express her aggressive, masculine side springs from a deep, underlying, unconscious need, and not from any mere whim. Possibly it has its origins in some early sexual trauma. In her case, indeed, the need is so pressing as to be a life-long obsession. There is little to be done, therefore, but to recognise the need and, ignoring all suggestions that she ought to try to be more 'feminine', to commit herself wholeheartedly to the world of male endeavour, where she may well turn out to be even more successful than the men themselves.

CENTAURS
= Satyrs (originally), Cheiron
See also DIONYSUS, SILENUS

A. Herd-instinct; group-aggression; mass militancy; mass-hysteria; communal erotic orgies; indiscriminate sexuality; inability to hold drink; drunkenness; vengefulness; vulnerability to HERACLES; collective Titanism (see PROMETHEUS, CRONUS); possibility (if persisted with) of a long final illness involving pain (e.g. arthritis) or poisoning in the legs.

B. Psychological balance; instinctive healing powers; strength in numbers; military effectiveness; individual wisdom and learning; ability as teachers and instructors.

THERAPIES Name, imagine and welcome the wild, animal Centaurs, fabulous creatures that are half-horse (or goat) and half-man, and always on the warpath; imagine, too, their wise old king, Cheiron, with his healing skills and his painful and incurable poisoned knee or left foot, caused by a stray arrow from the bow of HERACLES; sexual activities of all kinds; life in the wild; group-hunting (in whatever form — see page 79); horse-riding; bull-fighting; cattle-herding; military service; individual healing; medical practice; self-sacrifice; alcohol (WARNING: beware of addiction).

SYMBOLS Horse; hobby-horse; chaplet of grass; darts of fir; the constellation Centaurus.

Notes The Centaurs are a slightly older version of DIONYSUS and his Satyrs, with whom they were at one time considered to be virtually identical. Consequently they represent the emergence in the mass of instincts and urges which have long since been repressed by society in the pursuit of civilised living. Rather than drive them underground again, by far the best policy therefore seems to be to provide contexts, especially military ones, in which they can safely be given free rein. However, this approach cannot be applied forever: at some point the fighting has to stop. Soldiering is traditionally an activity for the first half of life, and many a soldier then takes up a second career.

In the particular form of the myth represented by the old healer and Centaur-King, Cheiron, however, it is an incurable illness caused by an accidental wound that eventually calls a halt. He, it seems, has pursued the military path for too long. Yet his suffering at least has the positive aspect that it allows death (see HADES) to be welcomed as a friend. Or possibly it is Centaurism itself that eventually becomes so painful that it realises that it 'hasn't a leg to stand on', and welcomes its own death for the sake of the posterity of PROMETHEUS, who represents human civilisation itself. (The agonised Cheiron, in the myth, consents to his own death in order that PROMETHEUS may become immortal in his stead.) Which, if so, would suggest that the Centaur syndrome tends in time to disappear of its own accord, provided only that it is allowed to do so. Its obvious Sagittarian symbolism suggests that it may be experienced most acutely in early winter.

Meanwhile, at the individual level, Centaurism also has its immensely positive, direct healing aspect. Soldiers, for obvious reasons, need to learn to cope with wounds. But the more general healing gift (so it seems from the myth) tends to surface at some point *after* the wilder manifestations of group militarism, and at about the same time as the unexpected emergence of a deeper, intuitive wisdom whose presence has hitherto been scarcely suspected. Midlife seems, on the whole, the most likely time for this development. Yet here the image is primarily of the 'wounded healer'. The implication seems to be that any healing undertaken by a 'Centaur' is likely to be at the price of the healer's own health, i.e. as a result of his actually having taken on himself the patient's symptoms. Admirable and self-sacrificial this may be — and an intriguing example of the scapegoat-phenomenon in practice — but it is an initiative that needs to be adopted, if at all, only after the most careful consideration of the likely consequences, lest the healer, too, should eventually discover that he 'hasn't a leg to stand on'.

CIRCE
See also MEDEA

A. Fatal seductiveness; jealousy; use of sex to manipulate others; arousal of men's worst instincts; misanthropy; drug-abuse; drug-pushing; witchcraft.

B. Hospitality; sympathy; understanding; premonitory dreams; prophecy.

THERAPIES Name, imagine and invoke the smiling, seductive Enchantress as she weaves her web on her magic island with its drugged wild beasts; isolation; island life; wilderness; early rising; hospitality; counselling; herbalism; free expression of grief; adverse circumstances; singing; spinning; weaving; pork; wild rue (WARNING: DANGEROUS TO

PREGNANT WOMEN, AND POISONOUS IN LARGE QUANTITIES: consult a reputable herbalist).

SYMBOLS Falcon; willow; alder; the moon.

Notes Circe the witch tends to have catastrophic effects on all men who encounter her. Only when she is resisted and even threatened do her more positive characteristics come into play. For the sake of her own good relations she therefore needs effective treatment. The root of her problems seems to lie in ancient traumas which have never been successfully brought out and worked through. These may well demand attention in the most dramatic ways during the midlife years. This, consequently, may be the point for her to forsake her isolation, at least temporarily, in order to seek safe emotional outlets and sympathetic therapies (such as co-counselling) in some highly supportive community.

CRONUS
= Chronos, Bran, Saturn
See also HADES

A. Ageing; dying; impotence; constriction; repressive attitude to own children; obduracy; rigidity; dogmatism; coldness; child-cruelty; infanticide; self-destruction through own misdeeds; continued resentment of parents; regret; nostalgia; introversion; melancholy; depression; insomnia; destructive attitude to new initiatives; fear of change; fear of the new and of the future; mania for order; obsessive counting; self-justification; rebellious sons; perjury; left-handedness; clumsiness; possible stroke, with paralysis of right side.

B. Precocious mental powers in childhood; intellectuality; administrative and organisational ability; good powers of self-healing and regeneration; oracular gifts; inspiration; eventual serenity based on happy memories.

THERAPIES Name, imagine and welcome the gloomy, materialistic old Titan, the murderer of his own father URANUS and usurper of his kingdom, but now threatened in his turn by his own children; literature; writing (e.g. memoirs); reflection; reminiscing; self-immersion in present interests; administration; planning; forecasting; harvesting; ponies; horsemeat; fire; sunset; autumnal oracles; spring festivities; high mountains.

SYMBOLS Crow; vulture; golden-crested wren; ass; horse; barley; cornel cherry; golden falchion (sickle-shaped short sword); the planet Saturn.

Notes Cronus is Old Father Time. He comes with his sickle to reap the harvest of life and make way for next year's seed. Provided that the task is acknowledged and co-operated with, his function is entirely healthy. His negative side, however, is nostalgia and chronic negativity — 'Old is good; new is bad' — the result of failure to co-operate with HERMES at midlife and to realise that death is the ultimate goal, and not the antithesis, of life. The result is a particularly repressive and heavy-handed old man, clinging on for all he is worth to former ways of thinking and acting, and living out the motto 'If it grows, cut it; if it moves, kill it.' This attitude in turn is liable, if persisted with, to provoke violent opposition from his children, leading to the forcible limitation of his power and freedom.

Astrologically, as the Roman Saturn, Cronus is most likely to make his presence felt at midwinter — whence his universal presence as the Spirit of Christmas Past. Untreated, he tends eventually to take on the character of HADES (q.v.).

CYRENE

A. Hatred of household tasks; anti-domesticity; love-shyness; wilfulness; irresponsibility.

B. Love of the outdoors, especially water and mountains; tomboyishness; love of strenuous physical activity; acceptance of challenges; love of high living.

THERAPIES Name, imagine and invoke this wild, untamable virgin Nymph with her passion for all kinds of physical activity; wilderness; animal husbandry; shepherding; cowboy-work; hunting; riding; wrestling; running; swimming and water-sports generally; marriage, possibly to an intellectually orientated husband (see APOLLO); motherhood; high living; being pampered.

SYMBOLS Lion; horse; bee.

Notes The spirit of Cyrene beats in the breast of every keen sportswoman and female athlete. All the while she can remain single that spirit is likely to flourish. Within marriage it may represent a problem. Marriage may thus be seen either as a cure or as a threat. There may be a choice to be made, and correct timing will in this case be of prime importance, if made more difficult by the constant, wolfish attention of men of the APOLLO type with a particular weakness for tomboys. It may well be advisable to send the children of any marriage away to boarding-school at an appropriate age — an action which may have some injurious psychological effects on the children, but is likely to pay off handsomely in terms of training, education and eventual all-round competence (see ARIS-TAEUS).

DAEDALUS
See also HEPHAESTUS

A. Tendency to over-confidence; professional jealousy; suspicion; paranoia; murder and its consequences.

B. Craftsmanship; invention; creativity; ingenuity; soaring imagination; transcendence.

THERAPIES Name, imagine and welcome the self-confident but slightly paranoid Great Inventor; crafts; industrial design; technical drawing; invention; escapology; flying.

SYMBOLS Partridge.

Notes Prominent in designers and inventors, Daedalus is really the spirit of human ingenuity, originality and lateral thinking. He is experienced negatively when the gifts he brings are regarded not merely as saleable commodities, but as personal possessions to be used exclusively in the service of the ego.

Personifying the archetype of transcendence, meanwhile, the soaring Daedalus comes to us as the spirit of self-confidence following a successful transition or a survived crisis (see HERMES). The feeling of having finally 'taken off' should be regarded with caution, however. As the associated myth of his son Icarus reminds us, we can still come badly unstuck if we attempt to fly too high too soon. Caution and avoidance of extremes are therefore recommended. As received folk-wisdom reminds us, pride and over-confidence often precede a fall.

DAPHNE

A. Pursuit by unwelcome suitors; fear of sex; possible lesbianism; panic flight from men — especially intellectuals (see APOLLO); constant washing; possible anorexia.

B. Spiritual awareness; sensitivity to nature; love of mountains and running water; devotion to Earth; love of female company; celibacy; virginity.

THERAPIES Name, imagine and welcome the shy mountain nymph and priestess of Mother Earth who is amorously pursued by APOLLO; ecology; gardening; geology and other earth-sciences; mountains; naked river-bathing; female company; flight and exile; laurel or bay-leaves (consult a reputable herbalist).

SYMBOLS Laurel tree; mare's head.

Notes From a particularly sparse myth a picture seems to emerge of a sexually attractive and virginal young woman who has found her niche in nature and wishes above all not to be disturbed by sexual entanglements, especially with intellectual men. Such men, in other words, could be either her downfall or her salvation. Since the former seems more likely, keeping her distance may well prove the best policy. She may, however, experience problems — or alternatively be forced to overcome her sexual hang-ups — if she takes part in mixed geological or ecological work. Since her natural context is consistent with maintaining her inner balance, there seems to be no special reason for changing it. Far better that she should have the courage of her convictions and simply disappear into the bush.

DEMETER
= Ceres, Isis
See also FURIES, PERSEPHONE

A. Nymphomania; resistance to marriage; withholding of favours when angry; unattractive 'mask' (see MEDUSA); tendency to scold; occasional temper; possessiveness; depression when children (especially a beloved daughter) die or leave home; resultant total lethargy and forsaking of home; neglect of appearance; loss of interest in clothes; deliberate disguise; refusal to eat, drink or wash; possible anorexia; absenteeism from work; absent-mindedness; lapses or parental attention; unintentional harming of others' children; winter depression.

B. Femininity; sexual love; fertility; good with children; gentleness; caring skills; healing presence; gratitude; generosity; underlying sense of humour; slowness to anger; love of peace; deep spiritual knowledge and insight.

THERAPIES Name, imagine and welcome this generous, but sometimes deeply depressed Goddess of the crops and of fertility, at first radiant and golden-haired, then black-robed and veiled, and finally radiant and golden-haired again; agriculture; flower-gathering; bread-making; growing and processing cereals (the word actually derives from her Roman name *Ceres*); corn-milling; wearing of rags, or self-disguise as old

woman (long black dress and veil), when depressed by children's departure, and especially by daughter's marriage; deliberate neglect of appearance; time off work; conscious release of daughter; formal decision to
come to terms with the new situation and share her with her new destiny;
nursery-nursing; youth work; handicrafts instruction; offering marriage
guidance; spiritual work of a pioneering character; self-transformation
initiatives; mirror-oracles; light; perfumed clothes; light or comic verse;
sex; avoidance of alcohol; barley-water flavoured with mint.

SYMBOLS Iris; ear of corn; fig tree; oak; dove; serpent; sow; porpoise;
bee; mare; horse's head; beautiful corn-wreath; flaming torches; serpent-
chariot.

Notes A former earth Goddess, Demeter brings with her many ideal
maternal qualities. Fulfilment and abundance follow her wherever she
goes. But this positive side to her nature is bought at the price of some
inner imbalance — an imbalance which tends to show at moments of
stress. It is at such times particularly — and above all when her favourite
daughter dies or leaves home to get married — that she needs all the
spiritual support that she can find. In the latter case her prime source of
healing may well lie in the time-honoured realisation that (to quote a
well-worn cliché) she is not so much losing a daughter as gaining a son.
Apart from this, her greatest consolation may well lie in contemplating
the theme of ongoing death-and-rebirth, or even of reincarnation — a
theme which her suggested work with the growing and processing of
cereals and other crops may well help to bring clearly to her attention.
Her inherent sense of humour, too, may have a valuable role to play,
especially in the latter stages. Whichever path she chooses, however, she
is likely to find eventual peace and lasting reconciliation with her
circumstances.

DIONYSUS
= Bacchus, Iacchus, Sabazeus, Zagreus, Krishna

A. Drunkenness; alcoholism; imagined invulnerability and prodigious
powers, especially when drunk; exaggerated optimism; over-confidence;
lack of inhibition; dissolute behaviour; chronic vulnerability to insidious
outside influences, especially of a materialistic kind; incipient or underlying feminine characteristics; bisexuality or transexuality, possibly with
special attraction to intellectual men of the APOLLO type (q.v.); uncontrollable erections; exaggerated show of masculinity; thwarting of
women's instincts; sensuality; sweet tooth; ephemerality; chameleon-like
changes of appearance; irrationality; untidiness; lop-sidedness; gaucheness; hysteria (especially in the mass); uncontrollable sexual cravings;

mental disorders; migraines (perhaps especially where the syndrome is repressed); skin-disorders; psychological or physical lameness; body-organ fetishism; sado-masochism; psychological disintegration leading to madness; social disruptiveness; proneness to drive those around him mad; hooliganism; vandalism; pandemonium; savagery; spreading of blind terror; murder.

B. Early tenderness; mother's boy; feminine upbringing, either by mother or by aunts; image of his father; enormous adolescent energy; passion; capacity for joy; humour; fluidity; adaptability; good relations with grandmother; attractiveness to girls and young women; sex-object; strong powers of recuperation; sexual balance and self-sufficiency; good psychological balance; eventual enthusiasm for spirituality; growing insight into the unconscious; growing respect for civilised values; eventual stable marital relationship with a woman of the APHRODITE or ARIADNE type or both; rulership, especially after the demise of a ZEUS (q.v.); faithfulness in marriage.

THERAPIES Name, imagine and welcome the tall, dark figure of the young, wild God of the Vine, horned and crowned with serpents, along with his even wilder attendants of both sexes; attachment to grand-mother, or to an older man of the SILENUS type (q.v.); sailing; swimming and aquatic sports; forests and woodlands; hunting (in whatever form — see page 79); flute music; spring festivities; frenzied dancing; late-night parties; festivals; dramatics; comedy; riotous activities generally; communal feats of endurance; spiritual group-pilgrimages, possibly to India; growing of beard; long robes; eventual city-planning and lawgiving; government and administration; honey; ivy leaves (CAUTION: ALL PARTS OF THE IVY PLANT ARE POISONOUS IN QUANTITY: consult a reputable herbalist).

SYMBOLS Horned serpent; bull; lion; panther; horse; ass; stag; ram; kid; trees generally; yule log; vine; ivy; laurel; phallus of fig-wood; golden apples; pinecone; phallic ivy-tipped staff; bull-roarer; winnowing-fan; dice; ball; top; wool; star; jewelled wreath.

Notes The mother-orientated Dionysus positively bubbles. As both the God of the Vine and 'the god in the wine', he is (quite literally) enthusiasm personified, whether in men and boys or in women and girls. In particular he is the spirit of youthful uninhibitedness, urged on by drink and convivial company. Since he tends, with PAN, to follow closely on the heels of HERMES (who is present at all life's major transitions), he is prominent not only in adolescents, but to a large extent in very young children as well. He also makes his presence felt — if in subtly transmuted form — during the midlife crisis of the so-called 'dangerous forties'.

Basically Dionysus needs a great deal of space in which to express himself safely and without endangering others. Given this, he is likely, like wine itself, to mature with age, eventually turning into a highly responsible citizen. In confined quarters, however, or if he fails to mature with time (perhaps through early blocking or repression), he is liable either to suffer painful internal pressures or to explode, in which case he needs to be approached with great care. Above all he cannot bear to be mollycoddled. Often his grandmother can cope with him a good deal better than his parents.

Collectively, the ephemeral Dionysus manifests himself as the spirit of adolescent mass-hysteria, whether as the goat-like *Satyrs* among youths at football matches (see also CENTAURS), or as the wild, shrieking *Maenads* among teenage girls at pop-concerts, excited by the throbbing of percussion instruments and ready at the drop of a hat to tear their male victims limb from limb. In the former case this phenomenon tends to be exacerbated by the fact that, in the male-dominated and sexually highly-differentiated West — and especially in the Anglo-Saxon countries — young male Dionysians are often disturbed at the god's revelation of their feminine aspect, and react with an exaggerated show of masculinity — 'just in case anybody should suspect', as it were. As a result, HESTIA (i.e. the housewife and mother) tends to be very much put out, and even displaced.

Still in the youthful context, the underlying theme of the Mysteries of Dionysus seems to have been that the god must be sacrificed in his younger form — or rather allowed the freedom to sacrifice himself to his own wild nature — in order that he may eventually reappear in his final, triumphant role as the mature leader and saviour of his people. Only by becoming lost will he eventually be found again. Only by being released is he likely to return safe and sound from his long and perilous voyage. Youth, in short, needs to be allowed its day, for only by working through it can the young ever hope to emerge into responsible and fruitful adulthood. And much the same applies to Dionysianism at whatever age it is encountered.

DIOSCURI
= Castor and Polydeuces (Pollux)
See also ARES, CENTAURS, AMAZONS, DIONYSUS

A. Cattle-rustling; gangsterism; group-mischief; plotting; dissimulation;

ambushes; murder; insults; taunting; danger of sudden death; possible
homosexuality.

B. Comradeship; *espirit de corps*; unselfishness; self-sacrifice; forgiveness; courage in combat; military expertise; energy; persistence.

THERAPIES Name, imagine and invoke the inseparable and ever-adven-
turous Heavenly Twins; soldiering; horse training; boxing; athletics; war
games; martial music; wearing of helmet; short hair or shaven head;
uniform; work as military instructor; coastguard and rescue work;
physically demanding activities; challenges of endurance.

SYMBOLS White lamb; white horse; sparrow; wild pear tree; spear;
white tunic; purple cloak; eggshell cap; the constellation Gemini; double
pillars linked by two transverse beams; Roman figure 'II' (the astrological
sign for Gemini); double amphorae entwined by two snakes.

Notes The Heavenly Twins are the spirit of youthful comradeship which,
whether by land, sea or air, takes young fighters off to war. Both Castor
the horseman and Pollux the infantryman know that the one may live
while the other dies, yet both know, too, that the other will willingly give
his life for his friend. Deprived of suitably constructive means of
expression, however, both are equally liable to turn to other outlets for
their urge for shared adventure — from membership of suitably helmeted
and uniformed motor-cycle gangs to actual group crime. Whatever the
context, their passion is to do or die together. Danger and excitement are
their stock-in-trade. And since nothing can quench this youthful enthusiasm, it is largely a matter of luck whether they or the passion die first.
Dioscurianism, in short, is an almost inevitable characteristic of young
men of martial age, and there is nothing to be done about it but to allow it
suitable outlets, ensure that they have good equipment, and trust that
their natural instinct for survival will take care of them until they have
finally grown out of this phase.
    Astrologically, the Heavenly Twins are closely associated with Mer-
cury (i.e. HERMES), and their prime time is early summer.

EARTH MOTHER
= Ge (Gaia), Oshoun
See also GREAT MOTHER, RHEA

A. Materialism; acquisitiveness; tendency to over-eat; fatness; heavi-
ness; anti-intellectualism; anti-spirituality; powerful unconscious urges;

terror-mongering; vengefulness; cold-blooded insistence on personal rights.

B. Fertility; motherhood; restorative and regenerative powers; soothing and calming influence; eventual discovery of higher consciousness; oracles; prophecy.

THERAPIES Name, imagine and welcome the dumpy and thoroughly down-to-earth Mother of the human race, the most basic and primeval of feminine archetypes; eating; homemaking; motherhood; wilderness; caving; mountaineering; fire; the arts; redress of grievances; laurel or bay-leaves (consult a reputable herbalist).

SYMBOLS Bee; dove; fern; laurel or bay tree; double axe; charcoal heap; *omphalos* or symbolic world-navel.

Notes The Earth Mother archetype represents all the most natural and basic maternal instincts. She even brings with her the natural human progression from early concern with the purely physical — indeed, positive opposition to such 'airy-fairy' concerns as spirituality, especially of the male kind — to a developing interest in the things of the mind and the spirit. Only if the inevitable negative aspects (mostly offshoots of the natural protective instinct towards the children) are out of all proportion, or prolonged too far into later life, does the presence of the Earth Mother call for therapy.

EPIMETHEUS
Brother of PROMETHEUS

A. Retrospection; regret; guilt; resentment, especially of hard work and ageing; incompetence; ineffectualness; profligacy; lack of planning-ability and foresight; heedlessness; unsatisfied passion; false hope; marriage as an attempt to escape inner problems; severe marital difficulties; psychosomatic illness; general health problems; vice; insanity; suicidal tendencies; morbidity.

B. See PROMETHEUS

THERAPIES Name, imagine and invoke this powerful, yet backward-looking and incompetent Titan; see PROMETHEUS.

SYMBOLS See PROMETHEUS.

Notes Epimetheus (whose name means 'afterthought') suffers from much the same problems as his more illustrious brother, except in reverse. Instead of always looking to the future, he indulges in the even more futile activity of living in the past. His most characteristic saying is 'If only . . .' Nevertheless, his basic problem is the same: avoidance of the present, and refusal to live *now*. Any suitable Promethean activity which helps to correct this attitude may thus prove useful.

ERIGONE
See also DEMETER, NIOBE

A. Depression, especially after bereavement; despair; projection of gloom; depressing effect on others; negativity; suicidal tendencies; self-destructive behaviour, possibly involving others too.

B. Motherhood; domesticity; tree-swings; wind-swung masks.

THERAPIES Name, imagine and welcome the bereaved daughter of Icarius, distraught after his murder by drunken shepherds; mourning; open grief; domestic tasks; maternal duties.

SYMBOLS Pine tree; the constellation Virgo.

Notes Erigone's archetype arises above all after personal loss or bereavement. Provided the grief is acknowledged and the natural mourning process allowed to happen, healing will come in time. Vigorous physical activity may be necessary to distract the mind in the meantime.
Erigone's association with Virgo suggests that, astrologically, early autumn could prove a particularly difficult time.

ERIS
Sister and female counterpart of ARES

A. Jealousy; rumour-spreading; vengefulness; trouble-making; strife; irrationality.

B. See ARES.

THERAPIES Name, imagine and invoke this twin and bloody-minded female counterpart of the ancient God of War; see ARES.

SYMBOLS See ARES.

Notes Eris's characteristics are very largely those of ARES, though there is a tendency for them to be exercised at second-hand. By and large it is a case of pushing *others* into conflict, rather than taking up the cudgels directly. For this reason, Eris may prove even more difficult to deal with than Ares himself, other than by devising symbolic 'war games' in which the problem can be reproduced. Encounter-therapy thus suggests itself as a possible treatment. A mellowing of the symptoms seems likely to occur with age.

EROS
= Phanes, Cupid

A. Lust; inflamed passions; auto-eroticism (see NARCISSUS); bisexuality or transexuality; incest; wildness; ungovernability; irresponsibility; immaturity; loud voice; cruelty; cunning; cheating; dishonesty; inability to hang on to wealth or property; seduction by mere glitter; fire-raising.

B. Energy; sexual potency; sexual attractiveness; creativity; spirit of self-sacrifice; idealism; wisdom; ardent love; ability to 'live lightly'; resonant voice.

THERAPIES Name, imagine and welcome the young god of primal sexual desire in all his winged, but self-willed beauty, the son (and thus younger version) of APHRODITE; sex; seduction; matchmaking; nocturnal wandering; sleeping out; hunting (in whatever form — see page 79; activities involving the making and feeding of fire; late-night barbecues; torchbearing; flowers; beautiful surroundings; idealistic and self-sacrificial initiatives; magic; pursuit of wisdom and truth.

SYMBOLS Rose; bull; ram; goat; lion; hare; cock; serpent; bee; goose; dolphin; cuttlefish; phallus; torch; bow and arrow; whip; axe.

Notes Eros personifies most of the bitter-sweet hallmarks of newly-discovered adolescent sexuality and physical maturity in both sexes. In him, too, emerge all those aspects of the psyche which were hidden during childhood. Yet these emerge only because they need to emerge, and so Eros must simply be put up with until he grows up a little more. Human development is not to be hurried, much as we may wish it otherwise. Nor, in the case of Eros, does it need to be, for he carries within him enormous potential for future development.

EUMOLPUS
See also HEPHAESTUS

A. Abandonment as a child; foster-upbringing; incest; guilt; rebelliousness; sedition; defeat and possible destruction.

B. Repentance; piety; priesthood; musical skills; good voice; teaching;
temporal power; empire-building.

THERAPIES Name, imagine and invoke this rejected and somewhat
maladjusted son of POSEIDON with his penchant for sublimation;
priesthood; religious Mysteries, especially of DEMETER and PERSE-
PHONE (the Eleusinian rites); esoteric cults and organisations; teaching;
administration; music (especially singing, plucked instruments and
flute).

SYMBOLS None known, but the infant Moses in his ark among the
bullrushes seems appropriate.

Notes At heart, Eumolpus personifies adult compensation for early
childhood rejection and disadvantage. His choice of therapy is best
determined by the way in which his problem is experienced. If feelings of
guilt are to the fore, as they may well be, expiation may be sought in the
sphere of religion and the various Mystery cults, not excluding Free-
masonry, Rosicrucianism, Theosophy and their various offshoots. If the
symptoms are less acute, teaching offers a way of ensuring that others run
less risk of suffering in the same way. The urge either to undermine the
establishment or to hijack it, however, suggests that no symptoms have
been recognised at all. While this may *seem* the best possible situation of
the three, in fact it is by far the most dangerous, for it means that the
problem is not being consciously addressed, with the result that the
sufferer may unwittingly be led into foolish actions that may harm both
himself and those around him. Consequently, since the problem is
unlikely ever to go away, the best plan seems to be deliberately to keep a
low social profile, as far from political power as possible, while using
music and religion as a source of self-expression and solace.

FATES
= Moira(e)

A. Sense of doom and gloom; pessimism; fatalism; fear of time; awareness of approaching death; false hopes of prolonged life or immortality;
insistence on rights; drunkenness.

B. Childbirth; knowledge of place in society; sense of propriety; awareness that 'there is a time and a place for everything'; literary ability; longevity; optimism.

THERAPIES Name, imagine and welcome the three relentless, white-haired females grimly spinning the thread of human destiny by the light of the moon; white robes; self-exposure to the weather; attention to the calendar and the progression of the seasons; observation and study of natural laws; spinning; realisation that one's fate is very largely in one's own hands; literature; singing; the moon; alcohol (WARNING: beware of addiction).

SYMBOLS Linen thread; moon; oak; brazen pestle; bee.

Notes The presence of the Fates is often signalled by a sense of irrevocable destiny, accompanied either by optimism or by pessimism. Both these last can of course represent problems, taken in excess — optimism because it is generally dashed, pessimism because, while things generally turn out better than expected, it tends to blight the present moment. The realisation that things are as they are, and that the future lies largely in our own hands, is not always easy to come by. Hence, no doubt, the hinted use as a therapy of the simple observation of the cyclic nature of time. The use of alcohol is no doubt intended mainly as a last resort: other soothing drinks may be equally appropriate and less health threatening. The Fates, it seems, are unlikely ever to go away completely, but at least it is possible to learn to live with them.

FURIES
= Erinnyes
See also NEMESIS, ORESTES

A. Over-active conscience; guilt; obsessive puritanism; subjection to maternal taboos; obsessive concern with family rights and duties; posse-sive, predatory nature; menstrual problems; hatred of human bloodshed; encouragement of sycophancy; weakness for flattery; 'martyr' syn-drome; bitchiness; scolding; anger; vengefulness; negativity towards all initiatives; hiding of face; deliberate change of appearance; refusal to eat or drink; anorexia; madness; exile; suicidal tendencies.

B. Righteous anger; insistence on others' rights; support of conventional morality; strong sense of family; matriarchy.

THERAPIES Name, imagine and invoke the three old, implacable Avengers, ever black of looks and clad in grey, but red in tooth and claw; physical or symbolic sacrifices or gifts (e.g. pig's blood); ecology and ecological campaigning; self-immersion in running water; policing; law; charity-work; flattery.

SYMBOLS Solemn matron; bat; bitch; serpent; flaming torch; whip; myrtle wreath; chaplet of iris; kerm oak.

Notes The Furies are the three (or possibly nine) ferocious bearers of society's mores as represented by maternal taboos. They represent the scolding mother, whose claims they support even when these are unjust. Loathsome, horrifying and destructive, they above all represent society's fear of internal disruption and bloodshed. Once present in women, they tend to be endemic, and therefore extremely difficult to balance out. In men (see ORESTES) they are experienced most strongly in the mother's presence, and their influence can thus be lessened — if not always eradicated — by distance. Confession, and close relationships with other, less Fury-orientated women, may also help.

GANYMEDES
See also ADONIS, NARCISSUS

A. Usurpation of women's privileges; tendency to stir up female jealousy; openness to homosexual advances by older men; subjection to pederasty and/or sodomy; liability to being kidnapped; aerial joy-riding.

B. Physical beauty; eternal youthfulness; love of flying; passive, easy-going disposition.

THERAPIES Name, imagine and welcome the comely youth whose beauty and easy-going ways turn the head even of ZEUS; catering; domestic service (or its commercial equivalent); passive homosexual relationships; wind-borne or wind-based sports; flying; sailing.

SYMBOLS The constellation Aquarius.

Notes Ganymedes, like ADONIS, is the spirit of arrested adolescence, the 'Peter Pan' or *puer aeternus* syndrome. In this case, however, his sexuality tends in the homosexual direction, and the syndrome is less likely to disappear with time. Nevertheless, provided that Ganymedes is fully accepted, and not suppressed, he is still capable of bringing with him a life of contentment and blissful fulfilment.

Astrologically, the Aquarian connection suggests that Ganymedes is above all a winter entity.

GREAT MOTHER
= APHRODITE, Inanna, Anat, Astarte, Ashtaroth, Ishtar, ATHENE,

= APHRODITE, Inanna, Anat, Astarte, Ashtaroth, Ishtar, ATHENE, ARTEMIS, Diana, Kali, Parvati, Lakshmi, Ma, Venus, Cybele, Isis, Freyja, Yemanjá
See also EARTH MOTHER, RHEA

A. Materialism; emasculation; usurpation of male prerogatives; negativity; unpredictability; anger; destruction; revenge; war.

B. Fertility; motherhood; love; generosity; unselfishness; self-sacrifice; grace; restorative and regenerative powers; sensitivity to unconscious needs; intuition.

THERAPIES Name, imagine and welcome the archetypal young Mother of the Gods, the source of all life and the very image of procreation, as she sits nursing her infant child that is humanity; reproduction; childbearing; parenthood; guardianship; self-sacrifice in a cause; animal husbandry; agriculture; close relationships with both sexes; work with charities.

SYMBOLS Corn ear or sheaf; Virgin and child; bee; moon.

Notes The Great Mother is the primal female archetype *par excellence*. Ambivalent and contradictory, she is almost impossible to tie down. As earth, she is the great giver and withholder. Yet she is also immemorially associated with the moon. Thus, she ebbs and flows, she waxes and wanes, she is ever-changing. Suffused in light at one time, she is plunged into deepest darkness at another. All that can be said for certain is that she remains, ever-reliable in her fickleness. As the great Mother Archetype, she needs to be accepted in all her moods. And when the demands of physical motherhood are past, she needs to be given other areas in which to exercise her considerable talents if her maternal instincts are not to take purely negative forms of expression.

Astrologically, her prime time is of course midsummer. Yet, for obvious reasons, she also resonates to a regular, monthly rhythm.

HADES
= Pluto, Osiris
See also CRONUS

A. Jealousy of own rights; possessiveness; hoarding; miserliness; reclusiveness; lack of compassion; dryness; stiffness; obstinacy; inflexibility; addiction to routine; puritanism; rare but sudden lusts; impotence; retrospection; nostalgia; lack of vision; blindness to higher truth; poor eyesight or physical blindness; unwillingness to see things as they are; refusal to accept death.

B. Consistency; predictability; rich psychological experience; delight in minerals, precious metals and jewels; monetary wealth; generosity; philanthropy; urge to set own affairs in order; destruction of the material spoils of a lifetime; clearing out rubbish; half-resigned anticipation of death.

THERAPIES Name, imagine and invoke the gloomy, hooded King of the Underworld; withdrawal from the world; reclusiveness; gloomy subterranean places; retrospection; discarding of rubbish; philanthropy; making will; sacrifices of black rams or ewes; mint; rosemary; myrtle (consult a reputable herbalist).

SYMBOLS Gold chariot drawn by four black horses; helmet of invisibility; black ram or ewe.

Notes Hades is the God of Death, who frequently haunts the elderly. Just as his name has come to be equated with hell itself, so his presence reflects a kind of underworld existence, a living death before the event. Typically, he tends to keep himself well out of sight, rarely emerges into the light of day unless hatted, and takes little or no interest in what is happening in the outside world. Instead, he is much more interested in events from the long-dead past. That having been said, however, he does represent the natural urge to die at the right time, and so is normally to be welcomed. Yet he can take over much too early, and this can perhaps be put down to a failure to deal adequately with CRONUS (q.v.) when he appears.

HECATE
See also ARTEMIS, MEDEA

A. Possible upbringing as only child; immersion in the occult; witchcraft; magic; hidden, unconscious powers; two-facedness; bitchiness; crude sexiness; extreme unpleasantness at times.

B. Psychic gifts; mediumistic abilities; restorative powers; gift for sacralising the profane; good luck; wealth; multifaceted personality; charm and attractiveness at moments of her own choosing.

THERAPIES Name, imagine and invoke the dark, winged, hag-like underworld Goddess of Witches in her gleaming 'Gipsy Rose Lee' headdress; shamanism; mediumship; counselling (especially of the dying and of pregnant women); midwifery; responsibility; supervisory duties; policing; road-walking; caving; the sea, the colours black, purple and mauve.

SYMBOLS Screech owl; snake; weasel; mare; cat; lion; she-wolf; dog;

bitch; Sirius (the 'Dog Star'); the moon; flaming torch; junctions of three roads; triple mask; gleaming headdress.

Notes Whether in men or in women, Hecate's most characteristic statement is 'I am psychic.' She is particularly prone to appear during the second half of life, possibly as a kind of mask — a way of coping with the temporary 'loss of identity' characteristic of the midlife crisis. Once installed, she is not to be driven out. With her she brings illusions of specialness and power over others which attract to her all the wrong kind of friends — basically, those who are prepared to bolster her illusions, and especially PERSEPHONE (q.v.). Nevertheless, the genuine gifts she brings can have value in bridging the gulf between conscious and unconscious. Her main danger lies in the temptation to hijack the unconscious for the exclusive benefit of the ego. Should she insist on involving herself in magic and other occult activities, she may indeed be queen for a while in her own kingdom, but it is likely to be an illusory kingdom, a dominion of the dead, and unlikely in the end to bring her much joy. And the unconscious, it needs hardly be said, will always have the last word, eventually confronting her with the stark reality of what she is doing to herself.

HELIUS
= Hyperion, Phaëthon, Helia
See also APOLLO

A. Over-eagerness; misplaced self-confidence; impracticality; carelessness; lack of observation; accident-proneness; tendency to draw the short straw / buy faulty goods / drop bread on the buttered side; inability to look after property; lack of control over own children; exaggerated conscientiousness; over-anxiety to please; doubtful dealing; tale-bearing; subordination to wife or mother.

B. Brightness; perspicacity; knowledgeability; acute vision; sudden insights; conscience; sense of responsibility; stamina; indefatigability; courtesy; purity; cleanliness.

THERAPIES Name, imagine and invoke the brilliant former Sun God as he drives his chariot confidently across the sky with less than due care and attention, eagerly looking anywhere and everywhere but straight in front of him; early rising; dawn; astronomy; astrology; intelligence work; spying; night-sailing; horse-driving; cattle-herding; supervisory activities; responsibility; fatherhood.

SYMBOLS Sun; cockerel; chariot drawn by four white horses or golden bulls; white cattle; poplar; alder; golden chalice; noon; sunset.
Notes The bright-eyed Helius, the historical predecessor of the solar

APOLLO, is something of a walking disaster-area, especially where property or children are concerned. He is a real trier, and full of goodwill — indeed, something of a 'Goody Goody Two-Shoes' — but at the same time he has an extraordinary inability to see what he looks at or to listen to what he hears. Yet he is quite prepared to broadcast it to others. And so this 'eager beaver' who is always on the go comes across as one with great knowledge who is nevertheless unwilling or unable to practise what he preaches, or as a father or husband who knows all the answers, but always manages to make a hash of things. Like Icarus (see DAEDALUS), he is especially vulnerable to disaster if (in his incarnation as Phaëthon) he attempts to fly too high. The opportunity for relaxation and quiet contemplation provided by some of the therapies suggested could thus have a valuable role to play in redressing the balance between theory and practice, between intention and result. A study of holistic therapies might also help. Somehow, it seems, the heat needs to be taken out of the situation. Some kind of 'step back' is likely to get things into less burning perspective and lead to calmer, more effective and competent action. Helius seems to have his female counterpart, too, in his daughter Helia.

HEPHAESTUS
= Thor, Vulcan, Ogoun
See also DAEDALUS

A. Childhood trauma or weakness, possibly following premature birth; psychological maladjustment; physical disablement; possible arthritis; dwarfism; ugliness; rejection by mother; possible violent fall; bad temper; unpredictable mood-swings; rebelliousness; negative mother-fixation; inability to relate successfully to women; lack of sexual control; tendency to rape; cuckoldhood; disappointment in love; liability to be victimised by rivals; attempted revenge; obsession with ensnaring rivals; manipulation of unconscious forces; pyromania; self-destructiveness; inability to hold alcohol.

B. Physical compensation for early weakness; strength; solidity; cleverness with hands; practicality; technical skill; imagination; creativity; inventiveness; artistic ability; perfectionism; cultural eminence and recognition; occult gifts; capacity for reconciliation and forgiveness; skill as peacemaker; use of self-mockery to defuse social tensions; understanding of women.

THERAPIES Name, imagine and invoke the lame, heavily-built Smith-God labouring at his forge; fire; vulcanology; building and construction; skilled manual work; crafts (especially jewellery and metalwork); invention; toolmaking; machine-tool design; robotics; midwifery; mediation; humour; subaqua diving.

SYMBOLS Sun; fire; cockerel; partridge; fine chain; hammer and tongs.

Notes Hephaestus is in many respects the spirit of adult compensation for childhood disadvantage and a difficult maternal relationship. Scars still remain, of course, but these are put to positive use. And although there are many setbacks and pains along the way, pre-eminence in one form or another tends to result eventually. Particularly prominent in the technical sphere, Hephaestus is thus a version of the 'local boy makes good' phenomenon. Highly-orientated as he is towards achieving success — he tends, as we say, to 'go at things hammer and tongs' — his main problem is not to allow his work and aspirations to go to his head to such an extent that he leaves no room or time for actually *living*. In later life he may well find himself drawn to compensate for this earlier imbalance through acts of charity and generosity. A deliberately Epicurean lifestyle may also help.

HERA
= Juno
See also PERSEPHONE

A. Fatal softness; gullibility; dependence; ill-treatment by husband and sons; shame; embarrassment; bickering; scheming; meddling; intrigue; lying; insane jealousy; use of sex as a weapon; 'unnatural' passions for animals; anger; ruthlessness; vengefulness; repeated desertion of husband; retreat into isolation; hatred of own children, adopted children, servants or agents; long periods of depression; temporary paralysis; rheumatism or back-problems; risk of death.

B. Beauty; femininity; fidelity; motherhood, tenderness; emotional warmth; pity; love of virginity; conventionality; insistence on monogamy; physical modesty; eventual reconciliation with children or adopted children.

THERAPIES Name, imagine and welcome the jealous and rather shrewish wife and twin of ZEUS, the cow-eyed leader of the female faction on Olympus and Goddess of Death and Resurrection; monogamous marriage; childbearing; midwifery; fostering, adoption; separation; divorce; all-concealing clothing; female athletics and gymnastics; back-stretching exercises (seek qualified advice); gardening; attention to calendar and the phases of the moon; swimming and bathing, espcially in clear spring-water; wearing of bangles, bracelets and anklets.

SYMBOLS Cow; cuckoo; apple tree; pomegranate; mayflower or white-thorn; double axe.

Notes Hera is a complicated character. Endowed with all the positive characteristics of a good wife and mother, she is at the same time so prone to feelings of jealousy that she is prepared to sacrifice and destroy everything she believes in — even her own life, if need be — in an attempt to re-establish what she believes to be her rights. Consequently her married life tends to be dogged by ever-growing crisis. In this she tends to be motivated more by her image of men than by the way her man actually is, and so tends to come into fatal collision with his parallel tendency to see only his image of woman, rather than the actual human being beside him. The victim of early paternal conditioning, she may thus do well to seek an alternative destiny outside marriage, and particularly in close proximity to nature.

HERACLES
= Hercules, Horus, Gilgamesh, Rama

A. Machismo; male chauvinism; antagonising of women; confrontationalism; combativeness; bloody-mindedness; providence-tempting; flouting of civilised conventions; wounding of mother; sexual excesses; promiscuity; unfaithfulness; enslavement to female sexuality; possible domination by wife; brief homosexual escapades; transvestite interludes; restlessness; evil dreams; bitterness; vengefulness; inability to settle down; temporary depression or madness; skin-problems; possible shingles or herpes; hypersensitivity.

B. Physical strength; youthful prodigies; heroism; sense of challenge; originality; all-round ability; urge to push back limits; persistence; opposition to cruelty; sympathy for living things; admiration of father; courtesy; aggression only when provoked; mournfulness; humour; sense of the ridiculous; sensitivity to omens; eventual recognition of own dispensability.

THERAPIES Name, imagine and welcome the archetypal hero and strong-man, always game for a challenge; competitive sport, especially athletics; women; hunting and shooting; animal-taming; physical challenges; hard manual labour; rescue work; military activities; expeditions; portering; austerities; feats of endurance; opening up new fields of endeavour; civilising missions; entrepeneurial activities; civil engineering; city-founding; little food at midday; isolation and darkness when depressed; auguries based on vultures; wild marjoram, cow parsnip (heracleum), henbane or aconite (WARNING: HENBANE IS POISONOUS, AND ACONITE INTENSELY SO: consult a reputable herbalist).

SYMBOLS Ox; club; lionskin cape; wild olive tree; poplar; aspen; upturned thumb; the Zodiac.

Notes Heracles is the archetypal hero (the two words are actually connected), and mythical founder of the Olympic games. He is the guiding spirit of male adolescence, most prominent from puberty until the early twenties. He glories mainly in physical strength and achievement, and may have little time for intellectual pursuits, let alone for spiritual matters. He loves the company of women, but his attitude to them is abysmal. In his proper time he represents a major development archetype whose promptings need to be acknowledged. He becomes a major problem only if not released when his work is done — and especially if he is persisted with after midlife, and in the face of the growing weakness of old age.

HERMES
= Mercury, Oshossi
See also HECATE, SILENUS

A. Insecurity; restlessness; obsessive nomadism; addiction to change; ephemerality; elusiveness; shiftiness; secret violation of rules; insolence; shamelessness; inconsistency; deception; dissimulation; lying; teasing; flattery; ambushing; banditry; cattle-rustling; secrecy; cunning; kleptomania; thieving; fraud; perjury; trickery; seduction; uncontrollable erections; bisexuality; apparent lack of compassion; contempt for clothes; regarded by women as a plaything.

B. Child prodigy; intelligence; self-recollectedness; self-awareness; learning-ability; adaptability; flexibility; cunning; hidden wisdom; perspicacity; eloquence; flair for word-magic; skill in foreign languages; young outlook; youthful good looks; adventurousness; keen vision; sudden insights; manual quickness and dexterity; open-mindedness; detachment; sexual frankness and lack of inhibition; originality; lateral thinking; luck; serendipity; opportunism; skill with animals and young boys; friendliness; kindness; gentleness; craftsmanship; athleticism; fleetness and lightness of foot; playfulness; healing ability; shamanic powers; flair for transforming hopeless situations; musical gifts.

THERAPIES Name, imagine and welcome the young, winged God of

Transitions and brother of APHRODITE, ever crafty and resourceful beneath his brimmed hat, and with a secret smile on his bearded lips; poetry; musical improvisation (especially on plucked instruments and flute); early rising; athletics; gymnastics; boxing; responsibility; work as a doorkeeper or watchman; domestic service (or its commercial equivalent); care of animals; work as a guide; escorting women; giving information and directions; travel; commerce; diplomacy; translation and interpreting; musical interpretation; orchestral conducting; administrative work; forecasting; forward planning; learning and civilised arts; rhetoric and philosophy; teaching; protective activities; the law; detective work; work in counselling; healing and/or psychotherapy; hypnotism; priesthood; ritual sacrifices; initiations; contact with the dying; attention to dreams, synchronicities and symbolic events; magic and alchemy; herbalism; dream-interpretation; games of chance; fire-walking; nocturnal wandering; naturism; nudity; siestas; dozing; sedatives; alcohol (WARNING: beware of addiction).

SYMBOLS Twin serpents or white ribbons on golden staff; brimmed hat; traveller's cloak; winged sandals; crossroads; frontiers; freshwater springs; whip; phallus; wild crane; gosse; dog; hare; tortoise; ram; lyre; fire; the number four; myrtle (consult a reputable herbalist).

Notes The elusive Hermes, who personifies the archetype of initiation in both sexes, is to be found working in the shadows at all of life's major transitions — and especially at adolescence, midlife and death. No doubt he is present at birth, too. Moreover, he has to be co-operated with if the transition is to be successfully made. This means accepting all the insecurities and contradictions, the regressions and retakes, the resurfacing of long-buried experiences and traumas, even the inability at times to see any way out. Once he has been allowed to do his job, he will depart, having demonstrated that — unlikely as it may have seemed at the time — he is truly the messenger of the gods, his magic staff the reconciler of the twin serpents of duality, the uniter of the above with the below, of conscious with unconscious, of man with himself. And at this point a kind of 'new childhood' tends to announce itself, characterised above all by PAN and DIONYSUS.

In the words of the crippled Roman slave-philosopher, Epictetus (c. AD 60-120): 'Come illness, come death, come penury and disdain, come mortal trial — all these shall be turned to good by Hermes' wand.'

Astrologically, as the Roman Mercury, Hermes seems most likely to make his presence felt in early and late summer. In that role he also acquires mercury, or quicksilver, as a further symbol.

HESTIA

= Vesta See also EARTH MOTHER

A. Stay-at-home tendency; exaggerated self-effacement; over-concern with personal security; rigid sense of values; conservatism; willingness to buy domestic peace at almost any price; characterlessness; obsessive virginity; Olympian detachment from external affairs; inability to cope with the wildness and animalism of teenagers; tendency to leave home when under extreme pressure from this quarter.

B. Virginity or celibacy; love of home and hearth; hospitality; moral uprightness; transmission of received culture; enjoyment of personal security and happiness; stability; sense of order; centredness; psychological balance; sense of focus or direction; determination; sense of belonging; sense of place; perspicacity; self-effacing nature; unselfishness; emotional warmth.

THERAPIES Name, imagine and invoke this least known of the Olympians, the colourless and rather straight-laced goddess to whom the Roman Vestal Virgins were dedicated; religious orders; giving of hospitality; open fires; home-making; house-construction; architecture; mead (WARNING: beware of alcohol-addiction).

SYMBOLS Hearth; fire; circle; *omphalos* or navel.

Notes Hestia's myth seems to have been devalued from the time of her symbolic displacement from Olympus by the young DIONYSUS. What remains of it, however, suggests that Hestia is in many ways the archetypal maiden aunt, the 'shrinking lily' perfectly happy with her way of life and unwilling to put it at risk by introducing new variables into it. In her married form she expresses herself in the home-loving mother with no detectable sense of adventure and no wish other than to fulfil her chosen role. As such, she is the hub of the family, the hander-on of received values, the ever-watchful bringer of order and stability, the focus of the family's sense of security and belonging. Since she clearly brings happiness and fulfilment, there is no need to regard her as a problem unless and until she starts to get in the way of the continuing process of personal inner development, or threatens the continuing cohesiveness of the family when the children start to reach adolescence. In this latter eventuality, it may prove useful for her to leave home temporarily, at least until suitable therapy can be set in train.

HIPPOLYTUS
See also AMAZONS, ARTEMIS, ORESTES

A. Incestuous attempts at seduction by mother or stepmother; subjection to wrongful accusations of rape; wild riding or driving; proneness to road accidents; narrow escape from death; exile; adultery.

B. Religious fervour and devotion; chastity; purity; severity; athleticism; marriage in second half of life; secluded and peaceful retirement.

THERAPIES Name, imagine and invoke the energetic bastard son of THESEUS, sublimated idealist, athlete and charioteer — and latterly adopted, for good measure, as a Christian saint; religious rituals; bachelordom; sport; athletics; driving; motor-racing and rallying; horses; hunting (in whatever form – see page 79); retirement in the wilderness, well away from horses and other forms of transport; deliberate disguise or change of appearance.

SYMBOLS Olive; myrtle; the constellation Auriga (the Charioteer).

Notes Rather like ORESTES, Hippolytus is pursued by his mother — or at least his stepmother — though in this case the attachment is a sexual one, whether hidden or overt. His response is to seek refuge in sexual sublimation, whether religious or athletic (his particular devotion is in fact to ARTEMIS, who generally supports him in a kind of platonic relationship). When matters finally come to a head he is forced to flee far from home, where the very wildness of his redirected passion nearly brings about his downfall. Only during the second half of life, possibly after his mother's death — and very nearly after his own — is he eventually able to settle down with a woman and find peace.

MEDEA
See also CIRCE, HECATE

A. Magic; witchcraft; deviousness; trickery; cruelty; poisoning; insane jealousy; bloodthirstiness; ambition for selected children; preparedness to destroy rest of family.

B. Psychic gifts; healing powers; constancy; determination; support for own children.

THERAPIES Name, imagine and invoke this cruel, archetypal witch and dark weaver of intrigues who murders her own brother and children to further her own ends; snake-charming; meadow-saffron (WARNING: HIGHLY POISONOUS: consult a reputable herbalist).

SYMBOLS Moon; winged serpent.

Notes Medea's myth is sketchy, but out of it emerges the unmistakable picture of a woman consumed with personal ambition, which she is prepared to pursue with utmost ruthlessness — even by proxy through her own children or, if need be, at their expense. This trait she compounds with an unhealthy passion for the occult. Totally ruthless and calculating, this spirit of untamed female egotism is thus a danger to herself, her family and everybody around her. Possibly that is why the surviving records have little to say about therapies. Apart from suggesting that she confine her activities to relatively harmless contexts, the best that can be done seems to be to attempt to concentrate on purely positive applications of such gifts as she has. Weaving, basketry and tapestry-work could possibly help. On the whole, the syndrome tends, if anything, to increase, rather than to disappear, with age.

MEDUSA
See also FURIES, PERSEPHONE

A. Possible youthful victim of rape or attempted rape; acquired ugliness; straggly hair; glaring eyes; unattractiveness to men; tendency to render men impotent; masculine characteristics; finds sex deeply disturbing (see POSEIDON); petrifying effect on others; sacrilege; iconoclasm; bossiness.

B. Cunning; self-assertion; impression of power; inwardly soft, gentle and sensitive.

THERAPIES Name, imagine and welcome the fearsome, Gorgon-headed monster who, for all her soft inside, turns all living creatures to stone; horse-rearing and training; moonlight.

SYMBOLS Gorgon mask, with scowl, glaring eyes, protruding tongue between bared teeth, and snakes for hair; the moon.

Notes There is no getting away from it: Medusa is ugly. Yet underneath her hard and unattractive exterior, she is quite remarkably soft and beautiful. She is also very vulnerable and sensitive. Possibly she has been deeply wounded by a man at some time in the past. At all events, she now insists on wearing a hideous mask, which has the effect of repelling not only men, but other women as well. Virtually ostracised, she thus turns very easily to negative and destructive attitudes which can all too easily reflect back on herself — whereupon *self*-rejection is likely to be added to her other problems. It is important, therefore, that she should find opportunities for putting her dragon-like persona to good and creative use. The reference to horse-rearing suggests that any profession which allows her to wield unquestioned authority over underlings may prove suitable. At one time she would have been welcome in the teaching profession, but nowadays policing, the armed services or hospital administration may well prove more appropriate. In time she may even find herself able to take on the mantle of ATHENE.

As the myth of PERSEUS suggests, Medusa is that aspect of woman (and especially of motherhood) that every young hero has to learn to disregard and disempower if he is finally to make the grade as a full-grown adult. He may even discover that he himself has taken on some of her force in the process. Medusa's association with the moon suggests that, astrologically, she may be at her fiercest at midsummer, while her aggressive tendencies may wax and wane to a monthly rhythm.

MIDAS
See also DIONYSUS, SILENUS

A. Love of pleasure; desire for riches; lack of taste; tendency to make an ass of himself; fear of having personal secrets divulged; digestive problems (possibly involving inability to eat or drink); possible anorexia; eventual horror of riches; possible suicide by poison.

B. Superabundance of riches; golden touch; luck; ability to fall on his feet.

THERAPIES Name, imagine and welcome the rather stupid king with the Golden Touch; executive power; entertainment; sensual pleasures; drinking sessions with old cronies; extravagant fiction; rose-gardens; grooming by servants; self-cleansing in river-sources.

SYMBOLS Ass's ears.

Notes Midas is really an adolescent who has never grown up, obsessed with the lures of materialism. Possibly he is over-compensating for early deprivation. After a vigorous and hopeful start, he brings with him all the social and cultural problems of the *nouveau riche*, and finishes up trying to cope with the even severer psychological problems of the millionaire recluse. He may have some lessons to learn from HEPHAESTUS but, failing that, he is heading for a gloomy old age whose misery is the direct reward for obsessive materialism prolonged beyond its time. The prospect carries with it its own clear lesson.

MINOS

A. Early homosexuality or pederasty; homosexual jealousy; determined and prolonged vengefulness; profanity; sacrilege; infidelity; unrelenting pursuit of young women of the ARTEMIS type (q.v.); venereal disease; eventual withdrawal behind multiple barriers; reclusiveness; possible mortal fever or scalding.

B. Luck of the gods; promotion to power; administrative ability; political charisma; sense of mission; good judgement; perspicacity.

THERAPIES Name, imagine and invoke the powerful and complicated king of Crete, semi-legendary leader of the federation of the Sea Peoples and subsequent judge of the dead; administration; justice; law-enforcement; complex dances.

SYMBOLS Bull; Minotaur, labyrinth; double axe; waxing and waning moon.

Notes Minos is a manifestation of the spirit of compensation and sublimation. Prominent in numerous world-renowned leaders, both in modern and in ancient times, he lies behind the transformation of many an inwardly tortured and complex individual into a leader and administrator of unexpectedly resplendent gifts. Symbolically, the labyrinth is his mind, and at its centre lurks a half-known monster which he dares not face. To it, in consequence, he would rather dedicate his greatest life-endeavours by way of sacrifice, sweeping along those around him in the process. True, his inner guilts and resentments will tend to catch up with him in the end, but until they do he can achieve a considerable measure of self-fulfilment and social usefulness which can, to an extent, offset and even defuse the inner situation. The *labrys,* or double axe, cuts both ways. *Destroying* the lurking Minotaur, however, is something which only the heroic THESEUS can undertake, and even he needs the help of Minos's daughter ARIADNE, who represents his rediscovery of his long-buried feminine side.

MUSES
See also APOLLO

A. Obsession with sex; promiscuity; orgies; sexual nightmares; proneness to lying.

B. Sublimation of sex-drive; aptitude for learning and training; artistic and poetic skills and discrimination; ability to produce both factual and fictional literature; oratory; acting; linguistic skills; healing powers; prophetic gifts; musicianship; astronomical knowledge; historical learning; good memory.

THERAPIES Name, imagine and invoke the nine bird-like mountain divinities and sophisticated patronesses of the arts; music (especially singing and flute); dance; drawing and painting; sculpture; architecture; literature; art criticism; astronomy; teaching; public speaking; animal husbandry (especially sheep); divination using pebbles.

SYMBOLS Tablet and stylus; book; roll of paper; lyre; plectrum; flute; tragic and comic masks; club or sword; shepherd's crook; ivy-wreath; laurel-wreath; staff pointing at globe; bee(s).

Notes The Muses are characterised by a deep inner contradiction. At basis they are intensely sexual beings, yet at the same time they tend, like both ACTAEON and SELENE, to be frightened by the sheer power and ungovernability of the sex-instinct. Perhaps that is why they bear with them their own therapies, personifying the imposition of cultural values on a nature which is otherwise purely instinctive, wild and uncontrolled. The result may well be a person who is vigorous, healthy and at the same time a lifelong model of civilised virtues.

NARCISSUS
= Hyacinthus, Hermaphroditus
See ADONIS, GANYMEDES

A. Possible subjection to pederasty, with special vulnerability to intellectual men of the APOLLO type; incipient bisexuality or transexuality; self-love; admiration of own beauty; narcissism; egocentricity; auto-eroticism; fear of emotional or sexual rejection; rejection of love by others; unsociability; love of sound of own voice; love of the unattainable; lethargy; back-to-the womb feelings; possible anorexia; death-wish; suicidal tendencies; self-destruction.

B. Eternal youthfulness; beauty; attractiveness to others of both sexes; silent admiration from gentle, passive women who are by nature afraid to make the first move; self-confidence; self-sufficiency; independence; idealism; quasi-sexual attraction to water.

THERAPIES Name, imagine and invoke the beautiful, languorous youth of sixteen summers gazing morbidly at his own reflection in the water; auto-erotic practices; masturbation; reflection; self-examination; pursuit of self-knowledge; rivers and lakes; plunging into clear water; acting; public speaking and entertainment; teaching; the church; narcissus or lily-of-the-valley; hyacinth (WARNING: NARCISSUS, LILY-OF-THE-

VALLEY AND HYACINTH ARE POISONOUS: consult a reputable herbalist).

SYMBOLS Narcissus; lily-of-the-valley or iris; hyacinth.

Notes The spirit of Narcissus haunts most boys at puberty in one form or another. Like ADONIS and GANYMEDES, he is liable, if persisted with, to become in later years an epiphany of the spirit of arrested adolescence (the 'Peter Pan' or *puer aeternus* syndrome). In this case, however — possibly as a result of parentally-inspired fears of rejection — he is stuck at the very early auto-erotic stage. The result may well be difficulty in forming adult relationships. Though beloved by others of both sexes, he is unable to respond adequately, and while he has great idealism, he may well have to pay for it with a full measure of despair and heartbreak. If he remains unrecognised for too long, Narcissus is likely to prove a danger to the patient who identifies with him. Recognised, however, this troubled spirit tends to destroy *himself* — so, at least, the myth seems to suggest. Early and genuine self-understanding is therefore important, and any treatment which tends to lead to this, be it psycho-analysis or some other form of psychotherapy, is to be welcomed.

The associated story of the fifteen-year-old Hermaphroditus (son, as the name suggests, of HERMES and APHRODITE) meanwhile reflects a form of the syndrome with a more hopeful prognosis. In this case the subject's narcissistic fascination with water is so strong that he literally prefers plunging into it to plunging into sexual liaisons. Yet therein lies his salvation. For in so doing he does contrive to express his ambivalent sexuality, albeit in substitute form, and so achieves not only sexual satisfaction, but inner balance and emotional serenity too. There is even a hint in the story that he may eventually find happiness with a like-minded women of a passive, soothing, domestic and above all totally dedicated disposition, and not at all like ARTEMIS.

NEMESIS
= Leda, Leto, Fortuna
See also FURIES

A. Negativity; cutting down to size; retribution; fatalism; pessimism; conviction that every silver lining has its cloud; sense of impending doom; violent rejection of, and flight from, advances by dominant, successful males; chameleon-like changes of character.

B. Fertility; sense of duty; justice.

THERAPIES Name, imagine and welcome this winged, yet pessimistic

Goddess of Death-in-Life with a chip on both shoulders; law; reform; revolutionary activities; pastoralism.

SYMBOLS Wheel; scourge; bit and bridle; apple-bough; ash tree; stag; goose; fish; swan.

Notes The records of the myth of Nemesis are scant, and a measure of interpretation has perforce had to inform the above details. Nevertheless they give a fairly clear impression of a fatalistic entity with an offended sense of fair play, possibly founded in jealousy or some kind of chip on the shoulder with its roots in bitter childhood experience. In the domestic situation Nemesis can thus prove extremely destructive with her constant taunt of 'It serves you right'. Directed into the social arena, however, her gifts can contribute considerably to maintaining balance and justice in society. This very approach, indeed, can help to establish within the patient the conviction that things are not foreordained and that something can, after all, be done. For that matter, historical and archaeological studies might help to convince her that, in the past, something *has*. Nevertheless, Nemesis is a persistent and obstinate character, and is likely vigorously to resist any attempt to drive her out.

NIOBE

A. Subject of attempted incest by father; possible frigidity; inordinate pride in own children; jealousy; egotism; boasting; cattiness; obsession with status; rank-pulling; snobbery; indirect destruction of own children; depression at their loss, or when they leave home; refusal to eat; anorexia.

B. Fertility; motherhood; love of own children.

THERAPIES Name, imagine and invoke the haughty and over-dressed Queen of Thebes with her airs and graces, who, bereaved of her children by APOLLO and ARTEMIS (q.v.), has now become 'Niobe all tears'; fine clothes; loose, long hair; weeping; mourning; open grief; fasting; sunlight on snow; springtime.

SYMBOLS Melting mountain snowcap; white swan-eagle.

Notes Possibly in compensation for her own ill-treatment as a child, Niobe is obsessed with status, and seeks it particularly through her children. As a result of spoiling them, however, she drives them from her, and so loses what she can least afford to be without. Since they are not to be brought back, it is vital that she should express her grief freely. Bright light is of particular importance to her in warding off any subsequent depression. And — who knows? — it may well be that once she has finally released her attachment to them they will return of their own accord.

ODYSSEUS
= Ulysses

A. Irascibility; anger; red hair; childhood trauma or sexual maltreatment; lameness; short legs; deviousness; craftiness; roguery; scheming; treachery in self-interest; boasting; pride; insistence on own rights; neglect of wife; take-it-or-leave-it attitude; restlessness; inability to settle down; obsessive nomadism; addiction to insecurity; courting of danger; tendency to dress in rags; secret worry; tinnitus (ringing in ears); possible asthma at times of deep disturbance; emotional vulnerability; masochism; feigned madness at times of own choosing; plotting; terrorism; violence; ruthlessness; victim of *grandfather's* hatreds; destruction by own success — or successor.

B. Respect for ancestral wisdom; puritanical streak; inconspicuousness; sense of honour; strong will; strong survival instinct; single-mindedness; leadership; planning; initiative; resourcefulness; versatility; originality; lateral thinking; adventurousness; inquisitiveness; caution; cunning; anticipation; prophetic wisdom.

THERAPIES Name, imagine and welcome the resourceful, determined and somewhat masochistic hero of the *Odyssey*; exploration; expeditions; the sea; navigation (both in company and single-handed); feats of endurance; low-profile military work; special operations; espionage; sabotage; ambushes; disguise; old, ragged clothes; life as a beggar or tramp; diplomatic work; negotiation; athletics; martial arts; retirement abode well away from the sea.

SYMBOLS Cockerel; the seaman's oar and the wooden horse of Troy might also be appropriate.

Notes While Odysseus is not himself a god, nor even an immortal, the myth of Ulysses which he expresses does seem to have a much older and more primal pedigree. And since every human being is perpetually engaged in some sort of symbolic odyssey, whether inner or outer, the myth of Odysseus is capable of speaking to all of us. At basis he is the determined, competitive, self-made man who relies on his wits, backed up by sheer brute force. Often insecure inwardly, and somewhat masochistic by disposition, outwardly he is the Man of Action, the Archetypal

Hero, the Triumph of Will personified. His motto is 'Don't just sit there: *do* something.' In short, he is the very model of the modern, go-ahead, dominant Western male. As in all heroic myths, however, there is (quite literally) a sting in the tail. Odysseus is destroyed by his own achievements — in this case, his own son wielding the tail of a sting-ray. (The sea, it seems, is a particular source of ultimate danger to him.) The moral seems to be that the hero-role, however personally and socially valid in its day, should not be identified with too closely or for too long. At the proper time it needs to be quietly allowed to drop. In particular, he needs to work the sea out of his bloodstream as early as possible, along with any associated domineering, ambitious tendencies and/or delusions of grandeur. In the words of the *Tao Te Ching*, 'Retire when the work is done.'

In the meantime, high altitude (e.g. mountaineering, flying) may prove helpful in easing any asthmatic symptoms, while any tendency to tinnitus may reduce in time of its own accord, especially if the inner ringing is *consciously listened to*, or if the ear is deliberately flooded with noise of a similar type.

OEDIPUS
See also HIPPOLYTUS

A. Abandonment as a child; foster-upbringing; hot temper; murderous hatred of father; patricide; incestuous love for mother; maternal suicide; unconscious self-condemnation; guilt; deliberate shutting of eyes to true state of inner affairs; blindness, whether real or metaphorical; blind rage self-punishment; exile; loss of self-esteem; nomadic existence; homelessness; swollen feet or legs; decline into senility and impotence; quarrelsome and ungrateful sons; pursuit by FURIES.

B. Physical strength; fighting skills; military ability; intelligence; intuition; insight; ability to solve problems; good relationship with daughters; heroism; glorious death 'in harness'.

THERAPIES Name, imagine and welcome the tragic former Prince and latter-day King of Thebés who successfully solves the Sphinx's riddle of human existence, but blinds himself after unwittingly killing his father and marrying his own mother; physical endeavour; combat; military activities; problem-solving; trouble-shooting; foreign travel.

SYMBOLS None known, but swollen feet and blind eyes seem obvious possibilities.

Notes As might be expected, Oedipus represents an extreme case of the so-called 'Oedipus complex', which according to Freud is normal in all young children. Under the terms of it, small boys are said to develop intense hatred for their fathers and overwhelming love for their mothers, while young girls experience the reverse. In the case of the real Oedipus, however, (and thus the Oedipus of theotherapy) the syndrome fails to develop fully until after the age of discretion has been reached. Possibly it involves a total rejection of the life of the head in favour of that of the heart, and/or a total capitulation of consciousness to the unconscious. Possibly, in other words, the subject commits himself to a life of impulsive, ill-considered action based purely on spontaneous whims, emotional urges and gut-reactions. Alternatively, it may be that he capitulates totally to his mother's control or to his inherited maternal taboos (compare FURIES, ORESTES). Either way, it seems that there is all hell to pay, and neurosis and even psychosis are never far away.

Oedipus's myth actually comes in two forms. In one, the former hero symbolically insists on remaining blind to what is going on within him, and a long decline to eventual catastrophe results. In the other, he recognises his inner reality and goes on to die gloriously in the attempt to regain his birthright of inner balance. The lesson is clear. Neither path is without its difficulties. Both may well lead to destruction, whether the hero-role is finally abandoned or not. But true fulfilment is more likely to come from a frank recognition of the inner problems than from deliberately avoiding them. And, perhaps, reading, watching or listening to the Oedipus plays of Sophocles may help cope with the situation.

Meanwhile, the myths hint at the possiblity of a further, quite unexpected outcome. For there is another old, blind man who comes stumbling out of Thebes. And his name is TEIRESIAS . . .

ORESTES
See also FURIES, ORION

A. Rigid adherence to duty; over-active conscience; haunted by maternal taboos; constant washing; inner conflict; self-punishment; self-mutilation; nail-biting; masochism; proneness to leprosy or severe skin ailments; madness; suicide threats; hatred of mother; vengefulness; heartless exposure of mother's faults and/or crimes; matricidal tendencies; liability to fall prey to ARTEMIS.

B. Strong sense of honour and justice; decisiveness in action; attraction to expeditions and idealistic initiatives; competence; planning ability; cunning; friendship with younger males.

THERAPIES Name, imagine and welcome the duty-obsessed son of the murdered Agamemnon, hounded by conscience for having wreaked due vengeance on the murderer — his own mother Clytemnaestra; deliberate disguise or change of appearance; association with younger males; self-punishment; nail-biting; symbolic sacrifices to the FURIES (e.g. pig's blood); self-sacrifice in idealistic causes; acts of patriotic daring; nautical expeditions; mountaineering; exile; open confession; self-purification in running water.

SYMBOLS Serpent; wool-wreathed laurel branch and chaplet.

Notes Orestes, apparently the latter-day vehicle of a much older myth, is a sad case — the victim, generally speaking, of a dominant and over-possessive mother. However hard he tries, he cannot get her out of his head. However much he tries to affirm his independence, his every action turns out to be either a capitulation to his mother's views or a reaction against them – more often the latter. Even the women he is drawn to turn out to be his mother in disguise. Consequently he finds it difficult to make real friendships, other than with younger members of his own sex. Only when the whole problem eventually comes out into the open is there much prospect of permanent relief, and failing any deliberate initiative to bring this about beforehand, this is likely to have to await the advent of HERMES in midlife. Until then the best that can be done is to concentrate on idealistic causes and far-out enterprises as far away from the maternal home as possible.

ORION
= Oshossi
See also ARTEMIS, ORESTES

A. Alcohol-induced rape or violation of own mother; self-exile; over-anxiety to please; attempt to buy love with service; earthiness; naïvete in personal relationships; misplaced trust in others; accident-proneness; vulnerability; possible intolerance to heat; fatal attraction to ARTEMIS, who is liable to destroy him psychologically; frustration; vengefulness; over-reaction; destructiveness; blind rage; possible temporary physical blindness (e.g. cataract); mental torment or disintegration.

B. Great size; good looks; hunting skills; love; loyalty; thoroughness; honest dealing; reliability; idealism; ability to learn from experience.

THERAPIES Name, imagine and invoke the mighty but socially naïve Hunter who exiles himself in blind rage when his amorous advances are rejected, and is eventually pursued by a monstrous scorpion when his subsequent hunting obsession threatens to lay waste the earth; hunting (in whatever form — see page 79); wild creatures; animal taming; dawn; early rising; sunrise; mountains; sunbathing; the sea; swimming; boating (especially rowing); navigation; travel; pilgrimages; alcohol (WARN-ING: beware of addiction).

SYMBOLS Wind; dog; Sirius the Dog Star; the constellation Orion; brazen club.

Notes Orion's myth is a confused mixture of several different stories, and harmonising its various elements has necessitated subjecting the literary record to a fairly broad interpretation. At basis, Orion seems to represent the 'What a good boy am I' syndrome, accompanied by a naïve tendency to take others at their word. The product of over-strict and over-protective parenting, and in particular of his parents' giving or withhold-ing of love as a form of discipline, he has great competence at everything but personal relationships. Consequently he needs to be exorcised early, if psychological pain and possibly disaster are not to ensue. Actual experience and being forced to see things as others see them can, it seems, act as effective eye-openers.

Astrologically, Orion ought theoretically to be most noticeable in late spring.

ORPHEUS
= Osiris, Oshunmaré

A. Excess of love; over-regard for women's sensibilities; tragic loss of wife or female partner; sublimation; repressed sexuality; bisexuality; potential destruction by fame and/or over-eager fans (see DIONYSUS), or possibly by philistines; proneness to retrospection and regret; depression; disintegration of personality; possible epilepsy; transcen-dence of persecution.

B. Love; fidelity; sublimation; celibacy; spirituality; knowledge of divine mysteries; monotheism; idealism; courage; self-sacrifice; musi-cianship; object of adolescent adulation and hysteria; regenerative and restorative powers; ability to soothe others' torments; pacification; persuasiveness; opposition to promiscuity; hatred of cruelty; sympathy for wild creatures.

THERAPIES Name, imagine and invoke the Divine Musician with his heart-shaped lyre, ever irrepressible and idealistic, yet also haunted by personal tragedy; music (especially singing and plucked instruments); literature; poetry; marriage; teaching; the caring professions; animal-taming; vegetarianism; avoidance of alcohol; sunlight and sun-worship; concentration on future action rather than past events; prophecy; monotheism; spiritual studies and discussion; asceticism; solitude; life as a hermit or monk; poppy (WARNING: SOME VARIETIES OF POPPY ARE POISONOUS; consult a reputable herbalist).

SYMBOLS Poppy; alder; black ewe; kid or lamb; the constellation Lyra.

Notes Orpheus is a sensitive musician, dancer and poet who is ever capable of plucking at the heart-strings and exciting strong, even over-whelming, emotions, especially in his younger listeners. In truth, he is something of a Pied Piper. Yet at the same time, paradoxically perhaps, he is an other-worldly idealist and religious revolutionary who makes trouble for himself by insisting on the primacy of his own distinctly puritanical (and even ascetic) beliefs and ideals over those of the estab-lished culture. His other main problems are his weakness in the face of the female will and his tendency to look backwards over his shoulder rather than forwards at where he is going — tendencies which, if persisted with, are likely to bring him much pain and grief. In particular, the habit of constantly asking himself 'Did I do that right?' or 'Can things really be as rosy as they seem?' is one to be avoided if possible. For the paradoxical truth is that the more obsessively he checks that good fortune is still with him, the more likely he is to lose it; while the less he struggles to hang on to it, the less likely it is to desert him in the first place.

At once loved and despised by those around him, and regarded by many as something of an oddity, Orpheus nevertheless enshrines within himself both the masculine and the feminine in almost equal degrees, and so is in fact unusually whole and complete psychologically. Yet his considerable influence especially on the young men around him is seen by some as suspect. The archetypal round peg in a square hole, he persists in his valiant attempts to make all the world round too. As a result he is subject to enormous psychological strains, yet immersion in his art enables him to go through hell for the sake of the truth within him that is his own feminine aspect, and to come out again on the other side still singing.

PAN
= Faunus,' Sylvanus, Satyrs, Shiva, Oshossi
See also DIONYSUS

A. Possible desertion by mother; early fear of the dark; panic; night-mares; breathing problems; suffocation; epilepsy; mental disorders; madness; unreliability; inconsistency; restlessness; addiction to all-night dancing; inability to get up in the morning; dislike of bright light (especially at noon); possible migraine; deceitfulness; caprice; devilish-ness; riotousness; noisiness; boldness; obstinacy; irrationality; fanati-cism; unbridled passions; uncontrollable erections; masturbation; rape;

bisexuality; dislike of clothes; hatred of washing; strong smell; over-whelming effect on initially interested young women, who tend to flee his advances and change character completely if cornered by him.

B. Nervous energy; strong survival instinct; uninhibitedness; sexual potency; passionate enthusiasms and opinions; musical gifts; music as a sex-substitute; conviviality; individuality; independence; sharp sight.

THERAPIES Name, imagine and welcome the grinning, horned goat-man and self-willed God of Shepherds (not the Christian devil, for the Greeks recognised no such entity; instead each divinity had his or her own negative aspect); animal husbandry (especially goats); hunting; wilderness; nudity; naturist communities; music (especially pipes and flute); laughter; relaxation; masturbation; sex of all kinds (i.e. auto-erotic, homosexual and heterosexual); dream-therapy; dark caverns; all-night dances; staying up until dawn; self-exploration.

SYMBOLS Goat; hare; ass; bee.

Notes When the natural instincts are in command, highly tuned to survival in the wild, Pan is in control. Civilisation and all its values are anathema to him. His reactions are gut-reactions. He is unpredictable. He can be convivial, but only with others of like mind. As the child of HERMES, he is most liable to appear (if fleetingly) in infants, among adolescents and young adults, and on the heels of the mid-life crisis. When firmly established in adults, he is the archetypal tramp or drop-out, fiercely protective of his independence and mistrustful of those who would reform him. And rightly so, for his salvation lies not in reform but in finding his right niche well outside established society and in close contact with nature.

When Pan appears in the short term, too, a spell in the wild may well be called for. Possibly, indeed, one function of the teenage camp or expedition, or of the annual holiday in the countryside or by the sea — an opportunity to 'let one's hair down' that is by now almost traditional in the nature-alienated West — is to act as a kind of prophylactic to forestall the disconcerting effects of his sudden appearance in the wrong context and at the wrong moment.

PELOPS
See also HEPHAESTUS, TANTALUS

A. Early paternal cruelty or psychic damage; seething resentment; fevers; childhood wasting disease or disfigurement; seduced by older member of same sex; difficult courtship thanks to opposition of intended's father; competitiveness; dirty tricks to achieve ends; ruthlessness; reneging on agreements; pride.

B. Goodwill; idealism; sense of propriety; magnanamity; canniness; fame; respect; power; wealth; wisdom; courage; fertility.

THERAPIES Name, imagine and invoke the misused son of TANTALUS who by hook or by crook manages to make good; administration; government; public works and services; speedboats; hovercraft; seabathing; philanthropy; rope-dances.

SYMBOLS Ivory human shoulder-blade; spear-sceptre; horse.

Notes Pelops — for whom the Peloponnese is named — is a classic case of compensation for early ill-treatment and disadvantage. In childhood he is 'eaten up' by those around him, all of whom tend to want a piece of him for themselves. Although, as an adult, he may have problems in achieving his aims, his sheer drive and ruthlessness tend to ensure that he eventually achieves power and status more than sufficient to offset anything that has gone before. All that is necessary in the way of treatment is sufficient outlets for his constant excess of energy. Mountaineering could well appeal particularly.

PERSEPHONE
= Proserpine, Kore
See also DEMETER, ARTEMIS, APHRODITE, ATHENE, HERMES

A. Gullibility; loss of innocence; proneness to abduction and rape; preference for female, rather than male company; possible frigidity and childlessness; vindictive attitude to men; possessiveness; strong unconscious urges; fear of snakes; winter depression; manic depression; periodic insanity; love of darkness; obsession with death.

B. Feminism; graciousness; complaisance; faithfulness; regenerative and restorative powers; mercy; admiration for real heroes; 'merciful' destruction of present circumstances; unwillingness to espouse death; ability to learn to love what she orignally hated; vulnerability to the spiritual or divine; eventual acceptance of death as a part of life.

THERAPIES Name, imagine and welcome the lost, depressed daughter of DEMETER and unwilling Queen of the Underworld; cosmology; self-transformation initiatives; self-development courses; weaving; agriculture; gardening; springtime; light; adoption; the moon, sacrifices of black rams and ewes; mint (consult a reputable herbalist).

SYMBOLS Black poplar; willow; aspen; pomegranate seed; narcissus; poppy; green corn; the moon; iris; black ewe; bat; flaming torch.

Notes Persephone, the feminine archetype of initiation, is the spirit of femininity in her most contradictory form, and may well reflect a decline from a former state of great energy, brightness and hope (see ATHENE). Once she has discovered the dark side of her own nature, she can be creative or destructive almost at will. Her moods change unpredictably. The men around her rarely manage to cope with her tendency to blow hot and cold. Moreover, she herself suffers from her internal contradictions, to the point where she is sometimes unable to cope at all. At such times she is all too likely to fall under the baleful spell of HECATE. Fortunately the natural world presents her with clear analogues of her inner tendencies. By directing her enormous energies into working with plants, soil, weather and moon she can start both to lower the internal psychological pressures and to objectivise her inner experience, realising as she does so that nature's contradictions, far from being arbitrary, have a valid place and significance within an overall cyclic plan. In this way balance and inner integration can gradually be achieved within a framework of ever-recurring change.

PERSEUS

A. Victim of grandfather's fears; infant hardship, possibly as outcast or refugee; youthful banishment; obsession with self-exposure to danger; confrontationalism; ill-considered, though short-lived opposition to DIONYSUS (q.v.), whether in self or in others; ruthlessness; deviousness; dissimulation; dependence on second-hand skills and ideas; destructiveness; over-willingness to use catastrophic weapons in self-defence; antagonism to unattractive or dominant women; tendency to be at loggerheads with grandfather and/or his age-group — eventually, perhaps, with unintended tragic effects on them.

B. Possessiveness towards mother; taste for challenges; dragon-slaying; adventurous spirit; sense of honour; courage; doggedness; thoroughness; physical strength; sporting or athletic prowess; survival skills; persuasiveness; pragmatism; willingness to make use of other's skills and ideas; fleetness of foot; soaring self-confidence; popularity; attraction to, and success with, beautiful women, despite their families' doubts; good luck and prosperity, both financial and political.

THERAPIES Name, imagine and invoke this restless and determined son of ZEUS with a taste for power, as he flies eastwards and homewards over the sea, triumphantly bearing the head of MEDUSA; challenges of all kinds; sports and athletics (especially discus); confrontations; enterprises involving self-exposure to danger; expeditions; sea and air travel; exploration; exile; marriage; politics; administration; government.

SYMBOLS Winged sandals; magic wallet; adamantine sickle of HERMES; bright shield of ATHENE; mirror; HADES' helmet of invisibility; head of MEDUSA.

Notes Perhaps in response to infant hardship and/or rejection, Perseus' story is one of constant high-risk endeavour and a literal living-out of the truism that 'nothing breeds success like success'. Never stopping to consider what danger he may be exposing himself to, he rushes headlong from adventure to challenge, from challenge to adventure. His youthful physical prowess even attracts the admiration and support of solid, middle-aged women of the stamp of ATHENE, as well as of the normally somewhat equivocal HERMES, i.e. the sceptics and turncoats. So infectious is his enthusiasm, indeed, that he is able to call on the very armoury of the aged HADES, and cunning enough to use it. And this despite the fact that his relationships with the elderly are not always of the best, and that he is particularly prone to make enemies of unattractive and/or forceful women. His transcendence particularly of this latter problem may turn out in practice to be a major source of strength for him, provided only that he can bring it off. But then, given his natural eye for the main chance, this is always quite likely.

At times, meanwhile, his sheer bravado, and the foolhardiness of his risk-taking, is enough to petrify even ATLAS. Yet, given time to mature, he will eventually find it possible to settle down into responsible domesticity, while channelling his still considerable energies into the high-profile social and political activities characterised by ATHENE. Here, by dint of borrowing ideas indiscriminately from right or left as circumstances demand, he is likely to remain as successful as ever, continually attended by the luck of the gods, and reconciled at last to the more formidable aspects of mature womankind.

POLYPHEMUS

A. Narrow-mindedness; simple-mindedness; slow-wittedness; poor sight in one eye; possible blindness; living in a rut; absence of creativity; forgetfulness of former craft-skills; self-pity; sullenness; moroseness; greed; huge appetite; inability to hold alcohol; drunkenness; gullibility; ignorance; lack of culture; philistinism; barbarism; brutishness; impotence; frustration; vengefulness; alienation from society; unsociability; reclusiveness; anarchic attitude.

B. Hard work; simplicity; great size; strength; ingenuousness; straight-forwardness.

THERAPIES Name, imagine and invoke the enormous, clumsy Cyclops with one eye in the middle of his forehead, holed up with his flocks in his vast cave, or hurling huge rocks at ODYSSEUS's ship; manual work (especially construction); sheep-herding; isolation; meat-based diet; alcohol (WARNING: beware of addiction); seek medical advice if the symptoms are of recent origin.

SYMBOLS Laurel or bay tree; cave; huge stones.

Notes Polyphemus is not so much a primitive as a cultural dropout interested only in his own material well-being. Possibly his attitude has its origins in actual physical illness. Over-developed physically and under-developed mentally, he now wishes only to wallow in his familiar routine. Since there is no obvious reason why he should not be allowed to do so, it is important for him only to stay well away from cultural activities that he does not understand, since he feels threatened by them and so is liable to disrupt and destroy them. In fact, though, his only real enemy is himself. Hard manual work is his preferred and ideal *métier*. As for relaxation, television seems almost designed for him.

POSEIDON
= Neptune

A. Destructive unconscious urges; barely suppressed savagery; ever-menacing anger; irrationality; surliness; bloody-mindedness; rebellious-ness; vengefulness; quarrelsomeness; power-mania; material acquisitive-ness; empire-building; jealousy of others' possessions; territorial dis-putes; indiscriminate extramarital affairs; rape; intervals of pederasty or homosexuality; involuntary nocturnal orgasms; provocation of women's masculine side; uncontrollable shaking; possible hypertension or heart problems.

B. Generosity; big-heartedness; defence of own; self-assertion; insistence on right to cater for own personal needs; discovery (in women) of own masculine side; inner masculine/feminine balance; political and/or com-mercial initiative.

THERAPIES Name, imagine and welcome the great Sea God, the dark-bearded Father of Earthquakes, armed with his mighty trident; rivers, springs, the sea and all things maritime; sports and occupations involving the sea and the air above it; bull-wrestling; horse-breeding and racing; farming; construction-work; city-building; athletics; sex; fatherhood.

SYMBOLS Trident; dolphin; fish; white bull; white horses; ram; ash tree; the constellation Delphinus.

Notes Poseidon represents the overwhelming power of the collective unconscious, liable at any time to erupt out of the depths of the psyche with irresistible subterranean rumblings and carve new kingdoms out of our experience. Whether we like it or not, he has to be co-operated with and acknowledged as the tidal force that even a whole race of puny Canutes cannot withstand. And this may involve us at times in conscious activities that shake us by their high-profile aggressiveness and go-getting self-assertion. In a sense, then, Poseidon represents not so much the undermining of the conscious mind by the unconscious (even though some severe shocks may be involved) as a definite push on the part of the unconscious to encourage the conscious mind to do one of the things it does best — namely to insist on the personal space and independence needed to carry through the next stage in the psyche's development. Failure to co-operate could well lead to actual illness.

Poseidon is always present within the psyche in latent form. As the astrological Neptune, however, he seems most likely to surface actively in late winter and early spring, while his clear association with life's major psychological crises (see HERMES) points to adolescence, midlife and the last few months of life as the most probable seasons of encounter.

PROMETHEUS
See also HEPHAESTUS

A. Worry; anxiety; mental and spiritual torments; 'pierced to the quick'; possible hypertension or heart-problems; devious or dishonest reasoning; head-orientated living; headstrong behaviour; craftiness; wariness; two-facedness; sedition; rebelliousness; belief in rights and principles; militancy; chip on the shoulder; support of revolutionary causes; chafing at physical limitations; frustration; temper; rage; belief in progress; undervaluing of the feminine; contempt for unconscious; chronic digestive disorders or hepatitis; possible back-problems, arthritis, or paralysis from the neck down.

B. Thought; reason; logic; anticipation; planning ability; wisdom; compassion; philanthropy; support of the underdog; craftsmanship; good recuperative powers; tolerance of cold; toughness; earthiness; eventual accommodation to spirituality; overcoming of health-problems through Herculean efforts.

THERAPIES Name, imagine and welcome the vigorous, wilful and cunningly subversive herald of the Titans who steals fire (i.e. the light of reason) from heaven for mankind and is condemned to be impaled on a stake (or chained to a rock) for his pains, while his liver is pecked out daily by a vulture (or eagle); crafts (especially those involving metal and clay); civilised arts and sciences (including architecture, astronomy, mathematics, navigation, medicine and metallurgy); backstairs politics; heroic endeavours on behalf of others; philanthropy; work for the underprivileged and underdog; blood-sacrifices; investigation of spirituality; sleep; probing of physical limits; the open air; mountains and hills; solitude; naked exposure to cold, e.g. snow baths (these and other associated activities such as cold showers or baths and year-round open-air swimming should be approached, if at all, gently and by easy stages; if other than young and fit, seek medical advice; desist at once if adverse side-effects arise).

SYMBOLS Fire; fire-drill; jewelled iron ring; crocus; willow; wreath of subjection; the constellation Sagitta.

Notes Prometheus, the Titan whose name means 'forethought' (or possibly 'swastika'), is the mythical creator of mankind, i.e. the entity responsible, along with ATHENE, for making human consciousness what it is. But there is a price to pay. His act incurs the wrath of ZEUS on behalf of the whole archetypal pantheon. It represents a kind of unilateral declaration of conscious independence, a split within the psyche — and this is a state of affairs which cannot be sustained for long, and which the unconscious will do its Olympian utmost to avenge, however long it takes. The inner state of civil war is duly reflected in the form of physical symptoms, which in turn serve as pointers to appropriate remedial action if illness is to be avoided. There seem to be hints that the subject may need to be literally shocked out of his state of inner tension. Indeed, the myth of Cheiron, king of the CENTAURS, suggests that there is some prospect of success, provided only that Prometheus's characteristic militancy can be quietly allowed to die.

Prometheus is not merely one of the most familiar daemons of modern Western males; he is the masculine guiding spirit of the whole of traditional Western civilisation. Consequently his myth has important lessons for all of us.

RHEA
= Diana (Dione), Nanan

See also EARTH MOTHER, GREAT MOTHER, CRONUS

A. Possessiveness; incestuous relationship with, or rape by, own son; over-protectiveness towards offspring; over-eagerness to promulgate divine mysteries; wifely frivolity; deflation; physical and mental illness; possible arthritis; danger of death.

B. Motherhood; knowledge of female mysteries; psychological integration; protection; restorative powers; healing; forgiveness; mediation; persuasiveness; canniness; worldly wisdom; down-to-earthness; promulgation of spiritual knowledge; shamanism; 'medicine woman'.

THERAPIES Name, imagine and welcome the ancient Earth Mother and dark-robed sister of CRONUS in her most possessive and yet most canny form — and notably as the grandmotherly guardian of much secret lore; motherhood; grandmotherhood; dark clothes; beekeeping; artificial respiration; first aid; water-divining; irrigation; metallurgy.

SYMBOLS Brazen drum; flute; cymbal; bull-roarer; dove; female snake; mountain lion; golden mastiff; oak; plane-leaf; the planet Saturn; non-ferrous metals.

Notes Rhea is the spirit of the woman who gives too much of herself and consequently smothers those around her with an excess of love. She has valuable spiritual gifts and a well-rounded wisdom, too, but is far too anxious to bestow them on others. Basically what she is looking for is love for herself, and the less she gets of it the more she gives. Outside her natural role as a mother, therefore — and even here her presence is a mixed blessing — she needs to discover that in fact love does not need to come from 'out there'. Charity, it has been said, begins at home. But this realisation is not easy to come by, especially as the problem generally has deep roots in infancy. The main role of the listed therapies seems to be to help take her 'out of herself' — a fact which might suggest painting as a further possible activity.

Rhea's association with her brother CRONUS suggests that the symptoms are likely to become more accentuated with age, and especially once the children leave home, though they may well recede again once the grandchildren start to arrive. Astrologically, the link with Saturn suggests that the problems are likely to be severest around midwinter.

SELENE
= Semele
See also PERSEPHONE, SIRENS, THETIS

A. Gullibility, naïveté; insistence on knowing would-be lover's innermost secrets; revulsion against full-blooded sex; menstrual problems; periodic depression; manic depression; love of darkness; possible alcoho⁼lism; spell-binding effect on men; elusive enchantment; shyness.

B. Beauty; sexual gentleness; keen observation; eventual regular menstrual periods; great fertility; re-emergence from depression (especially in the presence of DIONYSUS); cool skin; charm; spell-binding, soothing and healing effect on men.

THERAPIES Name, imagine and welcome the winged Selene, the shy, retiring, virginal Moon-Goddess; darkness; veil; all-concealing clothing; male bodyguards; low public profile; activities involving careful observation; alcohol (WARNING: beware of addiction); orgies; sleepy or unresponsive men; childbearing; horse-riding.

SYMBOLS Chariot drawn by twin bulls or horses; mule; stag; twins; not-to-be-opened basket; veil; menstruation; torch; diadem; dark cave; the number nine.

Notes Selene plays hard-to-get. Possibly the product of paternal over-protectiveness, she enjoys the sexual attentions of men, and is quite prepared to lead them on. But then she backs away in fright. Only very young men are likely to get past her guard, and then only by subterfuge, or with the aid of alcohol. In short, Selene is the spirit of female repression. She finds it difficult to let her hair down. In her tightly-closed basket — her 'Pandora's box' — she bears all those aspects of herself that she is afraid to let out. And it may take many years and a great deal of loving gentleness (both of course preferable to the last resort of alcohol) to persuade her to release her hold and commit herself to the kind of relationship that she secretly most desires. The effort is worthwhile, however, for her real destiny is to be the mother of a large family. Should she, by contrast, reach midlife with her basket still unopened, severe complications could well ensue.

SILENUS
See also DIONYSUS, PAN

A. Lewdness; randiness; uncontrollable erections; debauchery; drunkenness; fatness; female characteristics (e.g. women's breasts); laziness; sleepiness; romancing; inability to tell truth from falsehood.

B. Well-integrated personality; lack of inhibition; easy going nature; love of pleasure; musical gifts; abilities as a dancer; good humour; wide experience; general knowledge; raconteur; profound wisdom; prophetic gifts.

THERAPIES Name, imagine and welcome the fat, good-natured, tipsy, rumbustious Satyr and tutor of DIONYSUS, half-goat (or horse) and half-man; hills and mountains; teaching; music; wild dancing; humour; comedy; fiction; alcohol (WARNING: beware of addiction).

SYMBOLS Goat; horse; ass; hobby-horse; wreath of ivy, vine or fir.

Notes For all his dissolute and lazy behaviour, Silenus is in fact the very symbol of the well-adjusted human being. Totally at home both with his animal nature and with his intellectual abilities, he is unfailingly friendly and good-natured. Wherever he finds himself, and in whatever circumstances, he is completely at home. In the academic sphere, he excels without apparently ever doing any work. And while he has his fair share of human weaknessess, notably his continual randiness and his addiction to drink, this mythical Falstaff more than makes up for them with considerable strengths. An ideal companion for the young, whose Dionysiac tendencies he can understand and sympathise with, the knowledgeable Silenus — almost the archetypal university don — is thus hardly a problem at all. It is sufficient to allow opportunities for his positive characteristics to manifest themselves, and he will serve as a valuable, life-long friend.

SIRENS
= Harpies
See also ARTEMIS, FURIES, MUSES, SELENE

A. Obsessive virginity; proneness to group-hysteria; group-seduction, and then destruction, of men; public broadcasting of, and saddling of others with, own emotional problems; cruelty; heartlessness; anaemia; fevers; reclusiveness; self-destruction if scorned.

B. Feminine charms; sociability with other women; attraction to life in a female group or institution; attractive voice; musical gifts; calming effect; good appetite; love of good food; foreknowledge.

THERAPIES Name, imagine and welcome the two or more rapacious, bird-like female murderers who sing seductively as they lure sailors onto their fabulous island of flowery meadows (possibly Capri), only to devour them; isolation; living alone or in exclusively female company; singing emotional songs of love or death, especially in female groups;

spiritual or religious music; plucked instruments and flute; prayer; membership of a religious order; good food and plenty of it.

SYMBOLS Spoonbill; stork; bee or wasp.

Notes The Sirens are powerfully attracted to the opposite sex, but cannot satisfactorily relate to them. A collective and more dangerous version of SELENE with a touch of the FURIES about them, they yearn for love, yet cannot accept it, preferring instead to indulge themselves with rather more food than is good for them. Somehow their childhood conditioning is in violent conflict with their natural urges. The result is a series of catastrophic personal relationships, for the most part sabotaged by an insistence on remaining a female group or gang.

Unable to give themselves to another physically, yet well able to express their emotions in other ways, their most rewarding course is therefore to give of themselves in one of their stronger, non-physical areas, and yet one which is closely associated with their gift for sexual allure – namely the human voice. All the while, of course, staying well away from intimate contact with men, which could prove disastrous if persisted with.

A particularly valuable and rewarding way of applying their talents may well be to devote themselves to spiritual or religious music, where their services are likely to prove of special comfort to the bereaved, elderly or dying. All of which suggests that joining a closed religious order with a good musical tradition is a possibility well worth considering.

TANTALUS
See also PELOPS

A. Early pederasty or homosexual escapades; scandal-mongering; over-indulgence in rich foods and sweet drinks; nepotism; jobs for the boys; theft; fraud; perjury; inordinate desire for popularity; sacrifice of own children; infanticide; tremendous weight of guilt; inner torment; collapse of carefully constructed world; severe headaches; possibility of paralysis, either of legs or of whole body from neck down, accompanied by loss of feeling; great thirst; possible diabetes; chronic digestive problems; frustration at inability to enjoy the good things of life; fear of drowning.

B. Influential connections; high society; high life; attendance at glittering social events.

THERAPIES Name, imagine and welcome the ambitious royal father of PELOPS, always obsessed with status and self-advancement, and hung

up, starving, on a tree for his pains, with both fruit and water tantalis-
ingly just out of reach; high life; friends in high places; social eventing.

SYMBOLS Fruit-tree branches; the sun.

Notes Tantalus, like his son PELOPS, attempts to compensate for his
own inner burdens by constantly striving for success — in this case in the
social sphere. Above all he craves the attention and recognition that he
was denied as a child. His lifestyle constantly cries, 'Look at me.' But the
more he tries, the more he tends to undermine his own position. As a
result, he finishes up even more *tantalised* than before by the status which
continually eludes him. Unless and until he can be convinced that the
whole charade is unnecessary in the first place, and that his inner burdens
are largely self-imposed, the best that can be done seems to be for him to
enjoy while he can such social success as he does attain, in the full
knowledge that it is unlikely to last. Meanwhile he needs to take special
care over his choice of food and drink, and to treat any digestive
problems in their earliest stages.

TEIRESIAS

A./B. Early wanderlust; attraction to wilderness; bisexuality, hermaph-
roditism or transexualism; inner balance of masculine and feminine;
thorough understanding of both masculine and feminine *from the inside*;
accidental discovery of the primal forces and principles underlying
existence; deep experience of primal, unconscious urges; reconciliation of
conscious and unconscious; development of profound insight; indiffer-
ence or blindness to everyday, material events; possible physical blindness too; sixth sense; second sight; skill in prophecy; expertise in
interpreting symbols and omens; immense inner wisdom.

SYMBOLS Staff entwined by two serpents (compare HERMES and
ASCLEPIUS).

Notes Teiresias the blind seer is, in a sense, the joker in the pack.
Although an 'outsider', he can transform almost any situation. He is both
human and godlike. Indeed, he is more than a god, for it is he whom the
gods themselves call in to adjudicate their disputes. Thus (despite his
formal inclusion here) he stands beyond theotherapy, beyond treatments, beyond the world of dualism and the eternal dance of good and
evil. Harmony, balance and reconciliation are his trademarks. Buddha-
like, his eyes are closed. He does not even see the petty affairs of the
everyday world. Instead, his vision is a deep *inner* vision. And the world
that he sees is the world beyond appearances, the world of truth from

whose burning radiance the occasional spark falls to illuminate some small corner of the dark landscape of normal, mortal concerns. Almost inevitably, therefore, Teiresias also stands beyond time, for his is an ageless wisdom that appears in the briefest of flashes to generation after generation, whether of gods or of men.

Perhaps it is unsurprising, then, that Teiresias is not to be sought. He comes only when he is ready and when the time is ripe. His insights are not to be commanded. He is most likely to be encountered when he is least expected — often when the forest is at its thickest and the night at its darkest. And possibly, with the serenity of old age, and after a lifetime of inner endeavour, his soft footfall will be heard at the door, like that of a thief in the night, precisely at that moment when his presence is no longer striven for . . .

THESEUS
See also ARIADNE, HERACLES, ODYSSEUS

A. Selfish and self-seeking attitudes and behaviour; egotism; urgent need for feminine help; thoughtlessness for others; overdoing of heroism; brute force; unnecessary self-exposure to danger; engendering of suspicion and even rejection on the part of others; male chauvinism; cavalier treatment of opposite sex; subjugation of women; desertion of wife when the going gets rough; provocation of female opposition; a late 'season in hell'; eventual disillusion, defeat or destruction.

B. Manliness; courage, heroic impulse; daring; taste for challenges; intuitive capacity to solve intricate problems; supportive friends.

THERAPIES Name, imagine and invoke the swashbuckling, over-ambitious hero who slays the Cretan Minotaur with the aid of ARIADNE; athletics; expeditions; physical challenges; feats of daring and endurance; wrestling; bullfighting; diving and underwater swimming; marine salvage; rescue work; trouble-shooting; problem-solving; intricate mixed dancing; mazes and labyrinths; guidance by a trusted woman.

SYMBOLS Club; bull-sacrifice.

Notes Another version of the hero archetype — this time with early affinities to the young King Arthur — Theseus pushes his heroics rather too far. He is prepared to use anybody to serve his ends, and is not over-careful about whom he hurts in the process. Women in particular suffer from his bull-like behaviour, and consequently any activity which can constructively engage both his gifts and women at the same time can serve as a useful corrective. His competence at solving labyrinthine problems suggests that any area of intricate planning which can also involve women may serve him well in this respect. In the modern context, computer programming seems one obvious possible application. Such less blatantly physical activities also have the positive merit that they are less likely to be immediately ruled out of account at midlife, when the heroics are going to have to be quietly dropped if mental health is to be maintained. It is possible that one woman in particular may eventually be able to help him make this change towards a better balanced psyche, but he should not necessarily expect the encounter to mature into a close, long-term relationship.

THETIS
= Tiamat, Nereis, Electra
See also APHRODITE, SELENE, SIRENS

A. Over-attachment to foster-mother; fear of, or resistance to, sex; blackening of suitor's character; initial resentment of marriage; stormy resistance at first to sex with husband; harsh early treatment of sons in their own interest; later possessiveness; desertion of interfering partner; silent, chameleon-like changes of character.

B. Admiration of male valour; opposition to male aggression; rejection of sexual advances by superiors, in whom she is able to inspire fear of the consequences; petrifying defender of eventual husband; pacification; adaptability; forgiveness; late reconciliation; active compassion for the disabled and underprivileged; oracular gift.

THERAPIES Name, imagine and invoke this vigorous and slippery Sea-Goddess with a rosebud face, who has strong ideas of her own and an aversion to amorous advances; nude sea-bathing, dolphin-riding and diving; surfboarding and other marine sports; sea-rescue; navigation and pilotage; social or charitable work; midday siestas.

SYMBOLS Sea; water; dolphin; serpent; cuttlefish; lion; fire; rose-wreath crown made of gold and Indian jewels.

Notes Thanks to her mother-fixation, Thetis has difficulty in accepting her sexual role, and makes for a stormy marriage. She will resist any attempt to change her with every fibre of her being. Given time, however, she is capable of adapting, and her substitute love-affair with the sea and the creatures in it can help greatly in encouraging her to relax and accept her own physicality. Basically, she needs a man who will break through her considerable resistance and subdue her, for passionate hatred is, for Thetis, only a step away from equally passionate love.

TYPHON
= Python, Set, Shangó
See also DIONYSUS, PAN

A. Repressed unconscious urges generally; bad dreams; horrors; delusions; irrationality; pyromania; hot temper; blazing eyes; fiery words; muddled, incomprehensible utterances; fevers; murderous inclinations; temptation to rape; sabotaging of heroic impulse; direct opposition to spirituality; skin problems; possible hypertension and/or heart-problems; possible paralysis.

B. Great strength, at least while angry; healing dreams.

THERAPIES Name, imagine and invoke the violent, red-eyed demon of nightmare and spirit of the sirocco; permitted violence; wrestling and other forms of combat; storms; earthquakes; volcanic eruptions; activities involving fire.

SYMBOLS Ass; snake; volcano; fire.

Notes Typhon personifies the eruptive surfacing of repressed unconscious urges — the Freudian 'subconscious' red in tooth and claw. His special trademark is violence. The product of repressive parenting — possibly violent in its turn — he may appear only at times of crisis (perhaps in association with DIONYSUS), or be constantly in attendance. In the former case he is more liable to long-term illness: in the latter case he may be inherently healthier, but more dangerous to those around him. In both cases, therefore, he needs to be allowed suitable escape-valves if he is not to 'blow his top'. And in general this involves providing safe contexts in which he can express his inner violence with minimal restraints. Provided that he can be kept in balance for long enough, it is possible that he will eventually become, if not extinct, at least dormant. But it is likely to be a highly demanding task, as, in the myth, even the mighty ZEUS finds to his cost.

TYRO

A. Proud and ambitious father; cruel upbringing by stepmother; incestuous relationship with malice-motivated uncle; inability to express inner problems; retreat behind a wall of silence; loneliness; unrequited passion; love of the unattainable; social naïveté; liability to be seduced and raped by POSEIDON; abandonment or fostering-out of children; later quarrels among children.

B. Beauty; late reconciliation with children; eventual fruitful and happy marriage; fascination with water.

THERAPIES Name, imagine and invoke the repressed, embittered princess of Thessaly whose early incest with her uncle brings disgrace on her family — a burden which she tries to bear entirely on her own shoulders; weeping; free expression of grief; rivers; swimming and bathing.

SYMBOLS None known, but the weeping willow could be appropriate.

Notes Tyro's early life is blighted by an intolerable burden of grief and guilt which she is unable to express within her family. Once she has found a suitably supportive outside environment to allow her to unburden her soul — formal confession, possibly, or a mutual support-group of similarly afflicted people — her life can be transformed. In this context she could well find both free and 'sacred' dance to be excellent self-expressive therapies. But for all this it is essential that she should leave home and put her own needs first. Should she fail to do so, she must expect some kind of inner earthquake which will force her in that direction, probably at around the time of midlife.

URANUS
= Varuna, Oshala
See also ZEUS

A. Male domination; aggression; marital strife; paternal brutality; antagonising of sons.

B. Patriarchy; fatherhood; periodic reconciliation; foresight.

THERAPIES Name, imagine and welcome the bull-like original Father of Heaven, a tyrant who is eventually castrated by his earthy and rebellious son CRONUS; sex; fatherhood; family life; ageing (with consequent loss of sex-drive).

SYMBOLS Sky; mountains.

Notes Uranus's myth is fairly scant, and has clearly been deliberately devalued. In its received form it speaks of an over-developed paternal sex-drive, accompanied by an unnecessarily bull-like attitude to the rest of the family. A particular expression of the father-archetype, Uranus is at basis a petty, domestic tyrant. With time, however, his aggression is likely to mellow, and so a fraught relationship with his family (and especially his sons) is likely gradually to improve, first only in fits and starts, but eventually on a more permanent basis. Prolonged experience of life in a commune could conceivably help in this process.

Astrologically, Uranus seems likely to be at his most hawkish in late winter.

ZEUS
= Jupiter (Jove), Amun, Odin, Shangó
See also HERA, ATHENE

A. Male chauvinism; domination; dictatorship; fascism; aggression; rebelliousness; violation of over-possessive mother; patricidal tendencies; murderous and even genocidal inclinations; involuntary nocturnal orgasms; lust; rape; promiscuity or polygamy; intervals of pederasty; incest with daughter; bisexuality; mistrust of women; failure in love; unsuitability for marriage; quarrelsomeness; petulance; vindictiveness; ruthlessness; hot temper; bluster; paternalism; failure to understand own children; gullibility; pride; tendency to bite off more than can be chewed; cowardice; chameleon-like changes of character; dissimulation; dislike of, yet odd affinity for, snakes; paralysis in the face of the unconscious; possible paralysis or back-problems; disdain of sleep; ferocious countenance; petrifying effect on opponents.

B. Patriarchy; fatherhood; immense strength; powerful personality; authority; resolution; lightning decisions; effective action; reassuring presence; salvation and protection; unification; support of own children; generosity; magnanimity; pity; compassion; opposition to cannibalism; joviality; good humour; political tact; wide knowledge; wisdom; sudden shafts of insight and illumination; adaptability; organisation; managerial skills; divination; admiration of spirited women.

THERAPIES Name, imagine and invoke the resplendent Father and King of the Gods, the powerful and irresistible husband and twin of HERA; marriage; politics; government; the law; administration; planning; weather forecasting; rescue and protection; trouble-shooting; sheep-herding; trees; bathing in clean water; honey; milk; mead and wine (WARNING: beware of addiction).

SYMBOLS Thunder; lightning-flash; sun; sky; cave; oak; white poplar;

laurel or bay; crocus; white bull; stallion; she-goat; wolf; beaver; sow; golden dog; eagle; cuckoo; dove; quail; swan; bees; double axe; golden weighing-scales; the planet Jupiter.

Notes Born (like both Mithras and Jesus) underground at dead of night, the irrepressible Zeus has his origins deep in the unconscious. No mere reaction to conditioning, he is the spirit of paternalism, the primal father-archetype. True, his negative side is just as strong as his positive side. Were it not so, he would be unbalanced. And so, when his negative side appears well to the fore, a vast range of balancing activities is available. Since his spirit is common in present-day Western society, almost any activity or attitude chosen will fit comfortably with accepted ideals and norms. He is a born administrator and leader with a keen sense of justice, and is always likely to come out on top of the heap. Indeed, provided that he stays well within the framework of accepted law, he may well succeed in retaining his unquestioned supremacy for a good long time.

Astrologically, as the Roman Jupiter, Zeus is the ruler of Sagittarius, and so is in his element in early winter.

INVITATION TO THE READER

Theotherapy is by its very nature not a dead system of classification, but a living way of healing. As such, it is bound to be ever fluid, ever developing with the needs and experiences of those who apply it.

In order that the technique may be further developed and attuned to the needs of the late twentieth century, constant feedback from practical experience is therefore needed.

If you have any such feedback, insights or experience to offer, please feel free to contact the author c/o Element Books Ltd. A stamped, addressed envelope (or, where appropriate, an International Reply Coupon) will normally ensure a reply.

APPENDIX A:
A NOTIONAL CHRONOLOGY
OF THE GODS

(showing possible ages of onset)

Birth	0	Hermes? Poseidon?	Furies
		Pan Dionysus	
	Apollo Heracles		Artemis
	Helius		
	10		
Adolescence	Eros Adonis	Hermes Poseidon	Aphrodite Sirens
	Narcissus		
	Ganymedes Ares Pan		Persephone
	Actaeon		Nemesis Cyrene
	Dioscuri	Dionysus Typhon	Eris
	Orpheus Orestes		
	Heracles		Caenis Muses
	Centaurs Achilles		
	20 Eumolpus		Selene Daphne
	Perseus		Tyro Thetis
	Theseus Orion		Medusa
	Daedalus		
	Hippolytus		Earth Mother
	Hephaestus		Great Mother
			Circe Amazons
	30 Odysseus		Hestia Demeter
	Aristaeus		Fates
	Polyphemus		
	Asclepius		
	Prometheus		Niobe Athene
	Pelops Atlas		Ariadne
	Epimetheus		Erigone
	Zeus		Hera
Midlife	40 Atreus	Hermes Poseidon	
	Silenus Tantalus Pan		
	Oedipus	Dionysus Typhon	
	50 Uranus		
	Minos Midas		Medea
		Cronus	
Old age	60	Hades	Rhea
	70	Teiresias	
	80		
Death		Hermes Poseidon	

APPENDIX B:
PILGRIM'S GUIDE

A list of locations, mainly in Greece and Turkey, which are associated with the various gods and other mythical entities of ancient Greece (not all of whom are represented). Other sites may be found scattered throughout the Mediterranean basin. At some sites ruins of temples and sanctuaries still survive: at others remains are vestigial or non-existent. Consult a good guidebook for details.

Entries in capitals refer to major centres, generally of significance to a number of gods. Asterisks denote traditional birthplaces. Square brackets indicate that nothing more concrete than an anecdotal association now exists. Alternative names are given where the modern Greek differs significantly from the traditional form.

ACHILLES
Greek Mainland [Mt. Pelion]
Greek Islands [Skyros]
Elsewhere [Truva/Troy]

ACTAEON
Greek Mainland [Boeotian Orchomenos]

APHRODITE/CYBELE
Greek Mainland Argos, Arta(?), ATHENS (below SW corner of Acropolis), Ayia Sophia, Ayios Petros (Tripotana), CORINTH, Daphni, DODONA, Kaisariani, Kalpaki, Kithira, [Mt. OLYMPUS], Piraeus(?), Tembi/Vale of Tempe, Trizini/Troezen
Greek Islands Crete (Kato Simi, Sta Lenika, DELOS, Kos,

Kythera*, Lesbos (Mesa), Paros (Naoussa), Rhodes, Somathraki (Palaeopolis)
Turkey Aizanoi, Aphrodisias, Cnidus(?), Manisa (Mt. Sipylus), Midas Sehri

APOLLO
Greek Mainland Arakhova (Mt. Parnassus), Argos, ATHENS (Agora, Illissos), Bassae, CORINTH, Daphni, DELPHI, Demetrias, EPIDAVROS/EPIDAURUS, Glifadha, Kalpaki, [Mt. OLYMPUS], Palaio Bazari (Thermon), Perdikovrisi (Mt. Ptoon), Preveza (Promontory of Aktion), Sikyon, Tembi/Vale of Tempe (between Mounts Ossa and OLYMPUS, Vouliagmeni
Greek Islands Aegina, Anaphi, Chios (Kato Fana), Crete (Aptera, Drera, Gortyn), DELOS (Mt. Kynthos*), Evia/Euboea (Eretria), Kalymnos (Damos), Kea (Korissia, Poles), [Kos], Levkada/Levkas, Limnos/Lemnos (Charos Reef), Naxos, Paros (Naoussa), Rhodes, THASOS, THERA/SANTORINI (Anafi, Thira)
Turkey Alabanda, Claros, Didim/Didyma, Harbiye/Daphne, Milet/Miletus, Nemrut Dag, Patara, Pamukkale (Hieropolis), Side, Xanthos

ARES
Greek Mainland ATHENS (Agora), [Mt. OLYMPUS]
Greek Islands Crete (Sta Lenika)
Turkey Giresun Island(?), Nemrut Dag

ARIADNE
Greek Islands Crete (Knossos*), [Naxos]

ARISTAEUS
Greek Mainland [Kalpaki/Orchomenos], [Tembi/Vale of Tempe]
Greek Islands [Kea]

ARTEMIS/DIANA
Greek Mainland Aigani(?), ATHENS (Acropolis), Brauron, CORINTH, ELEFSIS/ELEUSIS, Kalkhis (Aulis), Kalpaki, Kalydon, Kionia, Levidhi, Loutsa, Messene, [Mt. OLYMPUS], Piraeus, Sparti/Sparta, Volos (Demetrias)
Greek Islands Corfu (Kanoni), Crete (Ayia Roumeli, Diktynna,

Falasarna, Limin Knersonisou, Polyrrhenia, Prinias), DELOS*, Evia/Euboea (Cape Artemision, Eretria), THASOS
Turkey Claros, EFES/EPHESUS, Izmir, Perge, Sart/Sardis, Söke (Magnesia), Xanthos

ASCLEPIUS
Greek Mainland ATHENS (Below south slope of Acropolis), CORINTH, DELPHI, EPIDAVROS/EPIDAURUS, Gortys, Kalivia/Pheneos, Kastro tis Doritsas, Larissa/Krannon, Orchomenos (Boeotia), Piraeus, Trikkala, Trizini/Troezen
Greek Islands Crete (Lenda), DELOS, Kos
Turkey EFES/EPHESUS, BERGAMA/PERGAMUM

ATHENE
Greek Mainland Alea, Argos, ATHENS (Agora, Roman Market and Acropolis — old temple, Parthenon and Erechtheion), DELPHI (Marmaria), Kastro tis Doritsas, Kavalla(?), Makrisia, Mikrothivai, [Mt. OLYMPUS], Philia, Sounion, Zeli (Kastro Lazou)
Greek Islands DELOS (Mt. Kynthos), Rhodes (Kameiros, Lindos, Rhodes), THASOS
Turkey Assos, BERGAMA/PERGAMUM, Didim/Didyma (Heracleia), PRIENE, Side, Truva/Troy

ATLAS
[Atlas Mountains, North Africa]

ATREUS
Greek Mainland Mycenae

CENTAURS
Greek Mainland [Mt. Pelion]

CIRCE
[Lussin Island(?) (N. Adriatic)]

CRONUS
Greek Mainland ATHENS (Ilissos)

CYRENE
Greek Mainland [Mt. Pelion]

DAEDALUS
Greek Mainland [ATHENS]
Greek Islands [Crete (Knossos), Ikaria]
Elsewhere [Sardinia, Sicily]

DAPHNE
Greek Mainland [Ayia Paraskevi and R. Peneios (Tembi/Vale of Tempe)]
Greek Islands [Crete]

DEMETER
Greek Mainland CORINTH, ELEFSIS/ELEUSIS, [Miloi], [Mt. Olympus], Neon Monastirion, Thivai/Thebes
Greek Islands Crete (Aptera), Naxos (Sangri/Alaunos, Paros (under church of Ayion Konstandinou in Paroikia), SAMOTHRAKI/SAMOTHRACE (Palaeopolis, THERA/SANTORINI (Thira)
Turkey BERGAMA/PERGAMUM, PRIENE

DIONYSUS
(Sometimes in natural caves and grottoes, and later much associated with the open-air theatres to which the cult seems originally to have given rise.)
Greek Mainland Arakhova (Mt. Parnassus), ATHENS (Chapel of Our Lady of the Cavern, temple and theatre below south slope of Acropolis), DELPHI, Dionisos/Ikaria, Kephalari, Kormitsa (Mt. Pagaion), Louksa, [Mt. OLYMPUS], Thiva/Thebes*, Thorikos
Greek Islands DELOS, Evia/Euboea (Eretria), Lesbos (Vatera), Skyros (under Church of Ag. Georgios), THASOS, THERA/SANTORINI
Turkey BERGAMA/PERGAMUM, Claros, Sigacik

DIOSCURI
Greek Mainland [Sparti/Sparta]
Greek Islands SAMOTHRAKI/SAMOTHRACE (Palaeopolis)

EARTH MOTHER
Greek Mainland ATHENS (Acropolis), DELPHI, Khalandhri/
   Phyla

ERIGONE
Greek Mainland [Mt. Pentelikon]

EUMOLPUS
Greek Mainland ELEFSIS/ELEUSIS

GANYMEDES
Turkey Truva/Troy

FURIES
Greek Mainland ATHENS (Areopagus)

GREAT MOTHER
Greek Mainland OLYMPIA
Greek Islands Limnos/Lemnos, SAMOTHRAKI/SAMOTH-
   RACE (Palaeopolis), THERA/SANTORINI(?) (Nimboreio)

HADES
Greek Mainland ELEFSIS/ELEUSIS, Kastri/Mesopotamo (Necro-
   manteion of Ephyra)
Greek Islands SAMOTHRAKI/SAMOTHRACE (Palaeopolis)

HECATE
Greek Mainland ATHENS (Kerameikos: Street of Tombs)
Greek Islands DELOS, SAMOTHRAKI/SAMOTHRACE (Pal-
   aeolopis)
Turkey Lagina

HELIUS
Greek Islands [Rhodes]

HEPHAESTUS
Greek Mainland ATHENS (Agora: 'Theseion'), [Mt. Olympus]
Greek Islands Limnos/Lemnos (Palaeopolis)
Turkey Chimaera, Olympos

HERA
Greek Mainland Argos, [Mt. OLYMPUS], OLYMPIA, Perachora
Greek Islands DELOS, Samos (Kolonna), THASOS
Turkey BERGAMA/PERGAMUM

HERACLES
Greek Mainland Abdera(?), ATHENS, (near Hill of the Nymphs),
    CORINTH, DODONA (under former Christian basilica),
    Heraklion, Kalidhromon, Marathon, [Miloi], Thivai/
    Thebes, [Tiryns*]
Greek Islands DELOS, Limnos(?) [Komil], THASOS, THERA/
    SANTORINI
Turkey Nemrut Dag

HERMES
Greek Mainland CORINTH, Glifadha, [Mt. Kyllini*], [Mt.
    OLYMPUS], Pilos (Koryphasion Promontory)
Greek Islands Crete (Kato Simi), DELOS, SAMOTHRAKI/
    SAMOTHRACE (Palaeopolis), THERA/SANTORINI

HESTIA
Greek Mainland [Mt. OLYMPUS], OLYMPIA

HIPPOLYTUS
Greek Mainland [Trizini/Troezen]

MEDEA
Greek Mainland [ATHENS], [CORINTH]

MINOS
Greek Islands Crete (Knossos)

MUSES
(Generally in out-of-the-way natural settings near springs and
    mountains)
Greek Mainland Arakhova (Mt. Parnassus), ATHENS (Hill of the
    Muses), Mt. Helikon, Mt. Zagora, Pieria (at foot of Mt.
    OLYMPUS), Pandeleimon, Thespiai (Palayopanayia —
    Valley of the Muses)
Greek Islands [Crete (Aptera)]

NARCISSUS/HYACINTHUS
Greek Mainland Sparti/Sparta, [Thespiai*]

NEMESIS
Greek Mainland Rhamnous

NIOBE
Greek Mainland [Thivai/Thebes]
Turkey Manisa (Mt. Sipylus)

ODYSSEUS
Greek Mainland [Kastri/Mesopotamo (Necromanteion of Ephyra]
Greek Islands Ithaki/Ithaca*
Turkey Truva/Troy

OEDIPUS
Greek Mainland [ATHENS (Areopagus)], [Mt. Kithairon], 'Schiste' crossroads (between Livadhia and DELPHI), [Thivai/Thebes*]

ORESTES
Greek Mainland [ATHENS (Areopagus)], [Mycenae*], [Trizini/Troezen]

ORION
Greek Islands [Chios], [Limnos/Lemnos], [DELOS]

ORPHEUS
Greek Mainland [Mt. OLYMPUS foothills], [Zone]
Greek Islands [Lesbos (Antissa)]

PAN
(Almost always in natural caves and grottoes, often quite remote from the nearest places named)
Greek Mainland ATHENS (Klepsydra — in northern slope of Acropolis), Glifadha, Kephalari, Marathon, Moni Kliston
Greek Islands DELOS, THASOS

PELOPS
Greek Mainland OLYMPIA [and Pelopponese generally]
Turkey Manisa (Mt. Sipylus)

PERSEPHONE/KORE
Greek Mainland ELEFSIS/ELEUSIS, Kastri/Mesopatamo (Necro-
    manteion of Ephyra)
Greek Islands Naxos (Sangri/Alaunos — under church), SAMO-
    THRAKI/SAMOTHRACE   (Palaeopolis),   THERA/
    SANTORINI
Turkey PRIENE

PERSEUS
Greek Mainland [Argos], [Mycenae]
Greek Islands [Serifos]

POSEIDON
(Often on prominent coastal headlands)
Greek Mainland ATHENS (Erechtheion, CORINTH, DELPHI,
    ELEFSIS/ELEUSIS, Isthmia, [Mt. OLYMPUS], Nikopolis,
    Omolion (Tembi/Vale of Tempe), Sounion
Greek Islands DELOS, Poros, SAMOTHRAKI/SAMOTHRACE
    (Mt. Saos), THASOS

PROMETHEUS
[Caucasus Mountains]

RHEA/DIONE
Greek Mainland ATHENS (Ilissos), DODONA
Greek Islands Crete (Psychro — Diktean cave)

SELENE
Turkey [Didim/Didyma (cave on Mt. Latmos)]

SILENUS
Greek Islands THASOS

SIRENS
Greek Islands [Crete (Aptera)]
Elsewhere [Capri(?)]

TANTALUS
Turkey [Manisa (Mt. Sipylus)]

TEIRESIAS
Greek Mainland [Thivai/Thebes*]

THESUS
Greek Mainland ATHENS, Isthmia, Stamata, Trizini/Troezen*
Greek Islands [Naxos], [Skyros]

THETIS
Greek Mainland [Mt. Pelion]

TYPHON/PYTHON
Greek Mainland DELPHI
Turkey Korykos/Corycia (Cave of Cehennem/Hell)

TYRO
Greek Mainland [confluence of rivers Enipeos and Alpheios], [Volos/Iolkos]

ZEUS
(Often on prominent mountain-tops or in mountain caves)
Greek Mainland Afikos, Argos, ATHENS, (Acropolis, Agora, and near Hadrian's Arch), DODONA (near Ioannina), Heraklion, Livadhia (Ayios Ilion), Mt. Karabola, Mt. Lykaion, [Mt. OLYMPUS], OLYMPIA, Sparti/Sparta(?), Stamata, Stratos, Valestin
Greek Islands Crete (Amnisos, Knossos, Olous, Psychro — Diktean Cave*), DELOS (Mt. Kynthos), Kalymnos (Cave of Kefalas), THASOS
Turkey Aizanoi, BERGAMA/PERGAMUM, Euromos, Labranda, Manisa/Magnesia, Nemrut Dag, PRIENE, Uzuncaburc

REFERENCE — BIBLIOGRAPHY

Dates refer to editions actually consulted or quoted.

1. Assagioli, R.: *Psychosynthesis* (Turnstone, 1975)
2. Berne, E.: *Games People Play* (Penguin, 1968)
3. Campbell, J.: *The Masks of God* (Penguin, 1976)
4. Capra, F.: *The Turning Point* (Flamingo, 1983)
5. Cooper, J. C.: *An Illustrated Encyclopaedia of Symbols* (Thames & Hudson, 1978)
6. Cooper, J. C.: *Symbolism* (Aquarian, 1982)
7. *Encyclopaedia of World Mythology* (Peerage Books, © 1975 BPC Publishing Ltd.), by kind permission of Macdonald & Co. (Publishers) Ltd.
8. Frazer, J. G.: *The Golden Bough* (Macmillan, 1957)
9. Graves, R.: *The Greek Myths* (Pelican, 1960)
10. Grimal, P. (ed.): *Larousse World Mythology* (Larousse, 1973)
11. Hamel, P. M.: *Through Music to the Self* (Element, 1978)
12. Harrison, J.: *Love Your Disease: It's Keeping You Healthy* (Angus & Robertson, 1984)
13. Hillman, J. (ed.): *Facing the Gods* (copyright © Spring Publications Inc., Dallas, 1980); quotation from p.iv by kind permission of the publisher
14. Jung, C. G.: *Dreams* (Princeton/Bollingen, 1974)
15. Jung, C. G.: *Man and his Symbols* (Aldus/Jupiter, 1964)
16. Jung, C. G.: *Memories, Dreams, Reflections* (Flamingo, 1983)
17. Jung, C. G.: *Modern Man in Search of a Soul* (Routledge & Kegan Paul, 1933)
18. Jung, C. G.: *On the Nature of the Psyche* (Princeton/Bollingen, 1960)
19. Jung, C. G.: *The Psychology of the Transference* (Ark, 1983)
20. Kerényi, C.: *Goddesses of Sun and Moon* (Spring, 1979)
21. Kerényi, C.: *The Gods of the Greeks* (Thames & Hudson, 1951)
22. Kerényi, C.: *Hermes: Guide of Souls* (Spring, 1986)
23. Leakey, R.: *Origins* (Futura, 1982)
24. Lemesurier, P.: *The Armageddon Script* (Element, 1981)
25. Lemesurier, P.: *Beyond All Belief* (Element, 1983)

26. Lemesurier, P.: *The Cosmic Eye* (Findhorn, 1982)
27. Lemesurier, P.: *Gospel of the Stars* (Element, 1977)
28. Lurker, M.: *Götter und Symbole der alten Ägypter* (Barth, 1976)
29. Miers, H.: *Lexikon des Geheimwissens* (Goldmann, 1981)
30. Miller, D. L.: *The New Polytheism* (Spring, 1981)
31. *New English Bible*, second edition, © 1970, by permission of Oxford and Cambridge University Presses
32. Post, L. van der: *Jung and the Story of Our Time* (Penguin, 1978)
33. Roscher, W. H. & Hillman, J.: *Pan and the Nightmare* (Spring, 1972)
34. Rossiter, S. (ed.): *Blue Guide to Greece* (Benn, 1973)
35. Russell, P.: *The Awakening Earth* (Routledge & Kegan Paul, 1982)
36. Saussure, F. de: *Cours de Linguistique Générale* (Payot, 1960)
37. Stein, M.: *In Midlife* (Spring, 1983)
38. Vaillant, G. C.: *Aztecs of Mexico* (Pelican, 1965)
39. Wilhelm, R.: *The Secret of the Golden Flower* (Arkana, 1984), by kind permission of Associated Book Publishers (UK) Ltd.
40. Ziegler, A. J.: *Archetypal Medicine* (Spring, 1983)